Remember the Moon

REMEMBER THE MOON
A Novel

Abigail Carter

Lemonbird

Seattle | 2014

Copyright © 2014 Abigail Carter

All rights reserved. This book or any portion thereof may not be reproduced or used in any manner whatsoever without the express written permission of the publisher except for the use of brief quotations in a book review.

NOTE TO THE READER:

This is a work of fiction. Names, characters, businesses, places, events and incidents are either the products of the author's imagination or used in a fictitious manner. Any resemblance to actual persons, living or dead, or actual events is purely coincidental.

Cover painting: Remember the Moon by Sheri Bakes
Cover design: Kelsye Nelson

First printing, 2014
Printed in the United States

ISBN: 978-0-9911050-1-4

Library of Congress Control Number: 2014917888

Lemonbird Press
P.O. 80102
Seattle, WA 98108
Lemonbirdpress@gmail.com
http://abigailcarter.com

For Olivia and Carter

CONTENTS

Chapter One - Going Home	3
Chapter Two - Cat's Eyes	18
Chapter Three - Floating Away	33
Chapter Four - March 6th, 2006	48
Chapter Five - No Return	54
Chapter Six - May 12th, 2006	72
Chapter Seven - Chopsticks	79
Chapter Eight - July 15th, 2006	93
Chapter Nine - Murmuration	97
Chapter Ten - July 23rd, 2006	114
Chapter Eleven - Tonal Education	120
Chapter Twelve - Therapy	128
Chapter Thirteen - The Psychic	148
Chapter Fourteen - April 10th, 2007	167
Chapter Fifteen - The Haircut	173
Chapter Sixteen - Art Opening	183
Chapter Seventeen - Blank Canvas	194
Chapter Eighteen - August 7th, 2007	212
Chapter Nineteen - The Plotting Process	220
Chapter Twenty - The Reunion	241
Chapter Twenty-One - Ponder	255
Chapter Twenty-Two - August 22, 2008	265
Chapter Twenty-Three - Full Circle	268
Other Titles by Abigail Carter	279
Acknowledgements	280
About the Author	283

Chapter One

GOING HOME

Fade away in moonlight
Sink beneath the waters
to the coral sand below
Now is the time of returning
- The Eleven, The Grateful Dead

Watching myself die, I felt no pain, no emotion, no fear. The grisly scene of my death faded and grew hazier, as if a dense fog had rolled in across the Sound, obscuring my view. The fog grew whiter and more opaque. I witnessed a unique clarity of light, like sunlight refracted through a diamond. For an instant, instead of being blinded by the light, my vision was clearer than it had ever been.

❊❊❊

My eyelids were heavy, the white noise of pavement clacking under the tires, lulling me at the end of a long day.

My spat with Maya still fresh in my mind, I knew I had been driving out of spite in order to join her and Calder on this family ski weekend, but I was determined to be the dutiful husband.

It was a clear night in February 2006, but construction for the upcoming 2010 Vancouver Olympics made the road treacherous. During a slowdown, I leaned my head back and closed my eyes for a few moments before a honk from behind jolted me into shifting gears and lurching on. I passed Horseshoe Bay and wound around steep hairpin turns in the dark, driving too fast, widening my eyes to keep them from drooping shut as the smooth hum of the car lulled me. I turned on the radio and fiddled with the tuner until I found a classic rock station playing Steely Dan's Aja. I cranked it.

The traffic thinned until only the odd car sped by in the opposite direction. Transfixed by the white dividing line, my eyelids fluttered shut for the briefest second. A crucial second. I missed a sharp curve, veered left across the oncoming lane, and launched through a perfectly aligned gap in the guardrail, fate having its way with me. My eyes sprang open. The arc of my ineffective coffee, suspended in time, splattered like a Pollock painting against the windshield. The car tilted downward, Steely Dan's Aja still blasting, ...there's no return...

The view of Howe Sound was particularly breathtaking. Tiny boats glowed against the black water. In the sky, a pale light of the crescent moon, ...double helix in the sky tonight. A voice that didn't sound like mine whispered "Oh fuck" just before the car made impact with the gnarled rocks of the coastline. The car rolled in deafening slow motion until it arrived at a precarious resting spot, teetering on the edge of the cliffside, fifty feet below the highway, a hundred feet above the water. The white edges of the waves crashed violently against the rock face. Still conscious, I couldn't feel my legs but could see that they were crushed beneath the dash. Something warm dripped down my cheek. I tasted blood. Christ. This was bad. I thought about Maya and Calder. If I made it out of this alive, I would stop being such an asshole. God. One weekend in Whistler. Why did I make it into such a big deal?

"You've gotten yourself into quite a pickle here, J.J." My father sat beside me in his Rolling Stones T-shirt.

"Dad? What are you doing here?"

"I told Calder to warn you."

"He did warn me. How did he know? Am I going to die?"

"You should've listened to your son, son."

I yelled a dry, hoarse whisper. Shit. I was hosed. I wondered if anyone had seen me go off the road. Darkness prevailed.

I awoke to a man's face leaning through the broken window, swinging slightly. I glanced toward where my father had been sitting, but he was gone.

"Hey buddy! Wake up! That's it." I forced my eyes open. Pain constricted the movement of my legs, forcing a moan from deep in my chest. He looked away for a second and shouted, "He's conscious!" Turning back to me he said, "Quite a mess you've found yourself in here. What's your name?"

"Jay," I croaked.

"OK, Jay. We're just going to try and get a line hooked up to the car and then we'll get you outta here, K?" I managed another nod.

"Just don't move. We're going to get you—" The car lurched another few inches, tilting now at a dizzying angle. "Whoa!" The firefighter swung free, his arms waving as he tried to regain balance and I realized he was suspended from above. He grabbed onto the door handle, leaning down to peer into the window.

"Don't move, Jay. K? Just don't move!"

"Tell my wife I love her," I whispered.

"You're going to be fine, Jay. We'll get you secured. Don't worry."

"Tell her to remember the moon."

"Remember what?" The car slipped another inch and I could only see his torso now. "I can't hold it!" he yelled up to the crew.

"The moon!" I yelled as loudly as I could. The car slipped away with a slight grinding of metal against rock.

"Shiiiit!" I heard the man yell. I closed my eyes and braced for the impact. A wall of water slammed into me through what was left of the windshield. The car bobbed for a minute, hood down, my entire body submerged. I gasped from the cold and sucked air into my lungs. When the trunk filled with water, my beloved Beamer and I plunged through the depths of black until my giant lead boot touched the sea bottom silently in a velvet nap of sand. My final breath escaped in tiny bubbles, jewels of iridescent light that rose, dancing languidly to the surface.

Gaping mouth, empty eyes, floating hair, legs crushed into my giant steel clamshell – I became a grisly sea anemone. I floated underwater, looking down on my lifeless body, limp hands and hair flowing with the current, my skin glowing an alien greenish-yellow hue.

A shape began to form in a fog – a body pushed against a thin layer of latex. A figure emerged through it, someone familiar.

"Hey J.J. Welcome home."

※ ※ ※

I was supposed to have taken Calder to a matinée after a short day at work, but there was a crisis at the office, as usual. Maya was pissed that I was so late. "I knew you'd do this, Jay," she said when I called on the drive home. The car ahead inched forward. I tilted my head back to lean on the headrest, eyes closed, willing patience. I rocked the clutch and accelerator, still in first, the car easing forward making a soft purr that sounded like a pent-up exhale. The choppy waves on the left side of the 520 bridge across Lake Washington were violent. Angry black water contrasted with sharp, white dragon's teeth crests, exploding into themselves in impressive plumes of spray that crashed over the low walls of the bridge. Two lines of cars were at a standstill. The water on the right side of the bridge was calm, mirror-like, pristine, as if unaware of the brisk February wind causing such havoc on the other side of the narrow four-lane strip of highway that floated on the water's surface toward Seattle. The cement sky grew darker, but sunshine poured through a hole in the clouds lighting up the Seattle skyline.

She had no right to be pissed. I couldn't help it. A client called in crisis mode, panicked. I had to calm her down. This client was important and if we were to lose her it could mean the demise of the small financial software start-up of which I was President. The company struggled financially as I desperately tried to get more funding or land a new big client contract. Fast.

I pretended not to notice the tone of disappointment in Calder's voice when Maya made me tell him the news. I'd promised to take him to the arcade downtown, then a movie and dinner at our favorite Mexican place. A guy's afternoon out during Calder's week-long school break. "We can still go to the arcade," I said, hoping to bypass a new mood he had fallen into lately, one I called "shut down." It seemed weird that a kid should be so morose.

"We may have to skip the movie, K. Beano?"

Calder replied with his newly learned refrain – "Whatever." Seven years old and already sounding like a cocky teenager.

Fucking traffic. Christ. Why were Seattlites such crappy drivers? The car ahead had at least five car lengths between himself and the car in front of him. I honked. The guy flipped me the bird in his rearview mirror. "Moron!" I revved the Beamer, and he slowed, increasing the gap to seven car lengths, allowing a car from the right-hand lane to move in ahead. "Screw that!" I pounded my hand against the steering wheel. Inexplicably, the traffic started to move again. A wave crashed ahead of me, sending spray across my windshield, blurring the view. I threw on the wipers, cleared the water, shoved the stick into second, then third. More flashes of brake lights ahead, back to second, to neutral. Christ. Another half hour passed before I pulled angrily into the driveway. In the kitchen, I flung my messenger bag on the floor and threw my jacket on a kitchen chair. Maya perched on a stool at the island, the paper spread out in front of her, a glass of white wine pushed to the side.

"Hey," she said, the word laced with sarcasm.

"Sorry."

Maya pursed her lips.

"C'mon, you know as well as I do how important this client is."

"I get it, Jay. You're stressed out about work. But he's really disappointed. He was so excited to be spending the afternoon with you."

"I'm still going to take him."

"I know. It's just... oh, never mind."

"What?"

"Oh, I don't know. Priorities I guess. I just wonder if yours aren't a little—"

"Please, Maya. I can't deal with it now, not after today."

"Well, I hope we can talk about it soon. This lifestyle just isn't working for me. For any of us. I feel like a single mother half the time."

"Please, Maya."

"OK. OK. I'm sorry."

"I'll talk to him." Erratic pounding and clanging noises could be heard coming from upstairs. "Not getting any better, is he? We need to get him some lessons."

"Hey, this drum thing was your idea. You find him lessons. Maybe that will help with the god-awful racket he's making now. What were you thinking, buying him that drum set?"

"Yeah, in retrospect not my brightest move, but it gives him an outlet. I know it helped me when I was a kid. To be able to bang stuff out. I guess I never realized the headache my mom had to put up with."

"I feel her pain."

I knocked on Calder's closed door.

"Hey dude," I said to the door. He couldn't hear me over the drumming. I opened the door and walked in. The room was dimly lit by the dinosaur lamp on the top of his tall dresser. He sat on the drum stool sandwiched into the corner of the room, pounding on the snare, part of the starter set I'd found on Craigslist. He did not look up. His hair hung limply to his shoulders, shrouding his face. His hi-topped foot hit the pedal of the bass drum, completely out of rhythm, no beat whatsoever, just noise. He looked up and saw me but continued playing.

"Hey!" I shouted. He looked up again but didn't stop.

"Can you stop drumming for a minute?" I yelled. He dropped his hands, holding the drumsticks at his sides, shoulders slumped. The quiet was a relief.

"I'm really sorry, Cald. It couldn't be helped. I had a really important call that could mean a lot of money for the company. You get that, right?"

Calder shrugged.

"But I'm here now. You want to get going?"

"Whatever."

"If you don't want to go..." I turned to walk out of the room, copying Maya's reverse psychology tactic.

"No! I WANT to go!"

"OK then. Let's do this," I said, resting my hand on his shoulder as we left the room, pleased with myself and amazed it actually worked.

❖❖❖

Calder sat in the backseat looking sullen. An old Grateful Dead song came on the radio, and I cranked it. I looked in the rearview mirror and saw him clamp his hands over his ears.

"OK, OK," I said, turning down the radio. "Not a Dead fan. I get it." Neither of us spoke for the rest of the ride. At the arcade, I handed Calder his tokens and he ran around from one game to the next amidst a dizzying array of flashing lights and loud electronic chiming noises, ignoring me completely.

"Hey, Calder, you want to do this shooting one with me?"

Calder shrugged his shoulders.

"What about the motorcycles?"

Another silent shoulder shrug. This wasn't how I'd imagined our afternoon together. I envisioned a laughing Calder grabbing me by the hand, pulling me around in excitement – shooting at muted pixilated enemies, careening across winding highways at nauseating speeds, punching at ominous street gang members. Things his mother would never let him experience.

"You hungry?"

A shrug.

"Come on, Calder. Throw me a bone here. You gonna be mad at me the entire time?"

Shrug.

"Well, maybe a movie then? We probably have time, though you might be a little late for bed. What movie would you like to see?"

"Borat?" He looked up at me, hopeful.

"Borat?! That movie is restricted! Where did you even hear of that movie?"

"I saw the commercial."

"Jeez. I thought maybe Curious George."

"I don't want to see Curious George. That movie's for babies."

"Fine. Let's get a burrito then." Calder said nothing but

followed me upstairs to the arcade's dining room. "Wings? Burgers? What's your poison?"

Shrug.

"We could just go home then."

Shrug.

"OK, what do you want?"

"I don't care."

"A hot dog?"

"I don't care."

"Fine. Let's go home." I turned as if to walk away.

"OK, OK! I'll have a burger."

"Great. A burger it is." I called the waiter over and placed our order. We didn't say anything for a while, Calder fiddling with the straw in his Coke.

"What the hell's up with you, anyway?" I asked.

Calder shrugged. His head bowed and his lip quivered.

"Are you crying?"

Calder wiped his face against his sleeve. "No!" He went back to playing with his straw and took a long sip before looking up at me. "Are you going to die?"

"What!? No. Christ. Thirty-nine is not that old. I have a lot of years in me yet. Why are you worried about my dying?"

"I had a dream that you died."

"Oh. Well, we all have weird dreams from time to time. It doesn't mean they come true."

"Grampa was in my dream."

"Grampa Willis?"

"No. The one who died in a canoe."

"Oh." I couldn't remember telling Calder the story about my dad, but perhaps Maya had. I realized I had never really spoken to Calder about my father and was surprised he would have a dream about him.

"He wore a black shirt with a mouth on it."

It took a second to register. There could be no way for Calder to know that my father had worn his Rolling Stones shirt the day he died. I can't imagine that Maya would have mentioned that detail to him.

"He said I needed to tell you to be careful. And to not go on that trip."

"What trip?"

"I don't know."

"Calder, it was just a dream. It doesn't mean it will come true."

"So, you're not going to die?"

"No, Calder. I'm going to be fine. Is this what's been bothering you? Why you've been so weird lately?"

"I don't know. Maybe." We were quiet the rest of the meal, though Calder seemed a little calmer. I was spooked. Like I'd been given a prophecy that, now stated, was set into motion. I reminded myself that he was a kid. Kids have irrational dreams all the time. I refused to let his dream ruin our evening.

"Hey, let's say we play that racing car game after we're done. I feel the need for some speed!"

Calder smiled and nodded his head.

***

I poured my second scotch and by the time Maya reappeared after putting Calder to bed, I lay on the couch, staring at the TV. Homer Simpson sat at Moe's having himself another Duff.

"He seems a little calmer," Maya said.

"Yeah. He told me about a dream he had, where I died. I guess it's been freaking him out for a while. I told him I was fine, that I wasn't going to die."

"He thought you were going to die?"

"Yeah. He said my dad told him to tell me to be careful if I went on a trip."

"Your dad?"

"Yeah. That was kind of strange. Did you ever tell him

the story?"

"Of how your dad died? No, I don't think so. Just that he died a long time ago. I didn't want to scare him about boats and water."

"Well, he seemed to know that my dad died in a canoe. And that he wore a black shirt with a mouth on it. Don't you think that's kind of odd?"

"I certainly never told him any of that. How could he possibly know?"

"Maybe my mom told him."

"I'd be very surprised by that. She never talks about it."

"I know, but it's the only explanation I can think of."

"Well, maybe your dad did come to him in a dream. And maybe you really are going to die." Maya widened her eyes into spooky eyes and laughed. I smiled nervously. We sat together on the couch for a while watching the last half of an episode of CSI Miami, the show's colors enhanced, showing death and Miami in equally vibrant tones. As we headed to bed, we peeked in on Calder, sleeping with one arm flung over the edge of the bed.

"I hope he doesn't have any more of those crazy dreams," I said.

"It really got to you, didn't it?"

"No, but how could he know those details? I'm sure you're right. My mom must have told him about my dad. Kids have dreams all the time, right? It doesn't mean it will come true."

"I hope not. We really don't need premature death to run in the family."

Later, Maya brushed her teeth while I languished in bed on the verge of sleep.

"It'll be good for us to spend this weekend together," she said. I groaned. I had forgotten about the trip to Whistler we had planned.

"You're still coming, right?" She poked her head out of the bathroom.

"Shit, Lene, I don't think I can go." I had taken to calling Maya Lene or Lenie after she told me the myth of Selene that night in Italy and somehow it stuck. I turned on my side to face her, any hope of sleep shattered. "And besides, Calder says I should be wary of taking trips."

Maya rolled her eyes.

"Please, Jay. This weekend makes sense. We can leave tomorrow since Calder's off school. That way, we can ski Friday and Saturday. It would be great for him and would allow us to spend some time together, all three of us, as a family." Maya disappeared back into the bathroom. I heard her spit toothpaste into the sink and then she reappeared at the bathroom door.

"So?"

"I just don't think I can swing it."

"I thought this is what we had planned! Ski school in the mornings for Calder, you-and-me time. Remember?"

I envisioned circling the icy parking lot, assembling gear from the trunk of the car, hauling skis, clomping around in those awkward, flat-footed boots, buying expensive lift tickets and ski school, an overpriced lunch at Merlin's, the restaurant at the bottom of Blackcomb. I knew there would be at least one bout of tears from Calder in the middle of a run. I didn't want to go. Why couldn't she see that I needed the goddamned weekends to relax?

"I have a big meeting with a new client tomorrow."

"Right. You knew we were planning this trip, but still you set up a meeting," she said, wagging her toothbrush at me.

"I didn't set it up, Lene. I didn't have a choice." In truth, I'd forgotten all about the trip, so absorbed in keeping the company financially afloat, determined to keep this business going. I had no desire to return to the slog of Microsoft if my business failed.

"Well that's fine, Jay. Calder and I will just go by ourselves then. I don't care if you come or not." Maya stormed back into the bathroom and turned on the water.

"Maya!" I yelled. "Christ. Gimme a break, would ya?" The water turned off and her head popped back out from the bathroom.

"No, Jay. You need to figure out your priorities. Clearly neither Calder nor I factor into your life much anymore. You didn't even come to see my last show and you missed Calder's soccer game last week. And I can barely remember the last time we made love."

"My priorities involve keeping food on the table, a roof over our heads, and the freedom to allow you to continue painting. I think my priorities are just fine, thank you. Jesus."

"I know you're working hard, Jay. And I know the sacrifices you make for Calder and me, but I guess I question what good those sacrifices are if we can't share the benefits together as a family once in a while."

"I hear you, Lene. I just have to get this company off the ground and then we can share the benefits all we want."

"Yeah, I've heard that before. But I'm tired of waiting."

The next morning I stood in the driveway in my slippers and bathrobe, a cup of coffee in my hand as Maya backed the car out, her expression a mixture of anger, sadness, and resignation as she swiveled in her seat to reverse. Calder waved half-heartedly. I waved back, feeling like a complete asshole. Maya didn't wave, her eyes avoiding mine. I could've rescheduled the meeting, but the truth was I didn't want to. I wasn't in the mood to make the drive to Whistler, wasn't in the mood to ski. I just wanted to spend a quiet weekend hanging around the house, sleeping in late, listening to music, puttering around in the garage. A whole weekend to myself. Why couldn't Maya see how badly I needed that?

Our conversation from the previous night played again in my head. Maya was right. I had missed her art opening. I should have gone, but I hated those shows. Standing around with a bunch of nambies in black discussing existentialism or some shit. Sure, I wanted to support my wife, but I could do it better by working hard so she could have the freedom to paint. Wasn't that supporting her art?

She had arrived home the night of her opening slightly tipsy from the cheap wine they served.

"Where were you?" she asked.

"Sorry, babe. I couldn't make it. I got stuck at work." I felt the heat of my second scotch.

"Of course." She went in the kitchen and began clearing out the dishwasher, slamming cupboards, crashing plates around. At one point I heard glass shatter.

"Shit!" she said. I took a deep breath and went into the kitchen, bracing myself for her barrage. Folded on the floor, surrounded by glass, she clutched a paper towel around her bloody finger.

"Jesus, get up! You're sitting in glass," I grabbed a broom from the closet. Maya just glared at me.

"I'm sorry, OK!"

I began sweeping around her, trying to clear the glass away from her.

"Do you want a Band-Aid or something?"

"No! I don't want a damned Band-Aid! I want a husband who actually supports what I do by showing up at my goddamned art opening! Is that too much to ask?"

"I said I was sorry."

"Marcus was there." Tears began coursing down her cheeks.

"What?"

"Marcus Pellegrino came to my opening."

"Why the hell would he show up?"

"To support me."

"I didn't know you two were in touch."

"He found me on Facebook."

"That's just great. Did he try to make a move on you?"

"Would you even care?" Tears started streaming down Maya's cheeks.

"Of course I would care. He's an asshole."

"At least he shows up at my openings."

"I said I was sorry!"

"A ton of people asked where you were. I felt like an idiot telling them I didn't know."

"What can I tell you? I'm sorry."

"I sold five paintings in case you wanted to know."

"That's great, Lenie!"

She stood up and stepped over the glass. I tried to pull her into an embrace as she passed, but she pulled away and I remained standing in the middle of the kitchen with a broom in my hand. I swept away the rest of the glass, put the rest of the dishes away, and resumed my place on the couch with my scotch, wondering what Marcus Pellegrino wanted with my wife. I awoke on the couch at five in the morning and got up and left for the office.

Asshole. You should have gone to the opening, I thought, still standing there in the driveway. I plodded back into the house and loaded a giant bag, along with my skis, poles, and boots into the back of the car and headed to the office. I would head north after work.

Chapter Two

Cat's Eyes

"The moon, like you, is far away from me, but it's our sole memento: if you look and recall our past through it, we can be one mind."
—Saigo, Awesome Nightfall

Fifteen years earlier, I literally fell over Maya in Pompeii on a hot Italian September day. My eyes on my guidebook, I strode along blithely, sweat dripping down my forehead. Not seeing her crouched in the middle of the shimmering hot road, I toppled over her hunched form. Lethargic tourists – their cameras slung around their necks like all-seeing windows into their souls – limped past trying not to make eye contact. I cursed and rubbed my knee. Mortified, she stammered words of apology as she stood. Surprised she spoke English, I reached up to take hold of her outstretched hand, noticing its softness as she pulled me up with surprising strength. I stood shakily, looking into her eyes, which were a greenish yellow, like an olive, but flecked with light brown and blue and with a dark purple ring around the iris. I might have overlooked them under different circumstances, but she looked directly at me, eyes filled with concern. Familiar eyes.

"Maya?" I hadn't seen her in ten years, on August 15th, 1981, the day my father died. She'd been my fourteen-year-old crush, an infatuation both light with innocence and marred by tragedy. I'd spent many summers at Maya's cottage, swimming in the lake, bunking in the boat house, playing Crazy Eights on rainy days. Two years older was an eternity to a sixteen-year-old girl in love with Marcus Pellegrino, one of her cottage friends from down the road. At eighteen, he trumped me with his fully matured biceps, deep baritone voice, and Italian-Irish confidence. The last I'd heard of Maya, she lived with Marc in a tiny apartment in Toronto while she studied Fine Art at the Ontario College of Art. He worked as an account executive for some big Toronto ad agency.

Meeting there in an ancient city-sized graveyard seemed impossibly ironic, as if death followed us here and arranged for this serendipitous meeting. Maya looked good. A little older without the baby fat, and her hips had filled out nicely. To me in that moment, she was as sexy as it got. She wore a tight tank top over low-slung utility shorts cinched with a wide leather belt, a brass star for a buckle.

"Jay? My god! What are you doing here?"

I continued to clutch her hand as she spoke my name.

"Hello, Maya. I could ask you the same thing. What the hell were you doing down there?"

She gave me a sideways glance, looking coyishly sexy. "I wanted to feel the ruts in the street."

I looked at her quizzically.

"I know it's weird. But I find them amazing."

I glanced down. Two parallel grooves – the distance between them presumably a standard ancient cart-wheel width – were deeply etched into the stone. The two lines wavered down the block until they seemed to meet far in the distance.

"Those ruts were formed by carts driving along this street thousands of years ago, and yet here they still are, as though a cart had just driven along this road yesterday," she said as she looked down at them, shaking her head in amazement. I could tell she wanted to touch them again.

I smiled. Maya's fascination with such a myopic detail was typical of her artistic obsession with details and textures. I remembered her at the cottage, always picking up stones and shells, rubbing them in her hand, passing them to me. But here in Pompeii, there was something more to it. As if by touching those ruts, she could transport herself back to another time and relive what had happened there. One couldn't deny one's mortality in a place that remained frozen in death – the grisly aftermath of a volcano's wrath, scant reminders of once-busy lives, instantly ended.

"Are you just traveling in Italy for the summer?" I asked. My open-ended post-college backpacking trip was my attempt to avoid being a grown-up and finding a real job.

"I came to Italy a year ago. I got accepted to this artists' commune at a monastery near Rome."

"Sounds interesting."

"Yeah, it has been. More or less." Maya's face clouded over.

"What?"

"Well, you remember Marcus?"

"Yes. I remember him." I hoped my voice sounded neutral.

"I've been living with him for the last three years in Toronto. When I got this fellowship, he thought it would be an adventure to come with me. Of course I was thrilled. I didn't want to leave him. I wasn't even going to come to Italy because of him. We were going to get married. Well, we talked about it... Anyway, he gave up his job in Toronto. He thought he might be able to get a job in Rome, but he didn't speak Italian. He took language classes, but then he found a motley group of Italian musicians to play with in a band. And then he found some cute Texan singer..." Maya shook her head as if trying to shake away the memory. "It hasn't ended well. He left two weeks ago. With her, apparently."

"I'm sorry, that must be tough."

"Yeah, but I've been doing some amazing painting. All that angst." Maya smiled.

"I'm really sorry, Maya."

"No you're not."

"I'm sorry to see you in pain, but no, I'm not sorry about Marcus. I always thought he was an arrogant prick."

"I know. You have a weird history with him. With your dad and everything."

"You could say that, yeah."

"But he's a good guy. Really. He's passionate and smart and..." Maya began to cry.

"I'm sorry, Maya. I really am." I patted her shoulder. Maya wiped away a tear and gave me a shy smile.

"Enough about me, what are you doing here, Jay?"

"The consummate bumming around Europe."

"I heard you went to Dalhousie. How was that?"

"I liked it alright. Got a degree in Computer Science. Have no idea what I'm going to do with it. I'm thinking about going to business school. What about you? I heard you went to Ontario College of Art."

"Yeah, I graduated from OCA a couple of years ago. I'm a painter. And an installation artist. I've even had a show at a tiny gallery in Toronto. You'll have to come to one sometime, when you get back to Toronto."

We both looked down and watched a drip of blood snake down my shin from a cut on my knee, threatening to seep into my one pair of clean sport socks.

"Do you need a Band-Aid or something?"

I smiled at her concern. "Nah, I'm fine," I said, brushing ancient volcanic dust from my shorts. Maya squirted my wound with water from her water bottle, causing a dusty, bloody mess to run onto my sock and shoe.

"It's OK. I'm fine. Really."

"I'm just trying to help." I'd forgotten her alluring pout, a tiny puckered rosebud. "I feel terrible I made you fall!"

I put my hand out for her water bottle, which she handed me and I took a swig. "So ruts in the road, eh?"

"I know, it's dumb." She squatted down to run her fingers over them once more. "They are proof of what was, a reminder of another world. And look at these." She reached over to point out a small, sparkly, inch-square tile embedded in the stone. "They're called 'cat's eyes'. They reflect the moon's light, guiding travelers at night. Funny how it took the rest of the world so much time to rediscover that technology." She stood up, grinning. "Oh, how I love Pompeii!" Her eyes flashed an excitement I remembered from when we were kids, becoming a deeper shade of green with contagious passion, drawing me in. "I could hang out here every day for a year."

"Yeah, I know what you mean," I said, my mouth strangely dry. I tore myself away from her eyes and crouched to pick my guidebook off the ground and shove it into my backpack. She blew a thick curl of reddish hair that had escaped her ponytail off her face. I noticed a few faint freckles across her nose. I had never noticed before that she possessed the same intriguing coloring of many of the people I admired in the region around Amalfi and Positano – that same deep shade of auburn hair, a complexion that turned coppery in the sun, and those green eyes. I remembered her dad Peter had the same coloring and now faintly recalled him talking of his Italian ancestry. It hadn't meant anything then.

"Have you seen any of the castings of some of the people who died that day?" she asked.

I nodded, grim-faced. They had spooked me. Bodies contorted, captured in their moment of death, trying to ward off the tons of ash about to bury them.

"They have some amazing mosaics and frescoes in one of the villas just down the road," she said, perhaps sensing my discomfort. "I was just heading there now. Would you like to join me?"

We spent the rest of the afternoon together, Pompeii a distraction from our intersected past. Only through some kind of divine intervention was it possible that I now sat with Maya Willis, ten years since I had last seen her, sipping freshly squeezed lemonade under the canopy of a giant fig tree, just outside the gates of Pompeii. The breeze, flecked with the sugary citrus scent of orange blossom, danced with her hair. This girl, now woman, knew my inner scar and shared my deepest sadness. She sat across from me, her elbows on the table, mouth pressed into an O around her straw, and looked into my eyes. I felt naked.

"I bet you never talk about it."

I pretended not to know what she meant. "About what?"

"Your dad, his death." She settled back into her chair, prepared to listen, eyes still locked on mine.

"What's there to say? He's dead." I began ripping the round cardboard coaster advertising Orangina into bits.

"Yeah, I know, Jay. I was there, remember?"

"Hey, that was ten years ago. I grieved. It sucked. And now I barely remember him."

She gave me the tiniest smirk, apparently expecting my reluctance.

"You sound like Marc. He wouldn't talk about it either." She turned to look at the tourists who streamed out of the entry gate trying to escape the late afternoon heat bearing down on the ancient, leafless streets. I watched a black crow hop around beside us, picking up pieces of popcorn off the ground with his beak.

A car horn honked. On the road below, a man drove by in a tiny red Fiat, waving at someone in the street. My father had once owned a pale yellow '67 Karmann Ghia with its smiling, friendly headlight eyes. At seven, I sat helpless in the

23

passenger seat in a motel parking lot beside a busy Toronto thoroughfare, my dad hidden slightly under the tiny hood. We'd been to a baseball game with his friend, Paul. We were speeding along happily, singing "Rocket Man", the words flying away in the wind when a loud clinking noise interrupted us and the car slowed. My dad managed to steer us to the side of the road. When we stopped, he looked at me with his lips and cheeks puffed out, eyebrows cocked in a look of resignation.

"We seem to have a bit of a problem, J.J. How 'bout you get out and push and I'll steer?" Cars whizzed by, their gusts rocking the car as he turned to face forward, his back ramrod straight, gripping the steering wheel at ten o'clock and two o'clock, waiting for me to hop out and push the car.

"I'm only seven, Dad." I was used to my dad's jokes. "I can't push a car!" He let out a howl of laughter.

"I'm kidding, Monkey! You steer, I'll push."

"Really?"

"You can handle it." He stood up on the driver seat, climbed over me and hopped over the side onto the shoulder. I climbed into his seat tentatively, holding the steering wheel tight until I felt the car lurch forward with my dad's push from the back of the car. Panicking, I twisted the wheel back and forth fast, veering the car toward traffic.

"Other way! Other way! Just hold it there! That's it!" Panic turned to thrill as the car slowly inched its way into the parking lot of the motel, its entire weight in my hands.

"OK, now put your foot on the brake!"

I had no idea which pedal was the brake, plus I had to lower myself off the seat to reach the pedals.

"I don't know which one!"

"The left one!"

I dangled my foot down, searching for a pedal, bending my head to look under the steering wheel. Finally I saw it and stomped on it. The car stopped suddenly and I heard the weight of my dad's body slam against the back of the car and he let out a groan.

"OK. Yup. You found the brake. Good job, J.J."

He came around the front of the car, popped the tiny hood, pulled out the long dipstick, and checked the belt, entirely exhausting his ability to diagnose the problem.

"Looks like we're going be late for dinner." He smiled. "Might have to find a place to have a burger. Good thing we're near a phone booth. I'll just go call your ma and a tow truck." When he came back, my dad told me to keep steering as he pushed me around the motel parking lot, laughing as I commanded, "Faster, faster!" I learned to brake smoothly that day.

The car honked again and I was back in Italy with Maya gazing at me expectantly.

"You OK?"

"Yeah. Fine. Just thinking of my dad. I haven't thought about him in a long time."

She turned her head and looked at me from the corner of her eye, suspiciously. "He was a great guy." She patted the top of my hand.

"Yeah."

We were silent for a while.

"Where are you staying?" I asked.

"Amalfi."

"We could get the bus back together. My place is on the way to Amalfi."

"That would be great, yeah," Maya said, smiling.

"Hey, I'm staying at this little pensione on the road between Positano and Amalfi," I said. "You can walk down to the water from there and swim in a tiny grotto. They also have amazing four-course dinners for next to nothing. Feel like a swim?"

"Are you trying to change the subject?" Her lips turned up in another sly smile.

"I'll take that as a yes." I laughed.

The bus deposited us at a stop a short distance from the pensione. We walked along the ocean side of the winding highway, buffeted by the wind of speeding busses that careened along the narrow road. We entered a gap in a long whitewashed wall just a few feet from the edge of the highway. A glazed oval tile adorned with red and blue flowers marked the pensione's name. We walked down narrow white steps that led into a tiny garden. On the ocean side of the garden, tall, pencil-thin Cyprus guarded the cliff's edge. A narrow set of steps carved into the rock face hugged the rugged cliff side as they descended crookedly toward the water.

"Oh, wow. That looks steep!" Maya hesitated at the top of the steps, but I knew she would not back down from the challenge.

"C'mon! Let's check it out!"

We descended the steps, Maya in front. She touched the rock face on her right for balance and held the flimsy rope rail. She avoided looking down to her left. Along the way, carved into the cliff wall, were tiny arch-ceilinged alcoves – shrines, tiled with images of Jesus and filled with candles. She stopped in front of one, caressing Jesus's shiny tiled face.

"Are these meant to mark the places where people have toppled to their deaths?"

"Wimp." I laughed. "Keep going. It'll be worth it, I promise."

At sea level, poised on a large slab of rock, we stood watching the huge swells crash just a few feet below us into the cliff side along either side of our platform. The true strength of the ocean expressed itself in the loudly pounding swells, the size of oil tankers.

"It sure is humbling, isn't it?" I said.

"Yes it is," she whispered. A shiver shot up the back of my neck as Maya took my hand.

"You ready?" I asked as I stripped off my shirt and shoes, wearing just my shorts.

"Oh. God. Won't those waves smash us against the cliff?"

"You have to wait until the wave is out, then jump in and swim to the grotto before the next wave hits. There's a ledge you can stand on just inside the entrance. C'mon, you can do it!" I pulled her closer to the edge. She tentatively removed her shorts, revealing sexy red panties that took my breath away. She then slowly unbuttoned her shirt and revealed a matching red bra. The bony child-like figure of my memory had grown womanly curves. Pale, untanned patches of skin created by her obvious habit of tanning in a bikini caused me to turn away to prevent myself from licking a pale coin of flesh between her breasts.

"Ready?" I asked. She took a tentative step closer to the edge of the rock platform and looked into the sea.

"Ready as I'll ever be..."

"One, two, threeeeee!"

We jumped, holding hands, just as a wave pulled away from the cliff wall. We were pulled away with it but swam toward the grotto's opening and a new wave pushed us into the cool dankness. Just inside, we scampered onto another outcropping of rock to avoid the full force of the wave as it thundered into the entrance. We sat for a few minutes breathing heavily, our skin goose-pimpling as our eyes adjusted to the dark. On the water's surface, pools of sunlight reflected onto the ceiling of the grotto, creating an undulating constellation. Long, limestone stalactites blistered down from the ceiling, threatening us with their menacing fangs. From their tips, large droplets of water fell into pools etched into the rocks by their Chinese torture dripping, creating a cacophony of high pitched tones, echoing throughout the cave in a methodic beat.

"Oh, wow!" Tiny flecks of gold reflected off Maya's freckled skin as she looked up at the ceiling. "It's so magical." Her voice reverberated off the walls.

"A temple of the sea, so to speak," I offered.

"It's very beautiful, but it's also kind of claustrophobic. I feel as if I'm in some sort of underworld."

"Maybe this is where you go when you die." I laughed. "I guess you don't want to see where some of these passages go, then?" I pointed to one of the tunnels leading off the main chamber.

"You can. But I think I'll stay right here, thanks." We sat together in quiet reverence, feeling both cradled and threatened each time a wave entered and then retreated. My heart began beating fast with my desire to pull Maya close and kiss her, each beat surely amplified throughout the chamber.

Maya turned to look at me, her eyes soft, and I leaned over and kissed her gently on the lips. It felt at that moment as if we had known each other a thousand years, a feeling I had never felt with any other girl.

"Wow," she said as she pulled away, closed her eyes, and took a deep breath. "I wonder what would've happened if we'd done that ten years ago?"

"I wanted to."

"You did?"

"Don't pretend you didn't know that."

"OK. I guess I did know. But you were just a kid to me then. A lowly freshman."

"Yeah."

We sat in silence for a long time, mesmerized by the iridescent mural of rock deposits painting the walls and ceiling of the grotto. I wanted to stay in this grotto forever, savoring the moment. Maya shivered.

"You ready?" I asked.

She nodded. "How're we going to do this?"

"Same way we got here. When a wave goes out, swim like crazy back to the rock platform." Her eyes widened, but she took a deep breath and looked determined.

"Ready?" I asked, as a wave began to move out of the grotto. Maya nodded.

"Now!"

Blinded, I re-emerged into sunlight. I looked around for Maya, who was already scrambling onto the rock. I swam over and hauled myself out, flopping into a puddle beside her prone figure. For a moment it felt as if I hovered a few inches above my own body, with nothing underneath for support, but still able to feel every lump and pucker of warm rock against my back. I closed my eyes against the bright light and clasped my hands behind my neck, trying to re-ground myself, the sun on my face pulsing red to the beat of my heart against the back of my eyelids. When I opened them, the sun seemed to have shifted, emitting a slightly different range of color, as if the Earth had begun spinning in a new direction during our time inside the grotto. Maya lay beside me, eyes closed, still breathing heavily, skin glistening, a large drop of seawater pooled in her navel. I wanted to lean over and suck out the water but remained rooted to the rock, paralyzed by the unusual sensations in my body. After some time, a minute or an hour, Maya wiggled towards me.

"Wow, I feel sort of dizzy, like I'm not quite a part of my body," Maya said as she reached out for my hand, rolling onto her side, her other palm flat against the rock, steadying herself.

"I thought it was just me," I said, pulling her into my arms. We held onto each other for a while, as if together we might be more successful reorienting ourselves in this brand new universe. Our eyes connected, transfixed, neither of us able to break the spell. Her eyes took on the indigo-green of the water crashing around us, eyes that seemed to reflect the possibilities of a million lifetimes.

※ ※ ※

Sometime later, hair still dripping down our backs and our dry clothes now pulled over our wet ones, we sat on the flowered seat cushions of the pensione's dining room, a vine-canopied rooftop balcony that teetered high above the ocean.

We held hands across the crisp white tablecloth. I didn't want to let go, certain that without her to ground me I might float away from her forever. Antipasto was followed by homemade spaghetti with a fresh tomato sauce.

"How did you ever find this place?" She took a sip of wine, hair brushed off her face and drying in the light ocean breeze. "It's so beautiful!" The ocean, draped in silky shades of mauve and tangerine, looked like a perfect Hallmark sunset scene.

"One of my dad's buddies, actually. Did you ever meet Gay Paul?" Maya shook her head. "He and a bunch of his friends come here. I trust his taste. It's a little more expensive than staying in a youth hostel, but cheaper than hotels in Amalfi or Positano because Praiano is on the highway between them and is harder to reach. Do you want me to see if they have an extra room for tonight? It would be a nice change from the youth hostel." Maya gave me a look, but didn't reply. I hadn't meant to assume something sexual between us; I simply dreaded the thought of having to say goodbye to her, now that I'd found her again. I worried I may have ruined the magic of the night.

"Sorry," I added. "I hope you didn't take my invitation to stay as a come on."

"Isn't it?"

"No... Well... Maybe it was."

"I kind of hoped it was."

"You were? It's not too soon since...?"

"Marc? He ran off with a beautiful singer from Texas named Annabelle. I don't even know where he is."

"Wow. That's harsh."

"Sorry, I didn't mean to imply—"

"That I'd just be your boy toy?" She looked horrified for a moment, until I grinned. "Kidding. I'll be your boy toy anytime."

"Then do I have to get a separate room?"

I laughed as heat shot to my groin. "Not at all!"

When the shiny gray skin of a white fish slathered in a lemony butter was all that remained on our plates and the tall glass carafe of the local Casavecchia was almost empty and we were feeling the heat of the day and the wine in the pinkness of our cheeks, we dragged our chairs closer together and held hands, sleepily taking in the view. The ocean was black now except for the diminishing highway of blue-white moonlight jetting between us and the giant sphere that rose high into the sky. I wondered what goofy smile was on my face, thinking how unbelievable this trip had suddenly become. What were the chances? Maya Willis of all people? Without Marcus Pellegrino? Suddenly I knew without a doubt that Maya was the woman I would marry.

"You know, this moon reminds me of the moon the night your father died. It was so bright that night. It didn't seem possible that someone could drown in such bright moonlight."

"Yeah," I managed, trying to catch my breath, not allowing my eyes to meet hers. I wanted my father to be far from my thoughts. I didn't want him ruining this night and yet, with my reunion with Maya came memories of him. I used the edge of my fork to scoop a chunk of almondine chocolate cake into my mouth, not knowing what to say.

"Have you ever heard the myth of Selene, Goddess of the moon?"

I shook my head, this time lifting my gaze to look at her.

"She had a lover. A mortal lover. An incredibly good-looking lover who was a hunter or possibly a king. The important part is that he was really good-looking." She winked, and again, heat shot from my face to my crotch.

"His name was Endymion, which in Greek means 'to dive in', so he is thought to be the personification of sleep or the sunset or something like that. Anyway, poor Selene fell madly in love with him. Blinded with love or maybe lust, she asked Zeus to give Endymion eternal life. She wanted Endymion to stay young forever so he would never leave her. Instead,

Zeus granted her wish by giving him eternal sleep. The only way Selene could see him was at night when he slept. He obviously didn't sleep much though, because they had fifty daughters together."

"That's a lot of daughters. How do you know so much about Pompeii and Greek mythology anyway?"

"Classical Studies. An art college pre-requisite. But it fascinated me. I kind of wished I'd taken classics at a regular university rather than art school. I think I would have loved those academic types. Anyway, when I heard the myth, it made me think of your dad. Maybe it was the moon that night. But I liked the idea of him resting in an eternal sleep. What do you think, Jay?"

I stood up and took her hand, pulling her in the direction of my room. I turned and took a last look at the moon over the water. It seemed to be smiling at me.

"I think I will never forget this moon."

The moon that night and the cat's eyes that Maya showed me in Pompeii that day, their iridescence lighting the way, guided a traveler through darkness. Those glinting markings and grooves in the road were all that remained of an existence now lost, routes once traveled, clues that led people to their journey's end. Each tiny coincidence, each chance meeting, each shared moon is just another reflective clue guiding our journeymen selves to our ultimate destination.

Chapter Three

Floating Away

As a dead man, I felt more alive than when I was alive. My vision had a peculiar clarity, allowing me the ability to see individual needles on the conifers that balanced on a high, windswept cliff all the way across the Sound, a mile away from where I had crashed. I detected a spectrum of color I had not seen before, minute shades of green, yellow, and brown. I knew I was dead – my drowned body below me bobbed under the water, strapped into the seat, my hands floating up over my head. I hovered over myself, both below the water's surface and above it at once. I reached out to touch a soft white-crested wave, surprised when the deep indigo wash disintegrated beneath my fingers, a dizzying, disorienting experience. Logic fell away, no longer necessary for comprehending my experiences.

I sensed my father beside me. My father who died when I was fourteen years old. I knew I should follow him, allow him to lead me somewhere, but I didn't want to go, didn't trust that this experience wasn't just part of a dream. He stood smiling, his hands held behind his back, barefoot, still dressed in his Rolling Stones t-shirt and khaki shorts.

It was strange seeing him, the same age as me, his curly dark hair disheveled, the same scar across his forehead from a teenaged bicycle accident, his wedding ring still prominent on his left ring finger. Dead at thirty-nine, I was the same age as my father was when he died. I had always thought of him as being older, the way a kid thinks of his dad, in that non-age sort of way. He looked youthful, boyish, younger than I did, with his dark shaggy hair and long pork chop sideburns in that consummate 70s retro look. The human me would have laughed or cried, given him a hug, or perhaps a punch in the arm for dying on me. But I was not myself. He too seemed different. No high fives, no whoops, no knuckle bumps. His self-possessed, steady calm and that knowing half-smile contrasted with the jumpiness I felt from the sensation of being outside my own body.

My dead body continued to bob lifelessly as a Coast Guard diver made a valiant effort to release me from the car. He floated up to the surface and shook his head. The futility was obvious. I felt a momentary impulse to leap back into the water, swim toward my body and climb back inside its limp form. My being seemed large outside the confines of my body, newly unfurled from its prison. I laughed unexpectedly. I could hardly imagine why I might laugh at the sight of my own dead body, but my weightlessness in the absence of my body had me feeling giddy, on the verge of hysteria – the way a kid might feel being thrown up in the air by an adult – at once exhilarated and terrified. *I'm too young. I still have so much to do! I'm not ready! Let me go back! I will be a better person!*

How many times had I cursed my father for dying young? Now I had done something equally stupid and careless, maybe more so. *Maya. Oh Maya. I love you so much! I didn't mean to leave you. And Calder. Will you ever forgive me for dying on you?*

I'm dead. I'm dead. I'm dead. Aren't I?

Yes, Jay, you are.

My father reassured me of my deadness. With my dad's confirmation, I felt my panic dissipate, replaced with an excited yet peaceful sensation. I sensed a duality within this new me – the panic of losing my body, and also the exhilaration of being released from it. I experienced a more distant feeling of calmness, that everything was happening as it should. I had no volume, mass, velocity, or any other physical attribute. I did not exist physically in space because a physical location no longer had meaning. I could float while Earth spun on its axis around the Sun, so that my relative position to Earth remained unchanged. My soul, even outside my body, maintained its identity as "Jay", though I didn't know how without any brain input. I had no concept of time, felt no pain. I felt sorry for my prone body, now a stranger.

I thought of the things in my life that now would never be – the second kid we had vaguely planned on having, the romantic weekend that Maya had been bugging me about, working out more, climbing Mount Rainier, jamming with Calder. Instead I'd made Maya a single mother to a seven-year-old boy. Only seven. Shit. He still had so much life to live and now he would have to do it without a father. I knew how hard that would be for him. Who would cheer him at his first little league game this summer? Who would kick his butt when he became a grunting teenager, or see him stand at an altar on his wedding day? I'd looked forward to nurturing Calder's musical abilities, his drumming, something I knew Maya had no interest in. The kid had talent and I was determined to help him discover it. How would I do that now? Damn it, I totally blew it. I thought of my mother, who would now be completely alone, her husband and her only son having abandoned her too young. I thought of never being able to taste chocolate ice cream again, or a drippy peach. Feel the sun on my face, the wind in my hair. I acknowledged these facts with a sad desperation, still hovering near my body in case it might come back to life. I imagined a rescuer suddenly diving into the water, hauling my dead weight back to the surface, rolling me up onto the rocky shore, and pumping my chest until I spewed up sea water. Might I suddenly open my eyes and laugh at my own dumb luck for still being alive, claiming to have seen a bright light and a tunnel? A small glimmer of hope for a life I knew could no longer be. I looked over at an actual bright light and a tunnel, and wanted to laugh at the irony of it all. I was gently tugged toward that light, almost against my will. I felt an overwhelming desire to go that I resisted with everything I had. Strange to long for both life and death at the same time.

The diver found my wallet and an officer called our home in Seattle, where Maya was wise enough to leave her cell phone number on the voice mail message. They called the cell phone and left a message. Time passed, and the divers suspended their recovery efforts until the following morning. They decided to haul the entire car onto a barge with a crane, a difficult maneuver that I looked forward to witnessing.

From my post near my body, I longed to be with Maya when she received the news of my death. With that thought I arrived at Maya's sister Bethany's condo in Whistler. But I could still see my body trapped beneath the waves. I didn't know how this could be and felt as if I had split myself in two.

I watched as Maya turned on her phone to check messages, saw her listen to the message left by the RCMP, saw the color drain from her face. Bethany walked in and, looking quizzical, mouthed, "What's wrong?" Maya shook her head and continued to listen to the end of the message, her hands shaking. She dropped her hands, still holding the phone limply.

"That was the Lion's Bay police. They want me to call. There's been an accident on the Sea to Sky Highway."

"An accident? Who?"

"I can only assume it's Jay, since they're calling me, but why would he be there? He said he wasn't coming."

Maya redialed the number on her phone.

"No," she whispered in response to what she was told. "No! He didn't come skiing. It's not him. You've made a mistake. He wanted a quiet weekend. It's not him. How can you even be sure it's him?" Bethany had her arm around Maya as she listened with tears streaming down her cheeks. Maya nodded her head without speaking, eyes wide, mouth slack, before she slid slowly down the lemony yellow kitchen wall until her bum reached the floor and she could slide no farther, her knees sticking up, her feet sunk into the goofy pink fluffy slippers her sister had given her for Christmas. The cell phone slipped from her hand onto the floor unnoticed. I longed to hold her in my arms, touch her smooth skin. I wished I could tell her one last time how much I loved her.

Later, I sat with Calder and Maya on Bethany's guest bed. Maya held a box of tissues on her lap, her shaking hands grasping it from either side, as if it were a shoe box containing a tiny fragile bird like the one that Calder had once rescued, that Maya had desperately yet unsuccessfully tried to nurse back to life with a medicine dropper.

"Calder, there's been an accident," Maya said. Calder looked up from his Gameboy.

"What kind of accident?"

"It's your dad. He's been in a car accident."

"Is he in the hospital? Do we have to go see him now?" Calder sounded panicked. Maya could only shake her head through her unending tears, making a sawing noise as she pulled a tissue slowly out of the box, quickly dabbing her chin to catch another falling tear.

"Is he.... Is he... dead?"

Maya cried harder and leaned over to hug him.

"Daddy's dead?"

Maya nodded, still holding him in an embrace. "I'm so sorry, sweetie," she whispered.

"Maybe he's just in space," Calder said. She smiled faintly

at his upturned, hopeful face.

"No, Calder, he's in heaven. We can't see him anymore."

I'm here, I'm right here.

"When he gets back from heaven, can we all go and get ice cream?"

Absolutely! Was it just last night that I had been such an asshole to him?

"Is Daddy still mad at me?"

Oh Calder, No. I'm sorry about last night. Please don't remember me that way. Calder cried loudly now.

"He needs to come back! Daddy, come back now!" Calder looked directly at me.

I want to Calder, I really do.

"I'm so sorry, Cald, he can't. But he loves... loved you very much." Calder seemed better able to sense me – perhaps children are naturally more psychic – making the permanence of my death incomprehensible to him. I touched Calder's shoulder lightly, making him shiver, frustrated that I couldn't take him into my arms. I kissed Maya's cheek, wanting nothing more than to feel its warmth, to look into her eyes one more time. To have her looking back into mine.

I told you you were going to die! You didn't believe me. Calder's thought was clear.

You're right, Buddy. I didn't really understand. I'm sorry I didn't listen to you.

* * *

Maya and I never discussed our wishes for funeral arrangements. It never occurred to us that one of us could die so soon, despite my own father's death at a young age. I suppose in my own denial of death, the act of planning my own funeral seemed like a self-fulfilling prophecy. No way *this* Cavor would die young.

My father had been cremated, and his urn sat for years on the ornate mantle that my mother had bought at an antiques fair and stripped of its hideous green paint. I loathed the idea of an open casket – over-rouged cheeks, waxy coral lips, hands folded over the person's chest, like a macabre wax museum display. Maya, I felt, was of the same mind. Closed casket then, if she went the funeral route. But then what? A funeral home? A church? We never frequented such places. I couldn't imagine Maya trying to choose a coffin for me, the types of wood, the color of the satin lining. Laughable. No surprise when she opted for cremation. Clean, neat, compact. The cardboard coffin was included in the price.

Days on Earth passed and I floated in a sort of no-man's land. The tunnel and its light continued to beckon; I continued to resist. I visited my body the moment before the box containing it was hoisted onto the sleek, stainless table, built to slide into a square door where I would be reduced to dust, baked at 1700 degrees Fahrenheit for two hours until I was the consistency of ash with bits of bone mixed in. I watched as the flames engulfed the box, imagined the smell as acrid, one of burning hair and flesh. I wondered why I felt so little emotion at the incineration of my body.

✢ ✢ ✢

Maya and a group of people stood on the bow of a boat, a yacht really, under a rare, clear March Seattle sky, a jaundiced eyeball of a full moon witnessing it all. The salt breeze pushed a wisp of Maya's hair away from her face and she pulled her long black wool coat tighter around her shoulders. Calder stood next to her, wearing his camouflage snowboarding jacket, whining.

"When can we go? I want to go home. I'm cold."

"I know sweetie, but I'm going to need your help sprinkling Daddy's ashes on the water. But let's go inside now and get warmed up first."

Inside the large cabin, a group of our friends and family were sitting in white plastic folding chairs that had been lined up in rows across the parquet wood dance floor, under a mirrored disco ball. My mother sat in the front row, knees clenching her hands between them, back slightly hunched, looking straight ahead. Her whole body appeared to be glowing, shoots of coloured light emanating from her torso. Muddy grays, yellows, and blues swirled around her and seemed to morph into warmer shades of pink and orange when I sat beside her. My own light blended with hers in tiny arcs between us. I realized that everyone in the room had similar rings of colour enveloping their forms, something I vaguely understood to be auras. I realized I could now see the vibrations of atoms, electrons, particles of every object in the universe. Even thoughts had auras.

Around the room a broad spectrum of electromagnetic radiation – microwaves, infrared light, and UV light flickered and danced like the flames of a candle near an open window in response to the energy emitted through people's auras. This light energy seemed concentrated around electrical outlets and light fixtures but also around those who seemed to be grieving most – Maya, Calder, and my mother - because their auras appeared to radiate more energy than everyone else's.

My mother shivered in response to my presence and turned toward me, as though about to address me, but then she looked through me.

I love you, Mom. I'm sorry. I know how hard this is, but I will see you again soon. I felt myself fill with love of her, and together we became surrounded by a now familiar white light. She seemed to physically relax, her shoulders slumped slightly, and I noticed a tear rolling down her cheek.

Damn you! I jumped. I heard her thought as if she had slapped me across the face. *First your father and now you. What kind of cruel world is this?*

I'm sorry, Mom. I am so sorry.

I drifted away from her, shut out by her sorrow.

Maya and Calder, their coats flung on nearby chairs and

cheeks rosy from being outside, stood now in a group with her parents. Maya wore a black turtleneck over a tight-fitting pink dress, something I loved seeing her in but that she rarely wore. I knew she wore it to my funeral especially for me, despite it being socially inappropriate in the way it pulled tight over the roundness of her beautiful ass, creating a sensuality out of place in the roomful of black suits. Her hair pulled back off her pale face, eyes red-rimmed and swollen and her lips lush and pink, beautiful even in grief, she gripped her glass of wine, whose blood-colored surface rippled with each tear that clung to her cheek before launching itself into the abyss.

Stone-faced, Maya rebuffed her mother, Estelle, when she tried to put her arm around her daughter's shoulders. I reached out in a habitual way to take Maya into my arms, to comfort her in a way I hadn't done, I suddenly realized, for too long. I wanted desperately to put my arms around her, to calm her, but without my body I was as successful at hugging her as a double amputee might be. Our auras linked, though she seemed oblivious. I sensed a purpose for my death, in both my life and hers, but it angered me to try to account for something so meaningless, unwilling to forgive my own stupidity.

Calder was tired and cranky, a seven-year-old teetering on the edge of a meltdown. Without trying to, I surrounded us all, wishing to be a whole family again, which transformed the yellowish ambient light of the dim room to a glowing spotlight. Calder sighed and seemed calmer for the moment.

And then I saw Marcus Pellegrino. He sat drinking a scotch in a seat in a corner, far away from everyone. His presence at my funeral surprised me. Had Maya invited him? I saw her look at him from across the room and then quickly look away, but couldn't tell from her expression if she too was surprised by his presence or expecting it. He wore a black wool coat and sat erect at the bar, talking to no one. His greying hair slicked back, he wore a heavy, expensive watch and polished Italian shoes. Marcus looked every bit the rich prick. Despite his obvious effort trying to make eye contact with Maya, she seemed to want nothing to do with him.

Distracted by feedback from a microphone, a sound that looked to me like transparent ripples fanning away from the mic, I lost interest in Marcus. Funerals were not called funerals anymore. This was a "Celebration of Life". I tried to think of things that could be celebrated about my life. Maya, Calder, yes. They were both reasons to celebrate. But had I been a good husband, a good father? I'd been focused on my job, took pride in each promotion, earned increasing amounts of money, but spent more and more time at the office, on the road. I spent more time with a bunch of twenty-something programmers than with my own family. I felt young with my employees, like an older brother, going out for watery beer and doughy pizza after a long day, feeling guilty afterward arriving home long past Calder's bed time. I had wanted to live that carefree young man's life again – no responsibility, no mortgage, no one waiting for me at the end of the day.

Jake and Miles now stood together, each holding the neck of a long brown bottle of Red Hook, watching a slide show of photographs, a window into their boss's life, a world they had never experienced in the time they knew me. A soundtrack accompanied the photos – Stevie Ray Vaughn, Steely Dan, Stones. My baby pictures flashed across the screen accompanied by Stevie Ray's "Little Baby". School pictures, ridiculous photos of friends and family, early shots of a teenaged Maya at her cottage. She was wearing a bikini, waving from the dock, me poised behind her, about to push her in, causing her to lose her top, much to the embarrassment of us both, but funny years later. I had sleepwalked through my whole life, waking up now as a dead man.

Maya moved some of the folding chairs from the front rows so she could sit on the floor with Calder on her lap. A couple of other small children came and sat down next to them, instinctively trying to comfort in that natural way the adults seemed to have forgotten.

Rob, my best friend from high school who had flown in from Toronto, stood up after the slide show, taking charge.

"I just want to say a few words." Tiny lines crept around his smiling brown eyes. His once thick dark hair was now white and wiry, and a slight paunch stretched the buttons of his suit jacket. I couldn't remember the last time I'd seen Rob, and the changes surprised me.

"I honestly can't believe I'm standing here. I can't believe Jay's gone. Shit, man. He was way too young." The room remained silent. "I can't help thinking about this time in grade ten at Jarvis. The shit... oh sorry... I mean the crap—" laughter poured from the audience "—that we got into! Jay never used to eat the sandwiches he brought from home. Instead, he would stuff them into his locker so he could 'grow mold'. The various types of mold that grew on those sandwiches did fascinate me, but I enjoyed the laughs too. The smell by the end of the year stank up the entire hallway!" More laughter. "He wanted to be a geneticist back then, before he got into that computer stuff. I figured he would discover the cure for cancer or something. I don't really know when he got into the software world." I did want to be a geneticist. I volunteered at a lab at the University of Toronto when still in high school and loved it, but when I got to University I learned how much political posturing went on in the profession at the academic level, it turned me off. I took some computer science classes and eventually found myself in Seattle working at Microsoft. Rob told the audience about my jazz band and how I got all the girls, which wasn't exactly true.

"But he only ever had eyes for one girl." Rob looked down at Maya, who looked up him and smiled. "And who could blame him? Maya was hot!" Maya waved at him dismissively, still smiling and now blushing. "Dude, I know I haven't seen you in a while, we've been pretty lousy at keeping in touch, but man, I'm sure going to miss you." The speech paused as Rob swallowed several times and licked his lips, fighting back tears. I was sorry we had grown apart. How had I let that happen? I should have been a better friend, should have called more often.

The screen came alive with a movie that I remember we made during my stag party: a bunch of guys getting high on 'shrooms and playing mini golf, a shockingly young, thin version of myself kneeling down on the fake grassy carpet lining things up, pretending to be the next Arnold Palmer. The sound of my own giggle surprised me and I realized I hadn't laughed like that for a long time. Maya still sat cross-legged with Calder in her lap, laughing at the movie, but also crying, an occasional tear landing on the top of Calder's head. People stood in a circle around her, passing down tissues. She seemed small and lost. I touched her hair, trying to feel its silkiness, the twist of a curl.

Damn you Jay! Damn you damn you damn you!

More slaps across the face. I shouldn't have been surprised by her anger, but oddly I was hurt. Was she even sad that I was dead?

Daddy, when are you coming home? I heard Calder this time. *You were supposed to help me with my science fair project. And you promised to drum with me.*

Calder, I am so sorry!

Tears filled Calder's eyes, and he turned in towards Maya and cried silently into her chest. She kissed the top of his head.

"I'm sorry this is so hard," she said, her own tears welling.

"Daddy was supposed to help me with my science fair project. And drum with me! Now he can't do any of it! Why did he have to die?"

"Oh, sweetie. I don't know. I'm mad at him too. But he didn't mean to die..." *Did you?*

Maya, of course I didn't mean to die!

Estelle came over and crouched down beside her daughter and grandson.

"Should we do the ashes now?"

Outside, on the deck of the boat, Estelle held the urn that contained my ashes and pried open the lid that Peter, Maya's dad, had previously forced open with a screwdriver. The plastic bag holding my remains had already been snipped open so the breeze carried a little of the dust into the air. Maya held the urn down low enough for Calder to see its contents. The grey powder held chunks of white bone. Calder looked up at Maya.

"Is that Daddy?"

Maya nodded.

"What do I do?" he asked.

"You can reach in and take a handful and then sprinkle it onto the water." Calder shook his head.

"I don't want to touch it."

"It's OK, Calder. It's just the ashes from Daddy's body." She stopped talking and looked at her mother.

"Calder, if you don't want to do it, that's fine," Peter said. "You do whatever feels right." Calder looked relieved. Maya put her own hand into the urn and scooped out a handful. She poked through it with her fingers, looking at the pieces of bone.

"It's so weird to think this is Jay. It's so abstract. I can't make sense of it." She tipped her hand over the rail and watched as the dust fell between her fingers and floated in the wind.

"I love you, Jay."

I love you too, Lenie.

The ashes settled in a dusty swath on the surface of the indigo water, alight momentarily before dissolving into the salty depths. My mother, Maya's parents, and Rob each took handfuls and released them, whispering their own farewells to me. There was a long silence after everyone finished and they collectively stared into the water.

"Well, I guess that's it," Maya said abruptly. People began to make their way to the cabin of the boat. Maya and Calder remained where they were.

I felt a tug, saw a pulsating glow on the bow of the boat that I hadn't noticed before. My father waited there.

I still need to help her. Help Calder. They both hate me!

You will be better able to do that from where you are going than from where you are now. My father's thoughts were clear, though I couldn't see how.

How can I possibly help them when I'm dead?

There's a ton for you to learn, son. You just have to trust me.

As the boat made its way back to the dock, only Calder and Maya remained on the deck, peering over the rail, where the light from the now-bright moon reflected on the waves. When they arrived at the dock, Maya took Calder's hand and led him back inside. She looked tired and drawn, but I could tell from the glances that she snuck toward the back corner of the bar that she wanted to speak to Marcus. People flocked around her to say goodbye with long drawn-out hugs as Maya stood mute, eyes glazed, patting them absentmindedly on the back until they released her from their embrace, tears in their eyes. When the crowd finally thinned and her parents had taken Calder home in their car, she walked over to one of the bar stools next to Marc and perched.

"What are you doing here, Marcus?"

"I came to support you."

"I'm fine, really."

"I'm so sorry, Maya."

"I can't do this right now, Marc. I have to go."

Maya collected her coat and purse and walked over to where my mom waited and whispered into her ear. My mom nodded and got up, put on her coat, and they were gone. Marcus slowly finished his drink and walked down the gangplank. He wandered in the direction of his hotel. I no longer cared about Marcus Pellegrino.

Without any effort on my part, I drifted away from the boat, weightless, suspended in air that wasn't air. Engulfed in a silky whiteness, a kind of brightness that doesn't make you squint, I had the sensation of lying on a warm, sandy beach, the sun on my eyelids creating a kaleidoscope of a million colors performing dances of light and form. I moved slowly toward a tunnel. I guess all those dudes who died and came back to life were right about the tunnel thing. I finally stopped resisting the insistent undertow and followed my father "into the light", as it goes.

Chapter Four

March 6th, 2006

Jay,

I superstitiously knock on wood against my bizarre thoughts of doom. God, you've been gone now less than a month and already I think I'm going crazy. You know it's not my style to be superstitious. Just before I fall asleep, or in those moments before waking, an image or feeling comes — a car crash, Calder being kidnapped, a fire. Some unnamed disaster, waking me in panic. I reach over to touch the bedside table as if a tiny stroke of its slick, cherry wood surface might calm the chaos wracking my mind. I wake up clammy, and the night's terror is reduced to a silly memory in the daylight. Maybe it was a dream, maybe a premonition. Either way, I live a nightmare. I wake each morning only to have to relive another day of you not being here, not being anywhere. I have to work hard to convince myself that you're not just on a business trip.

I dropped the pen and journal into my lap and lay back on the pillow. Would writing a letter to Jay really help anything? He was dead for Crissakes, but my therapist suggested it as a way to deal with my grief. It was 5 a.m.

again and I couldn't sleep, so I gave it a try, but it felt strange. I put the journal and pen on the bedside table and rolled over and pulled the duvet over my head to try and hide from the day. I lay awake for another hour until the alarm went off. Using sheer will, I rolled back over to sit on the edge of the bed, my frozen feet on the fuzzy rug that's meant to warm them. The effort to stand was unbearable and I waited there, prone, until I thought it might be possible to straighten my legs. My feet sank into the carpet as I stood, knees bending, hands on my thighs so I could use them to push myself to a wobbly standing position. I made my way to Calder's room to wake him. I felt like I was a hundred years old.

School was starting again for Calder today. He'd been off for almost a month, between the President's Day mid-winter break and his dad's death. As usual, it was nearly impossible to wake him. He turned toward the wall, wrapped in just his sheet like a long, blue cocoon. I had to think very hard to remember the order of my day. Teeth? Shower? Breakfast? Get dressed? The movements came from muscle memory, padding to the bathroom, scraping the shower curtain across the tub, turning on taps, fingers in hair. Tears were washed away, down the drain. Tears turned to sobs, and I doubled over in the shower, then crouched down to sit on the bottom of the tub, clutching my knees tightly as water and tears washed over me. Can you see me? Are you there, Jay? When I turned off the shower, I felt my essence flow down the drain with all those tears. I wrung myself out and re-pieced the mosaics of my being together with each article of clothing I pulled over my body. I stared at my face in the mirror, weighing the benefits, but ultimately rejecting the application of makeup, which my puffy eyes defied. A grieving widow should never wear mascara.

I poured Cheerios into a bowl and set it in front of Calder. His hair was in his eyes and he looked angry or sleepy, it was hard to tell.

"I can't eat. I don't want to go to school. Can't I stay home for another day?"

"No. It's time to go back. We need to get back to our routines," I said as I pushed oatmeal around in my bowl.

"Everyone's going to look at me," Calder said.

"It will be OK. If they look at you, it's because they want to help. It's because they care about you." It's because they pity you. I pushed the thought away. I faced the same fears.

"But they probably won't notice you at all and they will just be happy to see you back at school."

I'm not sure who I was trying to convince of this, him or me. I started spreading peanut butter on bread for his lunch.

"I don't want peanut butter."

"We don't have anything else." Grocery shopping was out of the question. I wished Bethany could come back and stay a few more days, but she had her own kids who needed to get off to school each morning. I couldn't rely on my sister for everything. She would know what to do, what to say to Calder to make him go to school.

"Can't I have pizza?"

"We don't have pizza."

Calder slithered under the table. I grabbed his arm and tried to drag him out.

"Stop this, Calder. I can't do this right now. We have to catch the bus."

"I don't want to go."

I pulled his arm, pinching him unintentionally.

"OWWWW! You're hurting me!"

He began to cry. Hot tears sprang to my eyes.

"Get out NOW!" I yelled.

His cry turned to a sob.

"Get up. We have to go NOW!" I was just as hysterical as he was now. He crawled out from under the table, still crying. I held his coat out for him and he put it on.

"Please Mama, don't make me go," he said through hiccupped sobs.

My heart broke for him. He sounded so pathetic and sad. I couldn't say anything because I knew I would cave in and let him stay home for another day. I knew I couldn't let that happen, that getting back to school was the best thing for him. I handed him his backpack.

"Please Mama!" He dropped to the floor face-down and continued his dramatic sobbing routine.

"Let's go." I picked him up and stood him on his feet and walked him out the door. We didn't say anything on the way to the bus stop. He kicked a rock along the sidewalk with his boot. When the bus rolled up, he turned and looked at me, a look of pure anguish on his face. I waved and turned away.

I drove to the gallery, blindly, on autopilot, stopping at red lights, accelerating on green, staying in the right lanes, uncertain how fast I should be going. I couldn't decipher the colors, shapes and words that bombard me, or make them appear meaningful. I didn't care anymore about my paintings and their display locations for this new show. The curator hugged me, muttering, "Sorry for your loss," before scuttling away as if grief were a contagious disease. I stared at my painting, so cheery in fuchsia and yellow, and tried to avert my glance from the picture of the three of us, collaged in the center, happy, carefree. I took it down. Every painting in that place was steeped in meaning.

Someone approached me from behind. I wiped away a tear and turned to see Manuel, the gallery's installer, giving me that horrible look of pity as he tried to hold my gaze like he wanted to read my soul.

"I'm sorry for your loss," he said. God, I hated that line.

"Thanks, Manuel."

"So, hey, I'm just wondering if you'd like to go out for dinner with me sometime?"

I stood in shock staring at him.

"Manuel, I appreciate the offer, but my husband died three weeks ago. It's going to be a long time before I feel like going out for dinner, with you or anyone." I couldn't help sounding disgusted.

"Yeah. I understand. Just wanted to put it out there."

He slumped off. This is what my life had come to. Christ.

Home again, I wandered around the house, not quite knowing what I was supposed to do next. More memorabilia assaulted me. The pen cup Calder decorated for me last year for Mother's Day. The tiny card Jay gave me on Valentine's Day two years ago, the one embossed with vines and flowers. He wrote, "To Lenie, don't know what to say, but I love you. Happy Valentine's Day – J." The heart-shaped rock perched on top of my stack of household bills that languished in their lateness. It was the stone he found on Vashon during that rainy weekend we spent at the B&B. We stayed in the loft of an old barn. I had spent weeks bugging Jay to get away for a few days. He was so absorbed in his work, staggering in from the office after dinner every night, barely in time to tuck Calder into bed. I convinced him we needed a family weekend away and he agreed, which surprised me. The weather cooperated and the sun poked shyly from behind the clouds as we held hands, making our way along the rocky low tide near the Point Robinson lighthouse. Calder ran ahead, crouching over tide pools, sticking his finger into the anemones to make them squirt. I loved seeing Jay relaxed and happy, in a good mood, one I hadn't seen in a while. He forgot his work stress, if only for a weekend, and that made me happy. The crease between his eyebrows softened, and I watched as he strolled down the beach, stopping to crouch beside Calder to point out various sea creatures. We made love that night, quietly, so as not to wake Calder sleeping in the next room. It was delicious and slow and afterwards I basked tangled within his arms and legs, my warm breath against his chest.

That memory stuck in my throat, along with the tears that were again threatening to erupt. I swallowed them down, sat in front of the computer to distract myself, clicked the computer mouse randomly. I had forgotten that man, the person I married. We were like driftwood, Jay and I, floating toward each other until a wave took us and floated us apart. Now that wave had taken him. He was gone and I was left to float alone, adrift. Is it me who is lost, Jay, or you? I'm not sure anymore. We were both present and absent, with form and without. Come back, Jay. Please come back to me.

That night in bed, I continued the letter. I didn't know where else to put the sadness and guilt I was feeling. Words on a page seemed as good a place as any.

Did you see Marcus at your funeral? You probably wondered why he was there. I didn't expect him to come. He had no right to be there. You will never know how hard he tried to get me back after I started seeing you. I never told you how he used to come to my studio when we lived in Toronto sometimes while you were at work and I was there painting. He'd take me out for lunch and tell me how much he still loved me, but I'd heard it all before. It was his story. Always the smooth talker. Besides, I'd fallen in love with you by then, Jay. I admired your ambition and the respect people had for you. A big change from Marc. Sure, I'd admired him, but I don't think I ever had the respect for him that I had for you. And maybe I never had the love for him either. I don't know. I thought I did. I wonder now what you thought of him. I don't know why I never asked you. Anyway, I guess it doesn't matter anymore, does it?

I hear your voice sometimes in my head, disembodied, spoken silently from within. Do I speak or do you? Are you hearing my thoughts? Reading this letter? Have we become one being? My body, your thoughts. Perhaps I'm going insane. I'm in danger of such insanity, I realize. I can hear you telling me I'm not insane, but what do you know? You're dead. Shit. Why the hell did you have to die? I need you, dammit. You got off easy. I'm sure there are no dishwashers to unload wherever you are.

Please come back,
Love Maya.

Chapter Five

No Return

My journey through the tunnel can only be described as disorienting and unexpectedly frightening. It was a dark, rock-like cave with an expanding circle of light at the opposite end. I hesitated before entering. It was foreboding, and I didn't want to leave Maya and Calder. But my father kept coaxing me, the way he did when I was little and he tried to get me to go on the roller coaster with him. "C'mon, J.J. It's no big deal. You can do this in a snap!" Except he did this without words.

I allowed myself to be propelled forward. For a time I could see nothing but blackness, a sensation similar to trying to wake from anesthesia. I heard singing but felt as if I couldn't open my eyes or move my body. I finally came through the tunnel and entered a patch of cloudy white fog. The stillness around me, the quiet, was striking, but periodically I heard chimes and drums, some sort of music I couldn't quite identify. I saw tiny lights flash by, headed in all directions away from me, like the sparks that fall off a firecracker. I sensed they were other soul-spirits. I could see their faces and could almost feel them inside me as each one flew past my line of vision.

I felt light and warm, as if filled with sunlight. I had become an orb of light, like those around me. I had no shape and as I moved I left a trail of glittery light. I later learned that only the most recent arrivals had glittery trails – the body's expended energy exiting this realm to fall back to earth. A profound sense of being understood overwhelmed me, and words came to me in a rush – power of thought, empathy, compassion, love.

I felt a euphoric sense of anticipation, as if about to join a party where I would be the guest of honor. I surrendered, letting an unknown power propel me in the direction I needed to go. I felt very relaxed as I floated through a gigantic crystal-like dome, built with a glittery mosaic of white ice particles. The layers arching above me seemed meaningful in their order. The space was infinite yet peaceful in its vastness. *I wish Maya could see this.* Abruptly, something stopped me – my thought of Maya. My father, still beside me, explained that I was about to be met by my guide, my "transporter", Alice. "She will accompany you to 'Intake'," he said.

"Don't I stay with you?" My sense of peace shattered. My illusion of being an all-knowing orb of light, replaced by my ratty Adidas and sweatshirt.

"I'll see you later, Jay. For now, you're in need of counseling."

"What? You mean I'm going to therapy? In heaven?! Why can't I continue being a ball of light like the others?"

My father's eyes looked sympathetic. "You still have a lot to learn, J.J. At Intake you'll take your human form in order to have a smoother transition. You've received a sensation of what it's like to be an orb as a sort of incentive. To give you a purpose to your learning. A goal to strive for. I know it seems ironic. Therapy in heaven. But it's not really therapy. 'Intake' is sort of a transitory place that newly dead spirits hang out in, while they get used to being dead. It's where you'll review your immediate past life on Earth, your life as Jay."

"You have got to be kidding me!" To say I was not pleased about having to analyze every nuance, every mistake, every triumph of my life on Earth was an understatement. Death was not at all what I'd imagined.

"Hello Jay. I'm Alice." Her voice was not audible. I heard her thoughts, and the gentleness in her eyes put me at ease. I could make out her features, perhaps by merely imagining them. Her soft-spoken thoughts made me think of her as a grandmotherly type with startling pale, watery blue eyes and an orb-like body, but with recognizable features like I had, though less formed than mine. She wore a nondescript, pale blue dress but seemed to have no arms or legs. Alice smiled more on the right side of her face, giving the impression she enjoyed some tiny irony, one I had missed. Tendrils of fine white hair ruffled around her head like a coronet. She was the sort of person who in her past life might have worked in a library – unassuming, knowing, immensely helpful.

"Why don't you come with me?" Alice said. I turned to my father, who somehow gestured his approval by moving back out of the way.

"I'll see you again soon." I tried to wave, but no gesture came, just the thought.

I followed Alice into an amorphous room, with shimmering opalescent walls and a not-so-soothing fountain made of brook stones in the corner. A window overlooked a harbor with sailboats bobbing in the water, seagulls squawking and swooping, a perfect blue sky. Alice gestured toward a white velvet couch, something my mother would have shuddered at and forbidden me to sit on for fear of marring its whiteness. But the couch, and for that matter the entire room, was a formality, since I couldn't actually feel its plush surface – another remnant of human life meant to put me at ease. Nothing about a white couch put me at ease. Alice looked at me and waited.

"Are you for real?" I asked.

She blinked. "Do you think I'm real?"

"You look real. But nothing seems to make sense here."

"You've had a shock. It's going to take you some time to remember."

"Remember what? Why the hell am I here?" It came out harsher than I had intended. Alice remained calm. Gentle.

"There is much for you to remember. Because of the nature of your death, its suddenness, we haven't had time to prepare you. It's going to take a little longer than usual to get you re-acclimated."

"Re-acclimated?"

"Yes. You need to spend some time getting used to being here again."

"Again?"

"Yes, Jay. You've been here many times before."

"I have?"

"In your sessions here, we will be reviewing your life, seeing where you may have taken a different path, what aspects of your life might still be holding you back. From remembering who you are."

"I know who I am! I'm Jay Cavor!"

Alice just smiled.

"Can I leave?"

"You can. It's up to you. No one here will force you to do anything against your will. You always have a choice, Jay. But know that leaving will simply prolong the process."

I slumped back into the illusional couch, exasperated.

"Why don't we try a simple exercise?" Alice suggested.

"Fine. Whatever."

"Think of a memory from your childhood. A simple one. A time that made you happy."

The room vanished and I stood on a bed playing Jimmy Page on a snowshoe with a bunch of girls singing into hairbrush microphones. One of the girls, a very young Maya, surprised me and made me laugh, landing me immediately back in the room with Alice.

"Shit! I forgot all about that day! We had a blast as kids at Maya's cottage that summer... At least until–"

The glass-like floor was a window into my life that played like a movie, with me an integral part of the action. It was a replay of my life in all dimensions. Thoughts, I realized again, were transparent in this realm. A thought equaled an action or a visual, and you could communicate thoughts without meaning to. Thoughts had the ability to show up right there on your own personal movie-screen floor.

"Very good," Alice said. "Now try a tougher memory. Perhaps one that made you very sad. What happened later that day, for instance?"

The floor grew dark then lighter, opening onto a familiar scene from the deck of the Willis's cottage on Georgian Bay, its breathtaking views of the water and crazy conifers forming a real-life Tom Thomson painting with their giant comb-like branches, acquiescing to the prevailing westerly winds. I stood on the dock where everyone hung out in bathing suits and flip flops, the girls' tanned skin shiny orange and flowery-smelling from the crumpled tubes of Bain de Soleil lying beside the beach chaises. The younger kids floated in the water wearing oversized lifejackets, learning to keep the tips of their water-skis up. My dad coached from the back of the boat, "That's it... almost... you're nearly there," flashing a triumphant grin when they finally took off, wobbly on bent knees and heeled over at the waist as my dad punched his fist in the air. "You did it!"

Later, he stood grilling hamburgers and hot dogs on the deck overlooking the water, taking swigs from brown stubbies of Labatt's Blue while the moms piled the table with condiments and potato salad, giggling from too much Chardonnay. After dinner, us kids scampered down to the boathouse where we slept, girls in one room, boys in another, blasting Pat Benatar's *Heartbreaker* on the cassette player, the girls jumping on the beds, holding their microphone hair brushes, wailing the words as loudly as possible.

The earlier memory replayed. I took an ancient snowshoe off the wall, strumming its animal-gut strings with a windmilling arm, crouching down on bent knee, the next Jimmy Page.

After some of the younger kids were asleep, Maya Willis and I snuck off to smoke one of the DuMauriers she had stolen from her dad. I'd had the hots for Maya for as long as I could remember, despite our two-year age difference. As luck had it, our fathers were good friends who got together often. But I knew she had a thing for Marcus Pellegrino, whose cottage was just down the road. I'd seen her swim all the way to the raft between cottages just so she could get a glimpse of him doing flips with his friends off the dock. We'd bumped into him and his brother a couple of times at the tennis court down the road. He was a few years older than Maya, and I could see the appeal of his broad shoulders and muscular thighs and the confidence he possessed as he walked down the gravel road with a cigarette tucked behind his ear. At fourteen, I was skinny enough to have to hold my trunks around my waist every time I dove into the water for fear of losing them. At the tennis court, Maya laughed every time she lobbed a ball and picked up balls without bending her knees so that we all got a good flash of her tennis-skirted behind. During one game, when the ball landed outside the chain link, she went dashing into the undergrowth to find it.

"Be careful of the poison ivy in there," Marcus warned.

"I will!" She rustled around for a bit and then we heard, "Found it!" followed by "Oh-oh." Marcus found some jewelweed that he insisted was the antidote and rubbed it on the inside of her thigh as she put her hand on his back to steady herself. I saw her close her eyes and inhale as if she could possess the very smell of him.

That night we were alone on the dock. She wore her yellow, over-sized Scooby Doo t-shirt, with just undies underneath and a shoulder poking out the neck hole. I tried not to look at her as she sat beside me, our feet dipping into the water, and so I leaned back on my hands, trying to look cool, watching the stars and the perfect, full moon.

We talked about people in our schools and passed the smoke between us. Our schools were close enough to play football against one another, and I had once seen her at a game, leaning over the railing of the bleachers shouting deliriously at one of the players, probably the quarterback. Her faded jeans were tight, but not coat hanger tight, like the ones my friend Brad's older sister wore. I once caught a glimpse of Desiree in her room, sprawled on the floor using a coat hanger to yank up the zipper. Maya's jeans fit just right, with a glint of silver from the safety pins she used to tighten them against her calves. When I spotted her at the game, I leapt from my school's side of the bleachers where I sat, waving my arms like a lunatic. She waved nervously before turning back to the game, probably hoping she never saw me again.

We heard laughter coming down the path toward us. We stood up quickly and I threw the butt into the lake just as our parents stepped onto the dock.

"Hey, Dad." My father didn't seem to notice the trail of smoke that escaped my nostrils. My heart sank when I saw Marcus come loping up behind them. Maya saw him too and pushed her hair behind her ear as she looked at him and smiled. Marcus smiled back.

"We're going to go for a little paddle," my dad said, a beer still in his hand, stumbling slightly as he hooked a foot into the canoe to bring it closer to the dock. "Do you guys wanna come?"

"Nah, I'm good," I said, hoping Maya would say the same thing.

"I'm not really dressed for it," Maya said, looking disappointed. "But I could change!"

"No, you stay with Jay," her dad said. "Three is enough for this tippy thing." Pete held the canoe as my dad tried to get in.

"Frank, be careful," my mom said, always the worrier.

"Jeez, Maggie, we're just going out to admire the moon, no biggie." Dad, balanced now astride the gunnel, winked at us. The canoe wobbled beneath his feet.

"Careful, Mr. Cavor," Marcus said, grabbing my dad's upper arm to steady him.

"I'm fine, I'm fine."

"Frank, seriously," my mom said.

"C'mon, Maggie, let's go have another glass of wine. The boys will be fine." Maya's mother, Estelle, put her arm around my mom's shoulders and led her back up the path.

We watched as the men paddled away and the canoe tipped severely as my dad tried to sit on the cross beam and grab a paddle.

"Whoa! Jesus!" I could hear Dad's voice clearly across the water. I turned to Maya and noticed, over her shoulder, the lifejackets sitting in a pile behind her.

"Dad?" A halfhearted call. I didn't want to interrupt what I had going on with Maya, stoked that she hadn't gone with Marcus in the canoe. We resumed our seats at the end of the dock, watching as the men disappeared into darkness. Maya hugged her knees inside her t-shirt. We didn't say anything for a long time.

"I'm glad the moon is full tonight," I said, finally. Maya shivered. "You cold?"

"No, I'm fine." She rested her chin on her knees.

"Hey, you can lean against me if you want." I hoped I sounded nonchalant but bit my lip to keep from saying something dumb when she wiggled herself between my legs and leaned back against my chest, her arms still hugging her knees. My wrists started to ache with the weight of us both, but I didn't dare move. We sat watching the moon reflect on the water, silent in our thoughts.

"Is that them?" Maya sat up a little so I did too, hoping for the chance to put my arms around her, but she struggled out of her cocoon and stood up. I squinted into the darkness and could make out a shape getting larger and the slight white of tiny waves made by paddling.

"Call 9-1-1!" The cry had an unmistakable desperation to it. Maya looked at me with horror movie eyes, recognizing her father's voice, and she bolted up the path.

On one knee, paddling hard, Pete, the most experienced canoeist, maneuvered the canoe towards the dock.

"Grab the lifejackets and get in!" I stood frozen. "Get in!" I leaped towards the lifejackets, threw them into the canoe, then stepped in carefully.

"Put one on!" Kneeling in a puddle in the center, I grabbed a lifejacket, almost falling backward as Pete pushed off from the dock with the paddle.

"Maya's calling 9-1-1," I told Pete as I struggled to wrap the pale canvas ties around the orange-covered floats of my life jacket. "Where's Marcus? Where's my dad?" Pete paddled behind me so I couldn't see his face.

"Jay, your dad fell in when the canoe tipped." Pete's tone was ominous. "Marc's diving for him, but we need help." His words made no sense to me in that moment.

"Marc's diving for him?"

"When the canoe tipped, only Marcus and I came up." We lurched forward violently with Pete's strong strokes. I fell back, my ass now soaked.

Marcus surfaced with a small splash in the distance, flipped and disappeared again into the patent-leather surface of the water.

"You stay in the canoe, Jay. You need to alert the police or whoever comes to help. I'm going to keep diving." I held both rails as the canoe tilted and Pete lowered himself into the water. Marcus came up, panting as he clung to the side of the canoe as Pete dove in.

"We'll find him," Marcus managed, too winded to say more. We watched Pete surface and dive a couple of times until I couldn't stand it any longer. I pulled off my lifejacket and, despite Marcus's protests, jumped over the side of the canoe, shivering with cold. I paddled toward Pete and took a deep breath. A rush of bubbles stinging my nose interrupted the underwater silence. For a moment my panic subsided, until in the blackness I lost my bearings, unable to tell up from down. A flash of something pale below my feet elicited an audible scream, my mouth filling with water as I kicked my way to the surface, gasping for air, coughing. I was a surprisingly long way from the canoe.

"Get back to the canoe, Jay," Pete yelled from about fifty feet away, the canoe just beyond him. "You were just meant to be our lookout and to help keep the canoe in position. We'll find him, I promise."

"But I saw something!" I dove again, this time better prepared. I could feel my hair floating around my head and see the whiteness of my own hand. I searched the blackness for what I had seen before, moonlight touching something pale, a fish or human flesh. *Don't let him be dead.* A muffled yell from above caused me to do a 180-degree swivel for one last look before breaking the surface. Pete, waving one arm, swam awkwardly toward the canoe, which now floated free, unmanned. I saw Marcus break into freestyle, heading toward Pete. I tried to do the same but instead flipped to my back in fatigue, twisting my head as I swam to stay on course, kicking hard.

By the time I got to the canoe, Marcus was already in, trying to pull my dad up while Pete and I each held an end steady. The canoe began to tip, but Pete held it and somehow Marcus got my dad's limp body into it. Marcus kneeled over my father, who now lay in the bottom, skin gray, water sloshing against his face. Pete pulled himself up and in, resumed his place in the back of the canoe, and picked up the paddle. Marcus was attempting to give my dad mouth-to-mouth and chest compressions. I wanted to jump in and knock him out of the way. I needed to be the one helping my dad, but I had to cling to the outside of the canoe. There was no room for me with my father taking up the entire bottom.

My kicks contributed little to our progress toward shore and I knew I created drag for Pete. We could see flashing red and blue lights off to the right, through the trees of the shoreline, making their way along the road. Marcus tilted my father's head back, pinched his nose and breathed into his mouth, desperation on his face as he waited a few seconds, then repeated.

"C'mon, c'mon, Mr. Cavor, breathe!"

I kicked like mad, every muscle in my body burning. At the dock, the police and paramedics were waiting. Two policemen held the canoe as the paramedics hauled my father in his cut-off jeans and black Rolling Stones t-shirt – the mouth and tongue mocking – onto the dock, where they began more chest compressions and clamped an oxygen mask over his nose and mouth.

"Damn him! Damn him!" my mother yelled behind them, held back by Estelle. "I told him not to go!" She bordered on hysteria. Estelle tried to steer her away, but my mom wiggled loose and kneeled on the dock just behind the paramedics, crying.

"Help him for godssakes!"

I wanted to go and comfort my mom, but I couldn't move, rooted to the spot. Maya had her head tucked into Marcus's chest and his arms were around her, comforting her. Later, after they took my dad away in the ambulance, after I sat with my mom in the sterile, submarine green hospital waiting room, after the doctor appeared, his jaw clenched, after I held my father's grey cold hand, his gold wedding band the only color, after the long, silent drive back to the cabin, I sat on the end of the dock, amongst the debris left by the paramedics – a syringe, torn plastic wrappings, a latex glove. The moon disappeared as the horizon turned a muted salmon-pink. I kicked my legs gently in the water, their undulating form below the surface tinged a pasty grey-green. I willed my dad to swim up, grab my feet, and laugh hysterically at his hoax. Peering down, attempting to see farther than humanly possible, I saw a flash of something move in the depths. I kicked violently, marring the image, lashing out at the sinister lake. A crow, perched high in a pine tree, cawed loudly at me. Still dressed in my damp Levis and t-shirt, I slid into the water, my eyes open, my heart pounding loudly, its weight crushing, yet oddly comforting, I urged the darkness to deliver me to my dad. Limply, I floated to the surface and took a breath of air despite myself. The crow cawed again and flew away.

My mother and I never went back to the Willis's cottage after that day and I only saw Maya once afterward, at a game. I didn't wave and she pretended not to notice me.

The floor blackened and I was back in the intake room, the fountain burbling ferociously. Alice sat demurely, waiting.

"That was rough. I had forgotten some of those details. I blamed myself for not being able to save him. I also hated Marcus for being there."

"Yes. And you were angry."

"Very, yes."

"Do you think your father's death was in any way related to your own?"

"What? No! Why would you suggest that?"

"Sometimes as humans we subconsciously create our actions. You realize that before you became Jay Cavor, you chose the elements of your lifetime as him? You chose who your parents were. You chose a life where you were unable to save your father from drowning."

"What?! That's insane! Why would I choose something like that?"

"In order to grow, Jay. You also chose to die the way you did, at the moment you did."

"Why would I choose to die in such a stupid way? Why would I choose to leave my wife and son alone?"

"Part of what you went to the Earth realm to experience was compassion and a sense of self-worth."

"How has dying helped me learn that?"

"Think about it, Jay. How have your feelings towards Maya changed since you died?"

The floor trick had me back in Toronto on our wedding day at Casa Loma, where I now found myself dancing with Maya in the courtyard. Her auburn hair fell in loose curls around her shoulders, which were bare and soft. She appeared ethereal in her wedding dress, made of heavy satin with many tiny silken buttons that began between her shoulder blades, and created a sensual line across her bottom. I wanted more than anything to run my hand over them, over her. She whispered the words of the Nina Simone song in my ear. *My baby don't care for shows, my baby don't care for clothes, my baby just cares... for... me...*

Our cheeks ached from smiling so much that day, and now as we danced alone in the courtyard, the wet stones of the old gothic stone mansion smelled fresh and damp, and the pollen from the canopied trees created a dusty yellow carpet under our feet. Faint strains of music came through the French doors, making our dance much more romantic now that we were not in the middle of the large dance floor in front of two hundred guests.

Reuniting in Pompeii after Maya's fortuitous breakup with Marcus, Maya and I traveled together for a few weeks before I returned to Toronto. She finished her program at the monastery and Marc seemed to disappear from her life. We spoke little of him. We married a year later and then waited a few years before deciding to have a child. When she told me she was pregnant, I was stoked, but sitting at work the next day I realized I couldn't just quit my job anymore if I didn't like it. My job and paycheck took on new importance. I needed to loosen my tie, stand up, and walk outside. I bought life insurance the next day. My father taught me that. I knew better than to leave Maya and a baby with nothing if I died a stupid, untimely death. A few months after my dad died, my mom was forced to sell the house, and we moved into a small rental cottage in the Beaches. Her work as a nurse at Toronto General was steady, but I worked as a bartender in the evenings to put myself through University.

I loved being a dad, though I wasn't great with the baby thing: incessant crying, poopy diapers, cranky wife. But I cherished those moments when Calder's tiny sausage-like body with its sour milk smell melded into mine and he fell asleep on my chest. And those belly laughs. I couldn't get enough of those.

I imagined what felt like tears form in my eyes as I remembered cradling his curled newborn body against my chest one more time, a tiny baby hand outstretched across my shoulder. In another memory I held his naked body in the bathroom mirror, a look of wide-eyed awe on his face, and I held his tiny hand as he learned to walk naked in the grass. I hid with him in the hollowed base of a giant shrub as Maya pretended to look for us, his giggles giving away our hiding place.

Once Calder started walking and talking, I found him a bit more fun. He laughed those great baby laughs when I threw him high into the air, a look of both terror and pure joy on his face that always made me catch him and clutch him into a big bear hug. Yet I'm ashamed to admit I was jealous of the bond Maya had with Calder, his begging to be pulled into her arms, something he rarely did with me. One chilly afternoon as I tried to put Calder's coat on, he pulled away and yanked the coat out of my hands, demanding 'Mama do it!' in that way kids do. I saw red.

"Are you teaching him to hate me?"

"What are you talking about?"

"He's such a mama's boy! Christ, he won't even let me put on his goddamned coat!"

"Jay, he's three."

"You're coddling him."

"I'm not. This is what babies do, Jay. They cling to their mamas." Calder stared at me across Maya's shoulder, as if to mock me. I stuck my tongue out at him and he began to cry.

"Oh great. Now he's crying. Maybe if you got home in time to put him to bed once in a while, or didn't spend the entire weekend doing your home projects or tuning out in front of the TV, you would have a better relationship with your son!" Her anger surprised me.

I sunk further into Alice's white couch.

"I took so much for granted. After that little spat, I did my best to make it home earlier, and Maya, to her credit, worked harder to find times for Calder and I to be alone together. God, what an idiot I was! Of course, she never took my shit, one of the many things I loved about her. Things improved when Calder turned four and he suddenly became Daddy's boy. We took trips to Home Depot where he rode the lumber cart, dove his hands into boxes of screws, and I taught him the names of all the tools. I guess that fight with Maya was a good lesson for me. Nothing ever stays the same for long. Shit. I guess I never fully appreciated how much I loved her. I took her for granted."

"Good, Jay. What about Calder?"

"I took him for granted too. Now Calder has a full life ahead of him and will have to live it with the difficulties of being a boy without a father. I hate knowing what kind of life he has in store. It sucks."

"It's a life Calder chose, Jay. From this world, before he was born. His spirit needed to learn through the difficulties of not having a father, in order to advance his own growth. He too has lessons to learn, lessons he will learn through your death."

"That's messed up."

"Not really. It will soon make more sense for you. Can you see how your death might have also helped Maya in her path?"

"No. She seems pretty miserable. I find it hard to get close to her, like she has a shield around her."

"Yes, that's common among newly grieving people. She

will be closed off for a while. But you can give her signs that you're around, watching over her."

"Signs?"

"You know: smells, lights turning on or off, music that comes on the radio that is meaningful to you both, dreams, that sort of thing."

"Huh. OK. How do I do that?"

"Like everything in this realm, Jay. With the power of thought. People who are experiencing the strong emotions that grief cause are often very open to these signs."

"She might not want to hear from me. I think she's angry with me for dying. Plus, I wasn't always the best husband."

"Why is that?"

"For a bunch of reasons..."

I wouldn't have admitted it in life, but our sex life suffered after Calder was born. We both seemed to lose interest. We were busy. Her pregnant body turned me off. It freaked me out that I might hurt the baby if we had sex. Then when Calder was born, Maya's focus was all on him. There was never a good time. Maya nursed Calder for a year and wore this hideous nursing nightgown, with slits cut lengthwise down the front, exposing her breasts with their wide brown nipples. I think after a while she just gave up trying to get laid, and I didn't push the matter, or try to seduce her in any way.

"That's perfectly normal, Jay." Alice's comment startled me, since I hadn't spoken my thoughts out loud. I kept forgetting about the mind reading. I really had no intention of telling Alice about our sex life.

"Childbirth is an intense emotional experience," Alice continued. "I'm sure Calder's birth reminded you of your own father and his loss in your life."

"Maybe. I never really linked my dad's death with Calder's birth before." I saw a brief image of Calder's tiny body, wrapped in a soft blue blanket and nestled into my arms as I lay on the couch. It was a moment I was overcome with emotion. Tears streamed down my cheeks as I looked into his tiny sleeping face. I couldn't have explained then what the tears were about, but my confusing emotions in that moment now made sense.

"Birth is a powerful reminder of the cycle of life and death. Witnessing the birth of your own child can elicit some pretty intense emotions that may have interfered with your sex life."

"I can't say I ever thought about grief much. After my dad died, I just threw myself into school and later, work. I worked harder than most people, maybe to prove to myself that I was better than my dad or something, as if I could make myself too good or too important to die."

"Working hard is also a good escape from the emotions of grief. You don't have to think about your loss."

"Yeah, that makes sense."

"Which is perhaps why the birth of your son caused you such anxiety. You no longer had control of your life."

"That's for sure."

"Perhaps in your mind, sex equated to a loss of control, potentially spurring messy emotions."

I cringed at her words. I hated all this psycho-babble. I had no desire to talk about sex with my afterlife therapist.

"Maybe…"

"You can still let her know how much you loved her. It's never too late."

"How do I do that?"

"Like I said before. With the signs. And in dreams. Let her know you're around."

"OK, I'll try."

Alice smiled. "There are endless possibilities, Jay. I think it could teach you both a little about yourselves."

"Teach us what?"

"Jay, I can't answer that. It will come from your experiences. You may also use the same techniques to connect with Calder. He needs your guidance. Don't you remember your grief after your father died?"

"Not really. I blocked it out. Is that why I'm in therapy for the dead?"

"Transitional Intake is a common path toward accepting your death. Most people experience some form of it."

"What do you have to do in your life to avoid it?"

Alice smiled.

"Oh, I get it. When I know the answer to that question, I won't need the therapy, right?"

"Something like that, yes."

"So what do I do now?"

"You look for opportunities to connect with your family in your new incarnation. Children are more easily accessible to us. They have not yet developed belief systems that block them from seeing what is right in front of them."

"Ha. You make it sound easy. Like I'm just going to hover over Calder's world and have little chats with him. Tell him what to do. Isn't that like trying to control his fate? I thought someone else had that job."

"Your job will be to direct your family toward opportunities that will enrich their lives."

"How will I know what those opportunities will be?"

"When it's time for you to know, you will know."

"That's vague. Can't I get something a little more concrete?"

Alice smiled again. "Well, Jay, that's it for today."

Chapter Six

May 12th, 2006

Jay,

    What to say to you exactly? I sit here in our too big bed, your imprint still visible in the ten-year-old mattress despite the four months you've been gone. I type my thoughts, my lap warmed by the heat of aluminum circuitry, thinking that you might hear in bits and bytes, a secret language of the dead. Your bathrobe still smells of your shaving cream and a sweetish smell like candy apples that was uniquely yours. Perversely, it is still flung over the green velvet chair in the corner where you left it that morning. I can't bear to move it. I run my fingers over it, or sometimes hold it to my nose, trying to infuse myself with your scent, as if that might bring you back to life.

    I can't decide between my bouts of pillow-muffled sobs if I am mad at you for dying or if this boiling emotion is grief. A surprising anger spreads across my being, a stain that refuses to be rubbed away. I hate you for dying on me, on us. I almost wonder if you did it on purpose, to be the martyr of our unresolved fight that morning, passing your guilt to me to bear for a lifetime. I know you didn't want to visit my sister for the weekend, but selfishly, I wanted you there. I thought your presence would prove your devotion to your family, to me. I am not *blameless. Did you drive spitefully, anger driving you right off that cliff? Damn you. So selfish to leave me with this guilt. Or perhaps I am irrational in grief, my anger and guilt unwarranted.*

The insurance agency called asking if Jay had been depressed, had been seeing a therapist, if he'd seemed different in the weeks before he died. It took me a few minutes before I fully understood why they were asking me such questions.

"Do you think my husband committed suicide?"

"No, no ma'am. Nothing like that. These are just routine questions..."

"Bullshit! I think I'm done talking with you. There is no way my husband drove himself off that cliff and I'm disgusted that your company would insinuate such a thing!"

I got off the phone and burst into tears. Could Jay have killed himself? Was he so unhappy in his life with me? Or was this just a big company trying to avoid a large payout? I chose to believe that Jay fell asleep at the wheel and didn't take his own life out of spite to get back at me. The thought had me laughing and then crying. Was Jay's life with me miserable? A momentary scene flashed in my mind. Jay, leaning over a steaming bowl of beef stew I had made, simmering it over the stove for an entire Sunday afternoon a few weeks before he died. He took large spoonfuls and tore into the rustic loaf of bread I bought to go with it, using it to wipe clean his bowl. When he was done, he sat back, reached over and grabbed my hand, to show his pleasure.

"That was amazing, Lenie. God. I am so lucky to have you!" I remembered the sensation of what I had felt at that moment, the warmth, the happiness, the contentedness. As we stood side by side by the sink cleaning up afterwards, I draped Jay's big arm around my shoulder like a heavy fox stole, warm and protective. I felt safe in his embrace. Surely that was not a man who would kill himself out of spite?

He was too devoted to Calder to kill himself. As proof, I

thought of the image of a baby Calder that Jay had installed as his computer wallpaper - the way he held Calder's chubby thighs as he thrust him up in the air, his two-year-old body rigid as he looked down at his dad, giggling; and Jay's pride at being there when Calder swallowed his first loose tooth with chewing on a bagel, Jay soothing his tears when Calder thought the tooth fairy wouldn't come. I can still see those crinkles in the corner of his eyes when he smiled that pleasure-smile, content with a life that always seemed to amaze him, one I knew deep down Jay never felt he deserved.

Jay was never the same after his father's death. It's strange that I was with him that day, a day indelibly burned into my childhood. It was the first death I had ever witnessed, the first funeral I had ever been to. It chiseled away my smug sense of security. I knew Jay had a crush on me then, but my 16 to his 14 was impossible math for a teenager and I saw Jay as something like a little brother. Still I was flattered he liked me, even though I had Marcus. Marcus was older and dangerous and perhaps toxic. I liked him, but he thought I was too young, or innocent, or something that made me not attractive to him.

Until the night of Jay's dad's death.

I tried to console Jay when he came home from the hospital that night, but it was like he didn't even see me. He pushed me away and walked down to the dock and I understood, but was hurt that I couldn't comfort him. I needed to be held and found my way to Marcus's bunk house, where we fell into each other in a strange, desperate way. I lost my virginity that night with Marcus, our lovemaking furtive and hungry and sweaty, and a little frightening.

The next day, everyone left the cottage and I didn't see Marcus for a few months. We went to different high schools. It wasn't until Homecoming that I heard from him. He called me on the phone. His voice, out of the context of the cottage, was unfamiliar, and it took me a while to figure out who it was. He asked me to his high school's dance and I felt my knees wobble when he said the words. We got serious after that night and dated during his whole senior year and into the summer. Marcus chose to go to the University of Toronto so he could stay in the city and be near me, but it didn't really work out between us. He wanted to hang out with his university friends and didn't want the embarrassment of a high school girlfriend. That was the first time he broke my heart.

I didn't see Marcus again for a couple of years. I was finishing my art degree and on a whim I decided to invite him to my senior thesis show. He hadn't always been incredibly supportive of my art. I didn't think he'd show, but then, as I stood talking to one of my girlfriends, he breezed in the door and my heart skipped a beat. His dark hair was longish and combed back; he wore a leather jacket and jeans and carried a motorcycle helmet under his arm. When he spotted me, I pretended I didn't notice him. As he approached, I turned toward him and saw a look in his eyes I could only describe as desire. The feeling was electrifying. No one had ever made me feel so desired. We went for Chinese food in Chinatown and caught up. I grabbed at pieces of barbecue pork with my chopsticks as he talked.

"I was an idiot, Maya. I should never have let you go."

"You're right. You shouldn't have. I was the best you're ever going to get," I joked, smirking at him.

"You're right about that." He wasn't laughing. He was dead serious.

"I was joking, Marcus. I was heartbroken, but I got over it. See? Look how well I've adjusted. I can even eat my food with chopsticks." I clicked them at his and then picked up another piece of pork and stuffed the whole thing into my mouth.

"I wasth the besth girlfriend ever!" I said, going for my most disgusting mouth-full-of-food-face. I gulped down some

Coke and then let out a giant burp.

"The best!" I said, laughing. He couldn't help himself and laughed too.

"So refined and cultured... and dainty!" he said. "That's what I love about you, Maya. Your daintiness. Like a flower."

Our laughter calmed and we continued to eat quietly.

"I've missed you, Maya."

I looked up at him, surprised. "You have? I thought by now you would have found some amazing med student to make beautiful, smart babies with."

"Med student? Nah. They're boring. All they ever do is study and work. I like the tortured, artsy types who lie around all day drinking bad red wine and talking about Neitze or something."

"Is that what you think artsy types do? This is not Paris, circa 1954, you know." I filled our tiny tea cups for the seventh time, emptying the metal pot. I tipped the lid and slid it toward the edge of the table where it was hastily replaced with a fresh pot.

"Do you want to try again, Maya?"

I cupped my hands around the tea cup to warm them, wishing I knew what to say.

"I don't know," I said.

"Do you remember our first night?"

"You mean the very first night? The night Frank died in the canoe?"

"Yeah. I think about that night a lot."

"We were in shock, Marc. I'm sure it was very intense for that reason."

"For me, there was more to it. I have always felt guilty. Guilty that I couldn't save him. I felt like it was my fault. It was my idea that we go for a canoe ride that night. I knew they were drunk, but I knew you were at the dock with Jay and I thought that if we went for a canoe ride, you would come with us, and I would win you over Jay."

"You went for a canoe ride because you were jealous of

Jay?"

"Yeah. I guess that pretty much sums it up."

"And then you did win me that night."

"Yeah."

"Shit, Marcus."

"Yeah."

"You didn't 'win' me as a result of Frank's death, but I can see how maybe that would be complicated in your mind. Maybe we both have a little of that guilt. God, Marcus, you've been carrying that for five years?"

"Yeah, I guess I have."

It began again that night. I went to his apartment in the Annex and we clung to each other. I wondered later if it was doomed again for the same reason. Frank's death. We clung to one another out of some misplaced guilt or shame or something neither of us could define exactly.

Marcus got a good job with a big Toronto advertising agency, one that demanded a lot of client lunches and drinks after work. He developed a habit for having a Scotch every night when he got home. It became several over time. We partied every night with his work buddies, drinking, clubbing, more drinking, and smoking. I didn't see how self-destructive his behavior was becoming, that the drinking was starting to get out of control. He kept a keg of beer in the kitchen and his drinking buddies came over almost every night. By then we were living together, and I would usually retreat to the bedroom to read or paint. I think I applied to the art school in Italy to escape that life. I knew I couldn't keep living it, but I didn't know how to get out of it, other than to leave. But then Marcus followed me, and the partying lifestyle just moved to Italy. I couldn't take it and when I found him with that girl, I finally had an excuse to leave him for good. Perhaps I had been looking for an excuse that I could explain. The drinking was somehow not enough of an excuse to leave him. I knew he wasn't serious about the girl, but I wanted out.

And then Jay fell on me in Pompeii. I couldn't believe the coincidence of it. How tied-in he was with the breakup I had just instigated, its roots in his dad's death. I could only imagine how devastating Frank's death was on Jay. He never said so, but I think he shouldered responsibility for not making them come back for the lifejackets that night. Or that it wasn't him who found his dad, but Marcus. In our ten years together, I could never quite help Jay over the hurdle of that loss. Perhaps my love was not enough. Calder's love came close, I think, and I am ashamed to say it made me jealous, the way Jay's eyes lit up for his son. Did they light up for me that way too? I couldn't remember. None of it mattered anymore.

I wonder if you can hear my thoughts. I wonder where you are, if you are anywhere. I sense your presence, though I can't describe how. The waft of your bathrobe scent, or the crow that flies by the window as I think of you, or the whispery breeze that comes from nowhere. I feel you watching me now as I type and so I will continue my clicking conversation with you, pretend I can hear your silent replies. Can you see the same moon that I see right now out the window? Bound by childhood, bound by loss, bound by the moon. Now it seems your losses have infected me - they follow me, they follow Marcus, they follow Calder. Will the legacy of an untimely death be true for Calder too?

The angry moment has passed and now I long for you, to touch the flesh of your earlobe, bask in the warmth of you sitting next to me on the couch as we watch another rerun of CSI. I long to step off this rollercoaster of emotion, long to sleep and wake up refreshed instead of re-entering the nightmare of our fractured family.

Oh Jay, help me to find my way out of this mire. They say you shouldn't move when you fall into quicksand, but immobility will only go so far and won't ultimately pull you free. I still need the hand that will pull me free. I don't know why I think you can still rescue me from wherever you are, but in grief anything seems possible.

Love Maya.

Chapter Seven

Chopsticks

I ran my hands over the grooves chipped into the glossy black servant's steps leading down into the kitchen, surprised that I couldn't feel the sharp, splintered wood. I sat on the bottom step, wishing I could smell Maya's famous Bolognese simmering on the stove, her secret ingredient – cumin – wafting up the steps around me. For a moment I forgot I was dead. Dragging my fingers through my arm caused nothing more than a parting of vapor, like walking through a cloud. I might just as easily have been in a dream – the corners of the kitchen were muted and ill-defined, making it difficult to see the fine lines of the bead board wainscoting that I knew was there. The scene outside the bay window was blurry, like looking through someone else's glasses, blobs of colour instead of the bucolic hedge of hemlock across the back of the spotted, mossy lawn littered with trucks and wagons and a variety of bright plastic toys. I might have been inside a memory, or a daydream. Or perhaps I was an integral part of the present, and Maya, in flip-flops, faded Levis cutoffs, and a white tank, actually stood in front of me at the stove, stirring. It looked to be summer, judging from her clothing and her slight tan, so I guessed I had been dead about five or six months.

Calder, ringed in an orangey haze that rippled away from the surface of his wrinkled t-shirt like waves of heat on a distant highway, entered the kitchen with two bamboo chopsticks, banging the walls, the countertop, a glass on the counter, and finally the stove around Maya, which made a satisfying metallic *ping, ping, ping*. From behind, I could see her shoulders tense. Her aura, a deep purple, seemed to pulse around her as if someone was playing with the knob on a gas stove and turning the flame up and down. Seeing auras around people was new, but I was learning how to tell the way a person felt based on subtle differences in the color, clarity, and thickness of their auras. Calder's orange aura was typical for a kid, free of inhibitions and so trusting. But today, the color was barely visible, telling me that his aura reflected the negative aspects of his mood – destruction and stubbornness. The giant Band-Aid on his elbow was testament to his latest skateboard mishap.

"Calder, please stop that," Maya said as she leaned over to taste the sauce and then grabbed the sea salt grinder to add more.

"But I need to practice."

Calder took a seat at the island to Maya's left, drumming now on both the glass and the salt grinder that Maya had just returned there. She too radiated negativity, outlined like a child's drawing in the color of a black tulip, indicating her feeling of being scattered, lost and depressed, which I guess you would expect from someone still reeling from the loss of a husband, even six months later.

"I don't think you need to practice all over the house. I think practice is meant to be done on your drum set in your room."

I sensed from their auras how unhappy they were, but I felt powerless. I longed to walk over to Maya and hug her from behind, kiss the back of her neck, tell her everything would be OK, and to maul Calder in a bear hug, tickling him into submission. Sitting there invisible on the back steps was pure torture. I needed to find a way to communicate with them.

"Calder, really. Please stop." Calder stopped but didn't look at her as he reached over and slid the bottle of olive oil over to line up with the glass and the salt grinder. The drumming resumed. Maya turned her back to him, grabbing a pot. She went to the sink and filled it with water, her lips pursed as she tried to ignore the noise. I couldn't help being impressed with Calder's ability. My boy had rhythm! He banged out a smooth pattern: glass, shaker, shaker, oil, oil, oil, repeat. The glass took on a high-pitched tone, where the plastic of the shaker had more of a dull *thwack*. The oil had a satisfying, deep resonance. Maya took a sip of wine from her glass, and when she put it down again, it became a part of the set, making the best sound of all: a high pitched bumblebee drone, one that took a while to fly away. Maya swiped her glass back and took another swig.

Maybe drumming was the answer to Calder's grief. Anything was better than riding his skateboard at crazy speeds. Only now, from this vantage point, could I see the meaning of Calder's unconscious drumming, the meaning of my own desire to drum as a young boy. Drumming, the most basic of primal sounds, connected humans with the rhythms of the universe.

"Calder, if you don't stop now, there will be consequences." Maya glared at him, her mouth set in a pursed grimace. She gulped her wine.

Encourage the drumming, Maya! That's it! I could feel Calder's drumming like a heartbeat, its even timbre resonating within my innermost being, just as when I was alive I could feel it deep within my gut. To the dead, a drumbeat mimics the heartbeat of life, a powerful reminder of our bodied forms. I wanted Maya to feel the magic I had just discovered within our son, to allow him to use his talent to communicate with the universe, to communicate with me. Drumming as an outlet has been used for as long as man has existed on earth. In ancient civilizations drumming was sacred: a voice to the heavens, a link that had the potential to provide a variety of riches, like immortality, solstice, water in the form of rain, and fertility. Drums echoed human existence. Instinctively, Calder called me and I came.

I could tell by Maya's voice that her threat wasn't one she would follow through on. She had yet to think of any consequences. Calder sensed the same but stopped playing for a moment.

"Like what?"

"Like... Like no dessert tonight!"

"We never have dessert."

"Then you lose a half hour of TV!"

"Fine!" Calder resumed his drumming.

"OK, then no skateboarding for a week!" Maya wagged a wooden spoon at him.

"That's not fair!"

"Well, if you can't respect me, then those are the consequences."

"I hate you!" Calder jumped down off his stool and went storming into the living room, drumming as loudly as he possibly could on the walls, the lamp, the hanging pictures, his aura now a fiery red. *Yes, Calder I hear you.*

Maya seemed to collapse with his angry words. She turned off the stove, took her glass, and plopped down in Calder's seat at the counter, silent tears dripping down her face. She had dark smudges under her eyes and a new streak of gray edging her hairline. I took the stool next to her, sitting as we often did when we ate a late dinner together after Calder was in bed.

Aww, sweetie, I wish you could hear me.

"Goddamm it, Jay. I can't do this by myself!" Maya whispered to herself.

I know, Lenie, I know.

"What am I supposed to do now? Our fucking kid has turned into a little shit! I bet he would have obeyed you! I can't stand the drumming! And the skateboarding scares the shit out of me." Maya finished her wine and refilled the glass.

Tell him you love him. And let him drum for godssakes! It's an outlet. Can't you see that?

I knew talking to her was useless, but I couldn't help it. Maybe somehow her subconscious could hear me. Maya squeezed her face into a mask of frustration and despair, flopped forward, and placed her head in her arms as she cried big uncontrollable sobs. I brushed my hand across her back, the layer of purple light rippling slightly. I was helpless, as she had closed herself off from me. I checked on Calder in the other room.

Hearing his mother's sobs, Calder stopped drumming. He kneeled facing into the couch, belly on the seat, pounding his fist into the cushions. I sat down next to him, wishing I could take one of the velvety throw pillows into my hands, to have something to hold onto. I could hear him muttering under his breath. "I hate her, I hate her, I hate her…"

C'mon buddy. Give her a break. She's tired and is trying to cook you dinner and you're in there banging away so loudly that she can't hear herself think. I know she doesn't give you the attention you need sometimes, but she's a good mom. She's trying.

Calder broke one of the chopsticks and then the other and threw them against the wall. He slumped down on the floor, back against the couch, and turned on the TV, his mind tuning away from me and onto SpongeBob Square Pants. *"Who lives in a pineapple, under the sea…?"*

Back in the kitchen, the phone rang, and Maya pulled herself together. I read the caller I.D. It said M. Pellegrino. Why would Marcus be calling Maya? She reached over and picked up the phone, staring at the name for a moment before pushing the button to talk.

"Hello?"

Suddenly I stood in a darkened room behind a man looking out a window to the full moon whose light flooded the street below. I couldn't imagine why I might be there. I wanted to be back with Maya and Calder. I didn't know this man until he turned around. It was Marcus. His graying dark hair was combed back, exposing a receding hairline, and there was a puffiness around his dark eyes that aged him even more. The slouch of his shoulders and the flaccidity of his skin gave him a mournful air, as did the clayish color of his aura. He had lost the arrogance he always exuded with his smug knowledge of the world. He seemed out of place in the almost empty room. The only furniture, an expensive-looking black leather couch and a chrome and glass coffee table that was littered with Chinese food containers and a crumpled can of Coke. A gleaming black and chrome drum set took up the area where a dining room might be. Beside it, against a wall, a table stacked with mixing equipment blinking with red and green lights. A muted football game filled the room with flashes of bluish light from the flat screen TV that occupied most of the wall opposite the couch. Hanging on the kitchen wall behind him, I noticed one of Maya's older paintings – a stark landscape. It looked stunningly beautiful in the room, against the white walls, in the bluish light of the TV, but I couldn't imagine why it was there.

"I miss you," he said into the phone.

On the couch, an old photo album was flung open, its red faux leather cover tattered, the stiff plastic that sealed the photos onto the pages yellowed slightly and pulling up in places. The page was open to pictures of Marc and Maya as teenagers at the cottage. Maya in mid-air, laughing hysterically, the split-second between when Marcus scooped her into his arms and Maya landed with a splash in the water. Another with Marcus standing behind her, his arms draped around her shoulders as they stood looking thoughtfully at a bonfire. Teenaged lovers. These were not pictures I had ever seen of my wife. Her life before me.

I never wanted to ask questions after she told me about her breakup with Marc that year in Rome. I knew it had been tumultuous between them. Although she never said so, I think Marcus following her to Italy showed a sign of weakness in Maya's eyes. She enjoyed her time in Italy without him, she told me once, surrounded by the type of people she longed to have in her life – painters, illustrators, filmmakers, and writers. Although he was a musician, he dismissed her friends as nerds or hippies. How she wound up with me, I will never know. I suppose I was supportive of her art, something that Marc seemed to have little patience for, which is why seeing one of her paintings in his kitchen surprised me. As far as I knew, she'd had very little contact with him in the years that followed. We heard from Maya's mother, who still talked to his parents, that he had bounced from job to job, never quite settling into any one career or place for very long. There had been many girlfriends, apparently, but he had never married or had children.

"Why are you calling me, Marcus?" The angry tone of Maya's voice coming from the phone that Marc held to his ear was unmistakable.

"Is it wrong to want to hear your voice?"

"Calder's still awake. I told you not to call during dinner time." Calder came into the kitchen and started tapping the counter with the broken chopsticks.

Marcus turned around, apparently to look at the clock on his microwave. "Oh. Sorry. I lost track of the time. It's just that I need to see you again."

"I can't."

My mind spun. *See her again?*

"I need to hold you in my arms." Calder's drumming got louder.

"I have to go," Maya said.

"Your kid has pretty good rhythm," Marcus said.

"Yeah. I guess. But I have a headache."

Marcus laughed.

"I'm hanging up now," Maya said, her tone tense.

"Wait, Maya—"

She hung up the phone and stood staring at it for a moment. I was back in the kitchen with her.

What the hell was going on?

She took a giant swig of wine and turned to Calder.

"That's enough now, sweetie."

Calder continued, louder now.

I wanted desperately to soothe her. I wanted her to know I was there. I wanted to know what was going on between her and Marcus. I blew a little on the back of her neck to make her shiver.

Jay? She stood perfectly still, listening for me.

I'm here.

What do I do with your son?

Kick his ass.

I bet you would tell me to kick his ass. She smiled despite herself and looked toward the ceiling, thinking I could somehow hover there against the ceiling rather than sit right here beside her. *The problem is, I forget, or maybe I never knew, exactly how you did that, Jay.*

Don't let him get away with shit. He's taking advantage of you.

I suppose you would tell me to follow through on consequences.

Exactly.

I just don't know if I have the strength.

C'mon Lenie, buck up. Or I'm going to have to kick your ass!

Maya closed her eyes. *I can do this. I can do this. I have to do this!* She took a deep breath.

"Calder, can you please stop drumming on the counter like that?"

"Why?"

The edgy skateboard dude on the front of Calder's shirt looked oddly menacing.

"Please come here and sit with me."

"Why?"

"Because I need to talk to you." Calder climbed up onto the stool next to her.

"Calder, this is not cool. Breaking things and being rude to me is unacceptable." Calder's expression was stormy, back in shut-down mode.

"If we're going to live together in this house and get along, we're going to have to respect each other. Do you understand what that means?"

Lenie, this isn't getting through... She stopped talking and looked at him.

"Do you understand?"

And there it was, the most useless line a parent can say to a child. The game-ender.

"I hate you," Calder whispered.

"I don't care if you hate me. You're going to learn to respect me. Your father would be disappointed and wouldn't tolerate this kind of behavior, so neither will I."

I am not disappointed with him, Lenie.

Calder burst into tears.

"I hate you, I hate you, I hate you!"

For a moment, Maya looked stricken but then her face softened and she pulled Calder into her lap. He struggled but she kept a tight grip on him. "It's not really me you hate."

"Yes it is!"

"No, it's your father you hate."

Hey! What the...? Calder looked at her, surprised.

"I know that sounds weird, but that's why you're mad right now. You're mad because he's not here. Do you want to know something? I'm mad at him too! He sucks for dying!" Tears were running down her cheeks now. She had Calder's attention now.

"Mama, are you crying?"

"Yes, I'm sad and mad too."

"I want him back! I want Daddy!" Calder started to bawl.

"I know, sweetie, I know." Maya hugged him tighter,

letting his tears come. His shoulders relaxed.

Not the approach I would have taken, certainly, but whatever works for you, Lenie. Once again, I had underestimated my wife. After a while, Calder's sobs subsided.

"I'm sorry I was mean to you, Mommy."

"I know, sweetie. We gotta help each other sometimes. We have all this anger inside us because Daddy died and for you it comes out when you drum things. Maybe we need to find you something to pour your feelings out on. You seem to like drumming. Would you like to take some drumming lessons maybe?"

Yes!

"Drumming lessons?" Calder sniffed.

"Yeah. What do you think?"

"Could I get a new drum set?"

"Maybe."

"Cool."

"OK. I'll look into it." Maya looked pleased. I could hear her thinking: *I am brilliant! Bring on the headaches!*

"K." Calder looked bored again. His thoughts were already back with SpongeBob.

"You know, your dad played drums and your grandfather was an amazing pianist. Perhaps you have some of their talent in your genes." Calder shrugged and tried pushing himself out of Maya's lap. Maya's grandfather, Albert, appeared above me, sitting at his piano playing a piece that I vaguely recalled as Handel. It seemed I had some competition. I wasn't the only musical influence in the family. When I looked up at him, he smiled down at me before fading away.

"Just for the record," she said as she kissed the crown of Calder's head, "your father would never have been this nice."

Hey! I resent that!

"He would be mad I said that." Calder looked up with alarm.

"Why? What would Daddy do?"

Take away the skateboard.

"I think he would have taken your skateboard away for a week."

"I'm glad you're not mean like Daddy."

Lenie, you break my heart.

Maya stood up and gave Calder a final hug.

"I guess we better get you some proper drum sticks." Calder shrugged again and walked back into the living room to resume watching his cartoon.

"Dinner in ten minutes!" Maya called to him as she turned on the gas and stirred the sauce.

See, Jay, I can do this. Even without you.

Yes, Lenie, you can. And you're doing a great job. I'm glad about the drum thing. But what the hell is going on with Marcus?

Maya and Calder faded from my view as I continued to sit on the back stairs. How had I gotten here? What was expected of me? Clearly, I had no influence over my family and seemed only to be remembered with a certain amount of resentment.

"Hard watching it, isn't it?" My dad now sat beside me on the step.

"Was I like Calder?"

"Angry? Hell yeah."

I sat now at our old dining room table. My mom, in a crisp white nurse's uniform, sat across from me at the stripped oak table in one of our chipped wooden chairs. I slouched as I picked out a rhythm on the edge of the table with my new Pro Mark drumsticks.

"Can you please stop? I'm trying to talk to you." I didn't care. A sixteen-year-old intent on driving his mother crazy. I continued to play the table. I recognized in my own face Calder's same grief-induced shut-down mode and almost laughed seeing our resemblance. Same slouched shoulders, same downward, stone-cold glare, same clenched jaw. My hair, honey colored and long, almost to my shoulders, curtain bangs that shrouded my inner turbulence.

"I'm trying to talk to you." My mom did a decent replica of my stone-like stare.

"Jay, we have to get this sorted out. You're failing math and barely hanging on in English."

"I KNOW! Jeez, you think I don't know I'm fucking flunking out of high school?"

"Don't swear at me. Something has to change. If it keeps up, I'm going to have to make you quit the band."

"But the band is the only thing that keeps me sane! I HAVE to keep drumming or I'll die! SCREW you!"

"You leave me no choice, Jay. You need to pull your socks up, and fast. From now on, you do homework before anything else."

"I fucking hate you." I whispered this under my breath so she couldn't hear me.

This brought me back to the step with my dad.

"I was proud of your mother that day. It was really hard for her to stand up to you like that. It took a lot of work on my part to get her to that point with you. But you truly needed your ass kicked." My father's eyes flashed and he smiled as his thought came through to me.

"Yeah, I guess I did. Wait, what? Work on *your* part?"

"I could see you were spinning out of control, hiding away in your room pretending to do homework when you were really drumming away on your bed and smoking pot. And those sticks weren't your only instrument, if you know what I mean."

"Jeez dad. You *saw* that?"

"Relax. I took about as much interest as watching birds fly. You'll see."

"I hope not. Will I have to see Maya... ugh. I can't even think of it."

"Really, Jay. It won't affect you emotionally. I promise."

"OK, so explain how you *helped* mom."

"Dreams. It's all in the dreams, J.J. my boy."

"What? You can enter people's dreams?"

"Not always. If a person is depressed or overly anxious and not sleeping, or using some kind of substance, like alcohol or drugs, then you're blocked. But otherwise, yes, it's possible to enter people's dreams."

"How?"

"You just have to have the desire. It took me a while to figure it out. When you started screwing up in school, I finally figured out that if I entered your mother's dreams I could get her to kick your butt and not put up with your attitude."

"Why didn't you just enter my dreams and kick my butt yourself?"

"Because in your anger, I couldn't reach you."

"Oh. I hated Mom that day, but I did get myself straightened out after that."

"Yes, you did. Straight A's as I recall."

"I should thank you."

"Nah. It was nothing! Just a dream!"

"I got to stay in that band, until we broke up after high school. I wanted to be a rock star so bad."

"I know, Jay. It just wasn't in the cards for you. Besides, you wouldn't have met Maya."

"Yeah. Or had Calder. I look forward to our reunion someday."

"Yes, I have to say it's been wonderful having you here. I look forward to seeing your mom again, too."

"And to think I thought there would be nothing after you died. I guess I was 'dead' wrong."

"Ever the crack-up, J.J."

"What's going on with Maya and Marcus, Dad?"

"One thing at a time, J.J. You don't need to worry about that now."

"What are you talking about? I don't need to worry that my wife is being stalked by an old lover? Did they have an affair? Is that what's going on?"

My dad just gave me a sympathetic glance and faded

away.

In Maya's dream that night I found myself in a snowstorm. A blizzard. Flecks of white glowed as they drew near and then rushed away leaving a trail behind them like tiny comets zooming across the sky. Except there were millions of comets all within touching distance. I found Maya huddled on a snow bank, peering into a vast green-black nothingness pocked with celestial dust. I took a seat next to her. Calder materialized before us, arms crossed over the skateboard dude t-shirt, chopsticks clutched in one fist, hair tousled, glaring. She reached toward him but he stepped away. She stood up and took a step closer to him and he stepped back onto a skateboard and shot out of sight.

"I can't reach him."

"Be strong, Lenie." She took another step forward, her silky iridescent white gown flowing behind her.

"I can't." She sat down again, her knees pulled up inside her gown. "Jay, I need you."

"I'm here, Lenie."

"I know you're here, but I can't see your face."

"I'm here."

A full, luminous moon rose quickly in the sky and from somewhere Beethoven's Piano Sonata #14 played by Grandpa Albert could be heard. Maya closed her eyes, listening to the music.

"Lenie, I'm glad you're letting him take drum lessons."

"Why can't I see your face, Jay? I want to see your face."

"I don't know, Maya. But I'm here."

"I'm sorry about Marcus. I didn't mean for it to happen."

"What happened, Lenie?"

She turned away from me, gazing dreamily into the comet storm. "Isn't the moon beautiful?" She stood up and walked into the falling stars, gown flowing behind her.

This dream thing would take practice.

Chapter Eight

JULY 15TH, 2006

Dear Jay,

I dreamed about you last night, but I couldn't see your face. It was frustrating. Calder was there too. He was lost to me, receding into a snowstorm. He still feels lost to me even now that I'm awake.

I heard Calder's skateboard and glanced over the computer screen and saw him – hair flying, no helmet – hurtling down the hill outside. I leapt up and tore out the door, yelling his name. He turned toward my voice and missed seeing a bump in the pavement, causing him to take a flying leap off the board and land on his knees. It took me a minute to reach him. His lips squeezed together as he held back tears and clasped his leg, a rip in his jeans exposing a scrape just beginning to bubble with dots of blood.

"Oh, Calder. Not again! And you're not wearing your helmet. I've told you again and again that you have to wear your helmet. That's it. No more skateboard!"

"Mama! Noooo!"

"Let's get you bandaged up." I worked to keep my voice

neutral and calm like the therapist taught me.

Be consistent, she said. *And in heightened moments of emotion, try to stay calm and keep your voice calm. The moment you get pulled into his emotion, you're sunk.*

I picked Calder up off the sidewalk, my hands in his armpits while he bent over to keep a tight grip on his knee, and hobbled him toward the house as he hopped along on one foot.

Inside, I dabbed his scrape with a wet paper towel, applied Neosporin and a wide, square Band-Aid, bought in bulk at Costco. The grey glue from the last bandage had barely worn off.

"Calder, your skateboarding is seriously dangerous. You not wearing a helmet is a big problem and if you can't play by the rules, then you will lose the privilege of skateboarding at all."

"Please Mama, I'll wear my helmet from now on!"

"No skateboarding for three days."

"Mama!!"

"Shall I make it four?"

Howling, he flung himself onto the floor. I walked away.

"It's almost time for your drum lesson. You need to wipe up your tears and change your jeans."

Calder cried louder.

"Now!" I yelled. I left the room, but heard him get up and sniffle his way upstairs.

An hour later, I sat in a dingy basement on a dilapidated couch, the banging of Calder on the drums barely muffled behind an unpainted, hollow wooden door. There were long pauses accented by low voices, mostly that of the college student teacher, Brandon. Upon first meeting, Calder had been intimidated by the kid's tight skinny black jeans belted with chains, his long, badly black-dyed stringy hair and ripped black t-shirt, but he'd given Calder a cool-guy nod and from the first lesson, Calder worshipped him. And had stopped allowing me to comb his hair. We toured every downtown department store looking for black skinny jeans in size 8, which were almost impossible to find. I finally found a pair online and Calder had barely taken them off, until today. I would have to buy another pair or patch the ones that were now ripped.

As I waited for the lesson to be over, I continued my letter to Jay in my journal.

The first lesson, Brandon had Calder pounding out rhythms and beats on a bongo drum. Now when he gets home from school, he dashes up the stairs two at a time to get onto his drum set. His face takes on a transcendental look, serene, angelic — that childish expression of glee, like the one he had when you gave him underdogs on the swing, and those giggles? I can't remember the last time I heard him giggle. I wish you were here to help me, Jay. You would know what to do or say to make him laugh. Although, thinking back, those giggles stopped before you died. Did he stop laughing or did you?

I envy him. I once knew that feeling of losing yourself in something you love and I want desperately to lose myself in that way again. To forget this world for a few minutes, and go back to living the life that someone else who looks like me is still living in some parallel universe. A life where you're still alive. I want to go there, and not be adorned with this heavy yoke of single parent widowhood that you have bestowed upon me. It's too much to bear. Maybe it's time to start painting again, but something about it makes me feel sad - a reminder of my old life that I so desperately yearn for.

Things weren't great between us when you died. I'm sorry for that, Jay. I'll live with that guilt forever, worrying that the problems in our marriage were my fault, that I nagged too much, always fighting for your time, your attention, your love. You hid a big piece of yourself from me, right from the beginning of our relationship, from the day of your dad's death, even. You shut me out. I tried to be there for you, but your father's death changed you. You never spoke of it. Will Calder grow up with the same malaise? Has he too been sentenced to a life of underlying sadness? I can't let that happen, Jay. I could never truly reach you, but I can still reach Calder. Maybe you can still reach him too. Help him, Jay. Show him the contentment you never found.

I need to tell you about Marcus, but I'm not ready yet. How do I ask a dead man to forgive the unforgivable?

The door opened, and a flushed Calder walked out. I quickly shoved my journal and pen back into my purse.

"Next week, Dude," Brandon said. He winked at me and I was horrified when I blushed.

"Don't forget to practice that scale I taught you, K?"

Calder nodded.

"You're doing great. You've got talent, kid. Just make sure you practice."

Calder smiled as he walked out the door in front of me.

Chapter Nine

Murmuration

The glossy chill of silk on skin. Popcorn, soggy with butter. A mouth-explosion of sour cherries yanked fresh from the tree. These sensations became memories, smooth as glass. Memories whose juicy tastes, aromas, and softnesses were tiny tortures. I stroked a silky curl of Maya's auburn hair or ran my imaginary finger along the peachy fuzziness of Calder's boyish cheek and felt nothing, not even warmth. Color in the afterlife world filled the void of human sensation – a spectrum of new senses, thought-based and linear. I slowly adjusted to deriving sensation from color. Cadmium red thoughts revived the sensation of heat, or the aroma of steak charring on a BBQ. The earthy green spectrum conjured the smell of juniper berries tinkling with ice in a martini glass. Yet I longed to inhale Maya's scent, to wrap myself in her aroma – taste her powdery floral hand cream mixed with the nut butter saltiness of her skin to which there was no corresponding color. I wanted to ruffle my son's hair, or punch my hand into his stiff new leather baseball glove to soften it, a pleasure I failed to pass on to him.

Runners kicked up the dust of the baseball diamond. Heat simmered the outfield where Calder stood, bent at the waist, hands on knees, flushed. I imagined the grittiness of dust in my own mouth as I watched from behind the mound. There was a popping sound as bat met ball which escaped gleefully into the sky. Calder looked up, searching, blinded by sunlight. He needed to move to his left but couldn't see this and the ball landed behind him with a *thud*, his opportunity for the heroism of a final out lost as Josh, a tall, loping outfielder, ran to scoop the rolling ball into his glove and flung it toward home. The ball went awry and landed between second and third base. Another score for the other team. Calder hung his head, a puppy who knows his mistake.

I hate this game.

C'mon buddy. Hang in there. It happens to everybody.

I should've been yelling from the stands, clapping my hands. "Good try, Son! Shake it off, C'mon now!" I watched Maya watching the other dads, their fingers hooked in the chain link as they coached their sons from the sidelines, her expression both sad and grim. She turned to one of the only other moms in the stands. A woman, intent now on her clipboard, marked the latest score, a tiny, smug smile betraying her affiliation. Maya looked out of place in her floppy straw hat, knees tucked up under her pale blue sundress and flip flops, tendrils of sweat-matted hair stuck against her bare back. With each inning, she looked at her watch, exhaling. *Why is the game of baseball so boring and so long?*

The coach, a leathery-faced, balding dad of one of Calder's friends, invited Calder onto the team, trying to do the right thing for a fatherless kid, but Calder spent more time on the bench or in left field than any of the other kids. He was younger than the other boys and lived in the wrong neighborhood to officially play on the team. On the bench, Calder slumped his shoulders, legs outstretched as he leaned back against the fence. He turned to Maya and pointed at the car, eyes widening in their plea, clearly wanting to leave. She shook her head. His face collapsed and he resumed his slouch. Max, another of Calder's buddies, struck out cleanly in three pitches. He flung his bat and plunked down next to Calder, looking equally dejected.

Maya walked over to the coach.

"Hey, Todd. Just wondering if maybe Calder can have a turn playing infield. He always seems to be either on the bench or in left field. I think he's getting a little frustrated."

Todd, distracted, dug around in an equipment bag looking for a smaller batting helmet for one of the players. "Yeah, Maya. No problem. I'll do what I can."

"Thanks so much, Todd. I really appreciate it."

As Maya walked back to the bleachers, she winked at Calder, thinking she had solved the problem, but in the next inning, Calder was sent back to left field. I saw Maya's mouth open, surprised that her request had been shirked. The inning lasted a long time, and the kids all seemed bored. Calder kept picking at one of the laces on his glove and then found a mound of dirt to kick. Mercifully, no more balls flew in his direction, because he definitely would have missed the catch. Finally, one of the opposing team's batters got tagged out and Calder's team was again up at bat.

"You gonna bat?" Tanner, the coach's son and clearly the star of the game, asked Calder. Calder shrugged and Tanner sat, bending at the waist, hands on his knees. He looked like a big leaguer, missing only the chew and spit. Within minutes, a batter struck out and another popped a fly to third. When it was his turn at bat, Tanner hit to first. Calder got a base run after a couple of strikes. I breathed a sigh of relief. Max struck out again in three pitches. The winning team came off the field kicking the dirt, slapping each other on the back and fist bumping. Calder walked from first base slowly, his one chance of excitement gone. He stood obediently in the cluster around Todd and flung his arm for the obligatory cheer for the opposing team and lined up for the handshake with all the lackluster he could muster.

"Goodgamegoodgamegoodgame..." Calder didn't stick around to laugh with his friends as they sucked orange slices, making monkey faces. Instead he stormed off toward the parking lot. Maya quickly gathered her things and followed him in a jog.

Calder flung his glove, hat, and water bottle into the back seat and before they had even pulled out of the lot, his face crumpled into tears.

"I hate baseball! Why do I have to do it?!"

"What do you mean? I thought you loved playing." As I sat next to Calder, I saw Maya bite her lip in the rearview mirror, a gesture I knew well. She knew this was not going to go well. I wanted to take them both into my arms and tell them it would be OK. Suggest ice cream. Turn on the radio. Something to distract them.

"I never get to play! All I do is sit on the bench while Owen and Tanner get to play every single inning! It's not fair!"

"Sweetie, you know that you're younger than the other kids playing and the coach has to play the kids who are really on the team. Tanner's dad let you join the team so you could learn the game and hang out with Owen."

"I already know how to play!"

Maya looked at him in the mirror. He dragged a sleeve across his face, wiping away snot and tears. "I know, sweetie. But this team has been playing together for a whole season already and you're just starting."

"I'm better than most of the other kids, but I can't even show them because I never get to play!"

"I know it seems that w—"

"I want to quit!"

Oh great. Now he wants to quit. What the hell do I do now? Jay?

"Calder, honey, you can't quit. You have an obligation to the team."

"No one would care! I'm quitting!"

Maya took a deep breath and swallowed, trying to hold

back tears. *I don't know what to say here.*

Let him cool down, Lenie. That tactic always worked with me.

Calder continued to sob, slumped in his seat, swiping at tears angrily. I reached out to touch his hair, but he had no reaction. I hated being invisible to him.

"Why can't I quit?"

"We'll talk about it later when we've both cooled down, K?"

Calder said nothing.

"Don't be so hard on yourself, Calder. You just have to be patient."

What's the right thing to say here, Jay?

You have it, Lenie.

"I hate being patient. I just want to quit this stupid team."

"I said we'll talk about it later."

Maya sighed and pulled the car into the driveway. Calder jumped out and slammed his door while the car kept moving.

"Hey! Calder that's dangerous!" Maya yelled, but Calder just ran onto the front porch, leaned his head against the front door and kicked it with a cleated foot. Maya turned off the car and sat there, needing a moment to gather her strength. She pulled a tissue from the armrest and wiped her eyes.

I can't do this, dammit. I can't do this!

You can.

God, Jay, where the hell are you? What am I supposed to do now?

We all have shitty experiences, Lenie. Let him cool off. And don't let him quit. He'll be fine. He's got to learn to be tough. Don't be soft on him.

Then Alice smiled her knowing smile, waiting for me.

"Hey! What's going on? I want to be with them!"

"I'm here with a suggestion. Think back on your own experience, Jay."

The floor disappeared and I looked down at my feet to see a kid's beat-up sneakers – royal blue with yellow zig-zaggy stripes – my old Adidas. I looked around. I was back at the Kew Garden, standing on another dusty baseball diamond, the grass surrounding it brittle, the color of wheat. I could feel the late August sun pulling the skin on my face tight across my nose. Later I would have a sunburn. A baseball rolled near my feet and I could see my teammates screaming at me to pick it up, but I was frozen. I could see them yelling, but I heard nothing. Another player ran toward me, knocking me hard as he scooped the ball off the ground and whipped it to home plate. The runners each slid into home, increasing their lead by another four. The kid who tried to save the play turned around and glared at me.

"What's wrong with you, man?" he said.

I felt hot tears threatening. Shame engulfed me. Another batter walked up to the plate. I prayed the ball wouldn't come to me. It popped up for a foul. Next, a hit to first. First and second bases safe. Sweat trailed down my forehead, pooling on my eyelashes. I shook my head and hid my nausea by bending over, my hands on my thighs, inhaling deeply. A *thwack* caused me to look up as the pitcher caught a pop-fly. The inning ended. I walked in slowly and sat down, my head between my knees in an effort not to throw up. I heard my dad behind me.

"What's up, J.J.?"

"Dunno, Dad."

"You tired?"

"Yeah. I guess. I dunno know what happened. I just froze out there."

"No biggie. Just have fun. Isn't that what a game is all about?"

"Yeah, but now everyone hates me."

"Why would they hate you?"

"Cause I dropped the ball? I stink at baseball."

"Son, no one cares that you dropped the ball. And you don't stink."

"I hate baseball. I'm going to quit."

"You can't quit, J.J. That won't solve anything. What's this really about?"

"Dunno. I just want you to be proud of me."

"Jay, I'll always be proud of you, no matter what you do."

I turned to look at him, to see his grinning face behind the chain link fence, but there was no one there. I thought I was hallucinating because of the heat or something. I walked over to the drinking fountain and took a long drink, then wiped my mouth with the back of my hand.

The images faded and I could hear the gurgling of Alice's water fountain.

"I thought I'd imagined that."

"No," Alice said. "That really was your dad talking to you."

"But my dad was dead by then."

"Did you feel his pride?"

"Not really. I thought I just willed him to say those words to me."

"In a way you did. But still, some of his pride got through to you, right?"

"It did, I suppose."

"You have the same ability to impart thoughts and feelings to the living, Jay. You employ thought. It'll be up to Calder to hear you. A person's grief or anger can sometimes block you from his mind. Then it's more difficult to be heard. That may be the case with Calder."

"Yeah. OK. He seems pretty messed up at the moment though. I doubt he's going to hear me."

"That may be true. But understand that his responses to the game may have something to do with his grief for you. If you are able to get through to him, you may be able to help him."

"He's a kid. He'll get over it. Maya just needs to be tougher with him."

"Is that how your mother treated you? Was she tough on you?"

"I don't really remember. She didn't say much. Just left me on my own, pretty much. Maya is at least aware of what's going on with Calder."

"Maya could probably use your help as well."

"I wish she wouldn't be so soft on him."

Alice smiled and said nothing.

Back in the kitchen, Calder was balled up in the corner against the lower cabinets, sobbing and hiccupping. Maya crouched down on her haunches, trying to tuck a strand of his hair behind his ear. He shook his head, as if annoyed by a fly and grabbed his hair in each of his fists and pulled.

"C'mon, Calder. You've got to stop. This's going nowhere."

"I caaann't. I hate my life!!"

"Calder, stop. I'm doing the best I can to make this a good life for you. I know it sucks that your dad died, but we both have to figure out now how to live without him. And it's really hard. It's not going to be easy."

Maya, be tough. Don't coddle the kid.

Calder stood, still sobbing, and leaned over the counter, head in hands. *Come on buddy. Hang in there.* I tried to put my hand on his back. He shivered. *Be strong, kid. So you're on the bench. So what? The important thing is you're in the game. You're learning. Don't get all messed up over it.*

Beneath him was the drawer of kitchen utensils. He opened it, still leaning over the counter, and took out a chef's knife. *Calder! No! Jesus!* He turned around, holding the knife, still crying. Maya turned and saw the knife.

"Ohmygod! Calder, what are you doing? Put the knife down!"

"Just kill me. I hate my life. I just want you to kill me!"

"Calder, I would never do that. Is your life really this bad? Let's put the knife down, K?"

"Yes! I hate my life!"

She reached out and took the knife from his hand and put it back in the drawer. Calder collapsed into her arms. She carried him to one of the dining room chairs and held him in her lap. I felt helpless. He was closed off from me.

"I'm not going to stab you."

"OK, then throw me off a balcony or poison me."

"Calder, I'm not going to do any of those things."

Jesus. Do moms have to do everything for their kids? Maya's thought made me smile.

She seemed to understand the drama was just Calder's cry for attention. She understood what I didn't. This was more than a kid needing tough love. I wondered what I'd be doing if our places were reversed? I'd be freaking out.

"Calder, I think you're having a really hard time with your dad's death and I think you need someone besides me to talk to about it."

"Who would I talk to?"

"Someone who talks to kids and helps them with really hard stuff like this."

Oh shit. He's not going to go for a therapist, Lenie. Maybe your dad or something.

"But I don't want to talk to anyone."

"Calder, you scared me just now with the knife. There are some things I can't always help you with, and sometimes I have to ask other people to help. I think this is one of those times."

"I won't do the knife thing anymore. I promise! But don't make me see someone. Pleeeeassse!"

"I sure hope you won't do that again."

And, here it comes...

Calder began to wail all over again, pushing himself out of Maya's arms until he resumed his fetal position under the dining room table. His aura was a deep brick red. Anger. Despair. Grief.

Damn this shit, Jay! Why does this have to be so hard?

I'm sorry Maya. I'm sorry you have to do this alone.

I absorbed Maya's frustrated thoughts, feeling her panic and confusion, but felt at a loss. My old human emotions took over my thoughts as they always had. I wanted to lash out at something. Swear. Punch. Tell Calder to go to his room. Tell Maya to be tougher on him. How could this kid ever learn to be strong when things got tough?

Maya left Calder huddled under the table, still sobbing. She walked into her studio, closed the door, and picked up the phone.

"It's me," she said.

"Is something wrong?" Bethany asked, kids yelling in the background.

"I'm having a crisis with Calder and I don't know what to do. He's under the table sobbing right now. I shouldn't be calling you, but…"

"I'm glad you did. OK. Tell me what's going on." Bethany listened as Maya told her about the baseball game and the knife.

"Shit, poor little baby. Poor you," Bethany said when Maya finished.

"Any suggestions?" Maya asked as she cracked the door to peek at Calder, still under the table, but quieter now.

"Seems like he's playing you," Bethany said. "Don't buy into it."

"I get that, but I don't know what to do now."

"Well, I'm not sure I can tell you that, Maya. He's a kid who misses his dad and doesn't know what to do with that. Some kind of weird behavior is to be expected. Maybe just try and be as normal as you can with him. Keep your voice calm when you talk to him. Don't get emotional. Just be matter-of-fact with him. Boys respond to that. He probably just wants things to feel normal again and he doesn't know how to express it."

"That makes a lot of sense. OK, I think I can do that. Thanks, Bethie."

"You're welcome. I'm here whenever you need me, Maya. You know that."

"I do. Thank you."

When Maya went back into the living room, she ignored Calder. She walked into the kitchen and started tidying dishes. Calder peeked out to watch her.

"It's time to get ready for bed now, Calder." Her voice was neutral, as if nothing had happened.

"I don't have to go see anyone, right?" Calder asked.

"I don't think either of us are in any shape to figure that out right now. You go get your jammies on and call me when you're ready."

Calder crawled out from under the table and disappeared upstairs.

Maya finished putting the dishes away and sat on a kitchen stool to have another sip of wine. "I can't believe that worked," she said out loud.

Nice job, Maya.

"Mama!" Calder called from upstairs.

"Coming!" Maya called back as she made her way to the stairs, grabbing a shoe as she went and tossing it into the basket in the entry hall.

After Maya turned out the light, I found Calder lying in his bed in the dark, hovering near sleep. I sat beside him. He stirred.

Hey Calder.

Daddy? Calder opened his eyes and looked around, blinking in the darkness, blind to me.

Yeah, it's me.

Aren't you dead? How can I talk to you?

Yeah, I'm dead. But you can talk to me anytime.

But I'm not talking out loud. I'm just thinking the words.

That's OK. I can hear your thoughts.

Is this a dream?

It might seem that way in the morning when you wake up.

Why can't I see you?

I'm not sure.

Will I remember that we talked?

I sure hope so. Otherwise I'm wasting my breath. Not that I have breath, of course.

Calder gave a snort. *What's it like being dead? Does it hurt?*

Nah. It's kind of fun. There's a lot of light and color. And I can see you and your mom.

Weird. Can you see me peeing?

Ha! No. I'm not really interested in seeing you peeing.

Is it like being in space?

Yeah, a little.

Cool.

You seemed to have a rough day today.

Yeah. I hate baseball. Calder fiddled with a wrinkle on his Spiderman duvet.

It's not baseball you hate, Calder.

It is so.

No. It's the fact that there were all those dads out there helping their kids and you don't have one.

A tear splashed onto Calder's pillow and he turned his head into the pillow to wipe it away. *I hate not having a dad.*

I know, Beano. I'm sorry I had to go and die on you. I want you to know that I am really proud of you…

He rolled into his pillow and another tear squashed under his cheek. *I just want you here, Daddy!*

I know, Cald. I'm here.

No, like, with me and Mama.

I know, I know. I wish I could be alive so I could be with you too. But I'm always here.

Like a ghost? That's scary!

No, not a ghost. Just… well, like a good friend who can talk to you in your head.

Well don't do it all the time. I might get confused about who's talking. I laughed. Calder smiled.

Beano, you need to let your mom get you some help, OK? Calder shrugged and hugged the pillow closer. *It won't be so bad. It might be really nice to have someone else besides your Mom to talk to.*

I have you, Daddy.

You know what I mean.

I guess… Calder struggled to keep his eyes open, his blinks becoming longer, his breathing deeper. I wondered if he would remember our conversation when he woke up. I wondered if I had it in me from this strange vantage point to fulfill Maya's wish and help our son from becoming the closed-off man Maya seemed to think I had become after my father's death. Had she ever articulated this to me? Did I know this was how she saw me, as a man burdened with underlying sadness? How then must I keep my child from being buried by my loss? Was his drumming the key? Why had I dropped it all those years ago?

The thought had me sitting on a small vinyl stool, a shaggy, Dorito-colored carpet under my feet, enclosed in a fake wood paneled box, the basement rec room of my best friend, Nigel. The drumsticks in my hands were smooth with wear, one tear-shaped end chipped, but the drum's thick white skin was impervious to sharp edges. I loved the snares – the chain-metal stretched across the bottom skin creating vibrations that produced ocean-waves-on-beach-pebble sounds. I needed to be careful of the rim, so I didn't gouge the stick further. Time ceased to exist as muscle memory made my wrists pliable and I held the rhythm of the song steady as Nigel squealed his Fender. His dark hair hung limply over his face, his lower lip jutted out in concentration, eyes closed, his body a question mark shape encircling his guitar, trying to reproduce a Hendrix complexity of shrill cries. I was his Mitch Mitchell, intuitively riffing off his sounds, collaborating my jazzy beats with his undulations. The amp turned to ten so our music could be felt viscerally – an external heartbeat pumping sound through our veins. No longer boyish, my knees and legs were still stick-like in Adidas shorts, but a yellow tank shirt sweat-stained with a rip near the belly button strained against my widening chest. My feet in red Chuck Taylors looked huge on the pedals and the size of my man hands startled me. Momentarily clumsy, I fumbled a beat, and Nigel's guitar squeaked painfully as he spun around to glare at me.

"We had it going on, man!"

"Sorry dude. Shit. I just lost it there for a sec. Should we take it from the top?"

"Nah, man. I've lost it. Fuck. That was so sweet."

"Yeah. Sorry, Nige." Nigel lifted the guitar over his head and leaned it against the wall. He walked over to the amp and turned it off. I laid the sticks across the snare and clasped my hands over my head, stretching backwards, banging my head into the wall behind me. I had forgotten how cramped the place was and how big I'd become. I felt like a giant, so different from my kid-sized baseball memory. Nigel flung himself onto the baby-shit-brown couch, the one held up in the corner by a stack of old encyclopedias, and flipped his head to the side in an attempt to get the hair out of his eyes, but with his straight, fine hair the flip achieved little. He peered at me with the one eye still visible under its curtain, looking uncertain.

"Man, I don't know if this is working out," he said.

"What? Practicing here?"

"No, man. You playing in the band."

"What? Why?"

"Shit, dude. I dunno. Mike always makes me do his dirty work."

"Dirty work?"

"Yeah, man. He's found this drummer dude. He's really awesome. He's played at the Horseshoe. Supposed to be some hot shit."

"But we have it going on."

"Yeah. I know, dude. It's nothing personal. It's Mike's band, you know?"

Mike was our lead singer. The girls went crazy for him. He had an imposing stage presence. Unruly curls, prominent lips with unusually white, even teeth, a nautical roped choker against his Adam's apple, wide leather wrist bands, and slim hips that gyrated in such a way that the girls that lined the high school stage where we played waved their hands at him, hoping to be noticed. He ignored them all except Felicity, our school's resident Bohemian beauty in smushed Chinese slippers, long flowing batik shirts, snug tank tops that pulled across her boyish chest, and a blonde pouff of waist-length hair that seemed to enter the room before she did. She draped herself on Mike, his pliable accessory, smug in her prowess over him. They were a single organism, morphing and reforming after each school-required separation. He was not at the practice, most likely because his long legs were encircling her naked torso in his own family's rec room, her pelt of hair spread across the shiny mattress covering of the pull-out couch. Not that I'd thought about them together. Or that I'd had my own fantasies about Felicity. Mike had it all. My popularity meter was directly linked to his. And now he was pushing me aside, out of the band.

"Holy shit! So just like that, I'm out?"

Nigel shrugged.

"And he can't even tell me himself?"

"Well, the new drummer is dropping by later, and Mike's supposed to be here... I just thought I'd better say something so it wouldn't be, you know, like, awkward."

"Yeah. I get it. Thanks for being such a good friend, Nige. Really appreciate it. Christ."

"Dude, it's not like that. Honestly. You're my friend. It wasn't up to me. I had nothing to do with it."

"Did you even stand up for me?"

"What the hell could I say?"

"I don't know. Maybe 'I quit'?"

"Why the hell would I quit?"

"Out of friendship. Shit, Nige, we've been friends since first grade. I thought there might be some kind of loyalty between old friends."

"Dude, this isn't personal."

"Yeah. K. Whatever. I'll be by tomorrow to pick up my set."

"Hey, Jay-man. It doesn't need to be like that. We can still jam."

"Nah. I'm good. I'm done with this drumming shit." I

didn't look back as I stormed up the basement steps, slamming the door behind me. I never went back for my drum set. I stopped hanging around with Nigel and Mike and found a new friend, Rob, when I joined the Rugby team. We all drifted apart after that. Mike went on to have a fairly successful music career, touring Canadian universities and outpost town halls. I lost touch with Nigel when he got accepted to Cambridge and moved to the UK. The last I heard he had a job working with Hewlett Packard in human design.

I remembered the twinges of regret that followed me through my life, regret that I had simply walked away, with so little provocation, from something I loved. I took the rejection personally. I allowed it to rob me of an intrinsic piece of myself, a purity of spirit I could see had always been with me. I neglected this part of myself, abandoned it like an abused dog that had been kicked and beaten into submission, one who cowers at the challenges life throws at it. I tossed away so many beautiful opportunities to savor those flavors and sensations in life that I now missed so profoundly.

Marcus had never stopped drumming; I knew from the drum set in his apartment. I didn't want to know the truth about what was going on between Marcus and Maya. I didn't want to think about how long it had been going on.

I was suddenly overcome with feelings of regret. Turmoil coiled around me, clasping, its grip tightening until I had to pull away into a moment of white-hot thought. I was released from the grip and felt the sensation of falling backward. Curiously, I saw my emotions – regret, despair, jealousy – floating away from me, a didactic painting, abstract, separate from me, and yet clear depictions of these thoughts. I stopped feeling that familiar gut-crushing sensation of emotion, experiencing instead a swarm of microscopic red lights that I inherently recognized as my sadness swirling within my aura of pale yellow light. Regret appeared in a slightly more purplish hue of lights than those of the red sorrow.

Awestruck, I reached out to touch them, forgetting I could not. The colors drifted around me, and I realized that each minuscule speck represented an individual thought, hovering, until without warning, the thoughts flared as a swarm and propelled themselves in a new direction, a colorful murmuration in an elaborate pedantic dance.

Emotion is habit.

The thought just came. Human emotion was a habit. I realized its truth. I had been hanging on to my human emotions and senses out of habit, remnants of my human self, once a comfortable home, now peeling and curling at the edges in its deterioration. I hung onto these emotions with the same tenacity that I clung to my senses, my last connection to my bodily form.

The swarms of thought disappeared as I separated from another piece of my humanness, and sunlight flooded my being. I laughed, realizing the obvious. So simple. How difficult I'd made my own existence. My need of emotion and sensation vanished. With their death, another freedom.

Chapter Ten

JULY 23RD, 2006

Jay,

Christ, it's been a nightmare week. I don't even know what to do right now. I wish I could talk to you about this knife business. That's the hardest part about parenting alone. You don't have that other person to talk you down. I so miss that partner thing we had. I miss having someone to tell about my days. This is such a lonely life.

Calder and I sat at the dining room table, me writing in my journal while he worked on his homework. He banged back into his chair and kicked the table.

"I can't do it."

"C'mon, Calder. This isn't hard. Let's read the problem carefully. 'In class today, only 18 of 26 students came to school. How many students were absent?' What's the first thing we have to do to figure it out?"

I read from the first page of a stack of stapled-together pages that represented a week's worth of homework that he could do at any time during the week. I had pulled few sheets of blank paper for working out the problems from the printer.

I took a pencil from Calder's pencil box, filled with partially chewed pencils and a well-stabbed eraser, and was poised for him to give me an instruction.

"I don't know!"

"Well, if we write 26 at the top like this…"

Calder was still slumped back in his chair, not looking at the paper.

"…and 18 under it like this, what do you think we have to do now? Do we add them or subtract them?"

Calder slid further down the chair until he landed in a puddle under the table. "I can't do it. I'm stupid!" "You're not stupid. You just have to sit up and put your mind on it. Help me figure it out."

"I hate math."

I leaned back in my chair and closed my eyes. Should I just let him be for a while? Write a note to the teacher?

"OK, maybe we should come back to this later."

"Nooooo! I have to finish my homework or the teacher will get mad!"

"OK. Then why don't you sit up and let's get to work. I will help you."

"I can't! I'm stupid. I don't know how to do it!"

Tears coursed down Calder's cheeks and he pulled his hair.

"Come here, sweetie. Come sit on my lap."

Calder made no effort to move, so I pushed my chair back and sat next to him on the floor and pulled him into my lap. At first he fought me, but then gave up and sat crying.

"Is this really about the homework, Calder? Or is something else bothering you?"

He looked at me quizzically. "Homework, I guess. I don't know what to do."

"Hmm. OK. Well I can help you, but you have to want my help. You seem to be upset about something. Maybe your dad?"

"That's dumb. I'm not upset about that. You always think I'm sad about daddy, but I'm not. He's dead. How can I be upset? I don't even remember him."

"That's not true. Of course you remember him."

"No I don't. I can't even remember his voice anymore." Calder began to cry again. And then he cried harder.

"Are you scared that you're forgetting him?"

Calder shrugged.

"I'm scared of that too sometimes," I said. "I have an idea. Why don't we watch the movie about him? The one they played at the funeral. Would you like to see it?"

"A movie about daddy? I don't remember a movie."

"Yeah. It's pretty silly. But we can watch it and it will help us remember his voice."

Calder wiped his tears and nodded. "OK."

We snuggled into my big bed and I popped the DVD into the player and soon images of Jay flashed across the screen.

I think it's time that Calder saw a therapist. What do you think, Jay? Crazy? I seem to recall that you hated your mother for making you go to a therapist after your dad died. I wish I knew why. Your input would be really helpful right now. I just feel like his behavior is out of my realm and my own therapist can only do so much to help. I'm trying to put one foot in front of the other, just to get myself through this grief. And now I have to find a kid therapist. Margie from across the street recommended a guy that she sent Isaac to after one of his high school friends was killed in a car accident. She thinks Isaac liked him OK. But you know high school kids. They don't tell their mothers anything. But right now, it's the only name I have. I'll give him a call tomorrow.

Calder was curled up on the couch watching TV when the doorbell rang. I had hired Chloe, a babysitter, to take care of him while I went to my grief support group. She was new, but came highly recommended from Molly, one of the women in the group. Chloe was college-aged with long dark hair and eyelashes, and a tattoo that bloomed from her collar bone, just under a black tank top.

"Hi, Mrs. Cavor. I hope I'm not too late. Your place is a little tricky to find."

"No, no. Come on in, Chloe. Thanks for coming. This is Calder."

By now, Calder was sitting up on the couch looking worried, but not saying anything.

"Calder, do you want to come over and say hi to Chloe?"

"Hi," he said quietly.

I showed Chloe around the kitchen and left her to get acquainted with Calder while I went upstairs to grab a sweater, but when I turned to come back down, Calder was at the top of the stairs with tears in his eyes.

"Oh no, Calder. Not again. I just have to go out for a little while."

"I don't want you to go."

Calder came and wrapped his arms tightly around my waist.

"I know Cald, but I won't be gone for long and Chloe seems really nice. Did you know she's a singer in a band? Maybe you could show her your drums. I bet she'd be interested. Let's go downstairs now and ask—"

"No, Mama! Please don't leave me."

I picked Calder up and he buried his wet face into my neck, and I started walking down the stairs, staggering a little under his ever-increasing weight.

"Calder is just a little sad that I'm going out," I said to Chloe when we reached the bottom. "But he's a drummer and I know you're a singer, and I thought maybe he'd like to show you his drum set."

To Chloe's credit, she immediately picked up what I was angling for.

"Hey Calder," she said to him, touching his hair as his head still rested on my shoulder. "I'd love to see your drum set."

Calder picked up his head and wiped his tears a little with his sleeve. "Mama, please don't go!"

I set Calder down, but he immediately grabbed me and held my t-shirt in a vice grip hold.

"Please let go, Calder. I need to go now."

"Hey, Calder, will you show me your room?" Chloe's voice was upbeat, but I could tell from her face that this was a little more than she had bargained for. She stooped down to squat near him, held his hand and gave me a nod.

I yanked Calder's fingers from my t-shirt and grabbed my purse from the bench near the front door, slipped on a pair of sandals and waved as I scrambled out the door.

"Be good, Cald—"

"Mama! Noooo! Don't leave!"

I slammed the door behind me and scurried to the car. I got in, buckled up, and burst into tears. I felt like the worst mother in the world. After a few minutes I pulled a tissue from the compartment between the seats, a new hiding spot for the ever-necessary tissues, and dabbed my eyes. I was thankful that I would soon be at Molly's house and would be greeted by large glass of Chardonnay. A crow flew into view and landed on the roof of the garage. It stared directly down into the car, at me, with a look that was either judgmental or sympathetic, I couldn't tell which.

"What are you looking at? Dumb crow. What do you know?"

I started the car and reversed.

God I wish you were here, Jay. I have to assume Calder's behavior is because of your loss, but maybe there's something else, something more serious. I don't know if I can do this. I feel like I'm breaking. I want to crawl into bed and never wake up. I want to cry and never stop. I want to scream or hit something. All this emotion has nowhere to go.

Could you give me a sign right now? Flicker the lights or something. Just tell me I'm doing the right thing.

Speaking of signs, I keep seeing crows and thinking of you. Is that weird? They seem to follow me, which is both comforting and slightly creepy. I hope it's you. I keep imagining myself walking up to them and having a conversation with them. See? I'm a nutcase. And since I can't go talking to crows in public, I'm thinking of seeing a psychic. I wonder if you'd come? I fear the emotional toll the reading might take on my state of mind. I'm still feeling pretty fragile and a reading might be really emotional. Do you think it will be positive or sad? What if it leaves me feeling even more empty and alone? What if a reading sets me back on the road of grieving by trying to connect with you again? What if the woman is a quack? Oh God. I think I'm going crazy. Maybe I'd be better off talking to crows.

I love you, Maya

Chapter Eleven

Tonal Education

My father morphs himself into my landscape, sitting on the black leather couch opposite me. In close-up detail I notice the stubble on his cheeks, a tousle of hair, that damned Rolling Stone's t-shirt, and smooth, unblemished hands. I'm unsure why I can still make out the human characteristics of people in this realm. I sense it is because I need these reminders of the living world during my infantile spirit stage, but they are beginning to seem unnecessary. Right now, though, I am glad.

My father is young and old at once. He could be in his twenties or his eighties. Both youthful and wise. His aura pulses emerald, a level well beyond my own pale yellow. I discovered the existence of levels at the Crystal Palace, as it's commonly called, a kind of port of entry for those transitioning from human to spirit form. From within the Palace's dome, it's possible to see the array of ordered color that signifies the varying levels of spiritual beings. The spectrum begins with pink for babies, progressing through yellow, orange, purple, royal blue, green, grey, light blue, and finally, white. Each level is seen clearly through the rest, like gazing into a glass prism, but one that takes up an entire skyscape like a multicolored Aurora Borealis whose clarity and depth makes it seem possible to see the entire universe at once.

Most people seem content to remain within the royal blue spectrum, the way most people on Earth are content with achieving an undergraduate degree. Newly transitioning souls usually come into their afterlife at the yellow level, but most progress quickly from there. A few go on to get their master's and fewer still get their doctorate. Apparently my dad had been busy up here and managed to get his doctorate in spiritual achievement, which impresses the hell out of me.

Apparently, I had become his apprenticeship project, as part of his spiritual doctoral thesis.

They decided to assign me to you, J.J., since relating to your own kin is a little easier for newly dead spirits. It's helpful to have a guide you feel comfortable with.

His first project was to teach me to "cycle up" my thought patterns, as I was still emitting at a frequency more in tune with Earth-bound entities. This was common with the newly dead and was the reason that as spirits we're more adept at contacting our loved ones on Earth in the first few months and years after we die. As we learn to cycle up, it becomes harder and harder to align the electrical thought processes with those of people on Earth.

We will try an exercise now, Jay.

OK. My dad's thoughts gave me a sense of warmth and well-being, a sense of being protected.

I'm going to hum and I want you to match the tone of my hum with your own.

All right. I'll give it a try. But why are we doing this?

As you master the ability to convert your thought processes to a series of high frequency tones, more of the voices around you will become audible to you. They will be your guides. Right now, you are not properly attuned to hear them.

You make me sound like an out of tune guitar.

Good analogy! You are exactly that, J.J.

Great. Thanks, Dad. I sensed his smile. And then I heard a tone, not unlike the *om* sound I used to hear coming from the lunch-time yoga session that some of the people from work did in the common room. I imagined myself opening my mouth to make the sound, but nothing happened.

Imagine it coming from deep within your throat rather than from your mouth. Then move the sound up through your throat to the top of your head until it comes out the crown.

I did as my dad suggested, but my memory-body struggled with the effort.

Concentrate. Rely less on your body memory and more on your mind.

OK. I tried again. This time when I heard his tone, I imagined myself singing with my mouth closed, singing into my eyes, into the top of my head, until finally I heard the most ethereal sound I have ever heard – a high-pitched operatic hum that, had I been in a body, would have brought me to tears. I realized this was not a new sound, but one I had emitted before. Long ago. In another lifetime. A life before the lifetime of Jay. I sputtered into silence.

Nice! Really nice, J.J.!

God. Wow. OK. Something just came back to me. I remembered something… like I've been here before… That was really weird.

Good, Jay. That tone is your entry back into this world. You have been here many times. As you practice your tone, memories of other lifetimes on Earth will come back to you. They won't always make sense. Just relax into them. Let them take you where they will. It's not your job to make sense of everything. It's your job right now to receive.

I can do that. I think.

Let's try it again.

This time it was easier to access the tone. I used less body memory and could move the sound out of the top of my being – no longer my head – much more quickly. My first impulse was to weep again; so intense was the sense of finding something beloved that had been lost, but was now found. How could I have forgotten this place? When had I forgotten?

My childhood hands rested on the blue gingham tablecloth of my grandmother's dining room table. The swirly handled silver spoon leaned against the rim of the cut crystal glass bowl that had, just moments before, contained my grandmother's homemade applesauce, heavy with cinnamon, her favorite spice. I imagined tiny apple worms squirming around in my stomach, as my grandmother always liked to joke that she may have left a worm or two in the sauce, "for protein". I rested my hands on the table because I felt unsteady, as if my legs had disappeared and I had nothing rooting me to the ground. I worried that I might float away. My dad, in his '70s style mullet, wore his lumberjack jacket at the table and argued with his father over someone called Nixon.

I heard unfamiliar voices laughing down the hall and I knew without looking that I would see a group of people gathered in the living room wearing old-fashioned clothes, clothes from the '20s or '30s. These people lived in the house long before my grandparents. I wanted to walk down the hallway and step into the living room so I could see them, but I couldn't move, seemingly glued to my spot. Instead I travelled within my mind to the door of the living room, but seemed unable to enter. I still couldn't see the old-fashioned people. I could flip myself between the present with my hands resting on the table in front of my applesauce bowl and that time long before, with those unfamiliar people I couldn't see yet knew were there. Behind the memory, a tiny hum, the kind that sometimes came into my ears without warning and then disappeared just as mysteriously. I wondered how I could slip through time, flitting back and forth between present and past and if I could always do this, or if it was possible to do this in other places besides my grandmother's gingham-clad dining room table.

Maybe the apple worms were hallucinogenic.

It wasn't the worms.

I smiled at my dad's thought. *I guess it wasn't. I don't remember ever being able to do that again.*

It's quite common in children. And the tinnitus, the ringing in your ears, is a reminder of this world.

I used to get it all the time as a kid.

And if you'd lived into old age, you would have had a recurrence of that. It acts as a tiny thread of memory, linking you back to this place. As children, we are closer to the memory of "home" and as we age, we again draw near enough to remember the place we will soon return to.

I remember reading of people who were terribly plagued by tinnitus.

Yes. It is a method we use in this plane to link the living back during times in their lives when they need to be reminded.

From what I read, it's a pretty annoying reminder.

Like all bodily ailments. All are reminders.

Reminders of what?

Ailments force us to remember our humanness, our lack of invincibility. Ailments come at a time when our minds and bodies are out of alignment. They remind us of what lies beneath the surface of who we are in our bodies.

And who are we?

In the Buddhist tradition, there is a story of an ancient Buddhist village that was about to be invaded. Afraid that their pure gold statue of Buddha sitting in the main square would be plundered, the townspeople covered it in mud. When the town was invaded, the invaders never took a second glance at the mud covered statue. The invasion lasted years and eventually anyone who remembered the gold statue died off. Finally, hundreds of years later, a young man prayed near the statue and noticed a tiny fleck of gold showing beneath the statue's mud coated surface and the pure gold statue was rediscovered. In myth, each one of us is that gold statue, covered in the muck and detritus of our everyday lives. Often in the business of going about our lives, we forget who we really are beneath all the masks and walls we build around us. But the reality is that we are pure gold.

I suppose as Jay I am still encased in mud.

Yes. Somewhat. But you've had glimpses. More than most because of your glimpses of me. Because of the effect my death had in your life.

Did I? I don't remember.

You chose not to.

Why would I choose not to?

I'm not sure. Anger?

I wasn't angry.

No?

"Happy birthday to you! Happy birthday to you! Happy birthday dear Jaa-ay, happy birthday to you…" Our table was surrounded by the entire wait staff of Lime Ricky's and I was pretty certain my face was the color of the cherry red aprons they were all wearing. The "cake" was one of Lime Ricky's famous key lime pies, to which I was addicted, and covered in sixteen candles. My mom clapped, pleased with her little surprise.

"Come on, Jay! Blow out your candles and make a wish!" I wasn't sure if she knew what I wished for every year, though I imagined she suspected. I imagined my dad sitting next to me now, slapping me on the back. *Fuck. Where the hell are you Dad?*

I'm here.

No you're not. You left, remember? You're fucking dead.

Jay, I'm with you always.

I'm sick of that pansy 'you're in my heart' shit. You're not here. You're not in my heart. You're not anywhere, asshole.

I hated birthdays. And this was the worst. Being sung happy birthday to by a bunch of prissy waiters at Lime Ricky's. Christ. I wanted to frisbee the pie across the room, punch the stupid singing, grinning waiters, and run. Get drunk. Smoke some weed. I gritted my teeth, which made my jaw ache its familiar ache. For months I'd been waking up with excruciating headaches, similar to the one that was now in full frontal lobe attack mode. I rubbed my temples.

"Jay? Are you OK?"

"Yeah, Mom, fine. Just don't have a wish."

"I'm sure there's something you want, sweetheart." I looked at her. She thought she knew what I wanted. *I want my dad.* But not this year. What the hell has he ever done for me? I blew. Hard.

I want a new dad.

Jay, you're killing me.

No, Dad. You did that all by yourself. I don't need your ghost voice in my head anymore either, thanks. I've got this.

As you wish, son. As you wish.

I felt my dad's mindful gaze upon me.

I continued to help you, though you were often closed to my guidance.

You were guiding me? How?

Yes. I gave you signs to show you the way.

Like?

Like getting Maya to bend down that day in Pompeii to feel the ruts in the road.

You did that?

Yes.

Why?

Because you and Maya were supposed to meet at that time.

Says who?

It's what you and Maya planned, Jay. Before you came into your lives as Jay and Maya.

We planned our lives together?

Yes, Jay. Try accessing your tone and you will see.

I settled into my tone. Shadowy images shimmered before me. One nondescript form I recognized as Maya, another as Calder. We stood before a group of entities, each positioned in front of what appeared to be thin plates of glass. Each pane acted as a portable viewing device with movie-like scenes playing in triple speed. The panes were suspended, hovering, but could also be merged together so the scenes would alter, adding new characters into the scene or removing them. Another pane seemed to alter the locations of the merged vignettes or the atmospheric conditions of the day. Eventually, we were watching as I stumbled over Maya that day in Pompeii. Her form turned to me and laughed.

Perfect! Maya's voice startled me. *This is right, Jay, don't you think? I'm glad we'll be together again.*

I felt myself wavering – a light about to flicker out. I needed to rest.

I suggest a period now of stasis.

You sound like HAL from 2001.

Funny, Jay. We talked about this last time, remember?

Oh. Right. Woo-woo meditation for dead guys.

Ratchet down your thoughts now, Jay. Think of darkness. Think of floating. Think of sleep. Remember this is akin to sleeping in human form. You need to put your thought process function to sleep. Like a computer.

See? You are *HAL.*

I began the process of cycling down that my dad had taught me. Not through tones like cycling up, but in conjuring an ebony darkness, an underwater silence, a monotonous rain. Sleep in the afterlife.

Chapter Twelve

THERAPY

I sat next to Maya on a couch in the therapist's office. Out the window, on a turf field, tiny girls in blue and white uniforms played soccer in the Indian summer sun. Calder slumped in a chair near the therapist's desk, an awkward arrangement. I could see why Maya might be invited into the first few minutes of Calder's sessions, but her attendance during the entire session had been going on for a month now.

"Do you like to play chess, Calder?" Mr. Ettinger, the therapist, asked. Calder made no reply as he sat cross-legged in the round swivel chair, picking at one of his shoelaces.

"Is there another game you like to play?" Still no reply from Calder. Maya breathed heavily. This guy wasn't getting through to Calder whatsoever.

"Uh, he likes computer games…" Maya tried to throw this guy a life raft, but in my book, he had already drowned. At the end of the session, Calder waited outside in the waiting room while Maya and the therapist spoke alone.

"I want to suggest that we try Calder on some meds. I know he's young, but they may help him to rewire his brain. I think they may help with the depression and the anxiety."

No way my son is going on meds, buddy.

"Meds? Like what kind of meds?"

"Something like Prozac. Prozac helps increase the levels of serotonin in the brain. It's possible the trauma of his father's death altered Calder's brain chemistry to a point where he's becoming wired for depression. The serotonin may help to reverse that trend. Give him a sense of what being happier feels like, perhaps giving him a little more control of his emotions."

"But he's so young."

"He is young. We would just try it for a while and see how it goes. I'm not thinking it will be a long term solution. I admit there is very little research that's been done on the effects of these SSRIs on the brains of children, but I've seen some great outcomes with many of my patients."

"So you think Calder's depressed?"

"I think he's in grief, and grief can bring on depression and anxiety in anyone, including children. From what I've observed, he seems withdrawn, prone to tears, easily frustrated, and from what you've told me, he's somewhat hyperactive at home and destructive to himself with the skateboarding. You've also told me how difficult it is for you to leave him at school or with a babysitter."

"Impossible, yeah…" Maya reached over and pulled a Kleenex from the box and wiped her eyes. "I just don't know what to do anymore."

"Those are all symptoms that could be helped with a medication like Prozac. I'm suggesting we try him on a low dose and see how he does. If there's no change, we can try something else."

"I just worry about what meds could do to his developing brain."

"Maybe take some time to think about it, do a little research, and we can talk again during the next session."

In the car on the way home, Calder started crying. A

sudden gust of wind blew a flurry of fallen leaves across the windshield as the autumn sky turned an ominous color with the threat of rain. A murder of crows flew overhead.

"Why do I have to go to dumb therapy? I hate that guy! He's stupid!"

"He's not stupid, Cald."

"All he does is ask me dumb questions about what games I play or who my friends are and stuff."

"I know it's hard to understand, sweetie, but I think you should keep going, at least for a little while longer."

"Noooooo! I hate therapy! I hate my life!"

Calder's right, Lenie. The guy's a crock. What kind of therapist has a mom sit in on every session? Calder's not going to open up with you sitting there. And meds? That's bullshit. He just doesn't want to do any real work. Find another therapist, Maya.

"Do you want to get a Dick's burger for dinner?"

Calder wiped his face with the back of his hand. "Do I still have to go to a therapist?"

"I don't know. Let's talk about it again later."

"K. Can I get a cheeseburger? And a chocolate shake?"

I wished I could go with them. Taste that gooey burger with its fake orange cheese, juices squirting as I took a bite...

"Having fun fantasizing?" Alice smirked at me. "You're just making it harder for yourself, you know. Clinging to human desires."

"I can't help it. I miss my desires. I miss Dick's burgers."

"Not my thing. I'd prefer a sliver of foie gras on a cracker with an excellent Merlot."

"You are a mystery, Alice. Who are you really?"

"If you must know, in one of my lives, I was quite aristocratic. I got used to the finer things, you might say."

"The mystery deepens. Why were you assigned to me?"

"We were paired because we could challenge one another. We have a lot we can teach each other."

"I'm learning from you, that's for sure. But what could you possibly be learning from me?"

"Besides patience?" Alice smirked, showing a small dimple in her right cheek that I hadn't noticed before.

"Hey!"

"I'm learning to have fun."

"You have a sly sense of humor, Alice."

"Thank you, Jay. You're teaching me that a sense of humor can have a place in the spirit world. You've helped me see the positive qualities of being human. My focus until I met you was about trying to extricate the human qualities from the spirit. In my work with you, I am beginning to see that the two can never truly be separated. Human and spirit must coexist even in this realm. I see there are benefits to being in touch with your humanness as a spirit, just as there are benefits to being in touch with one's spirituality as a human."

"I'm glad my failings as a spirit can help you out."

"No, Jay, that's not what I—"

"I'm kidding, Alice. I get what you mean. And I think you're right. No spirit can completely lose their humanness."

"Indeed, humans are flawed. A human is driven by an ego that's represented by the human body. The ego cloaks a human's True Self, that expanse that can't be seen, the expanse you are now discovering. An ego is like the tiny tip of an iceberg that's visible above the surface of the water, but the True Self is the mountain of ice that hides beneath."

"Nice analogy," I said, eliciting a smile from Alice.

"Thank you. I'm glad you understand. But enough about me. How are you coming along with Calder?"

"Not great, I'm afraid. The therapist has been a flop. He wants to put my son on anti-anxiety meds."

"How do you feel about that?"

"It's a complete crock. Meds are the last thing Calder needs."

"Why are you so certain of that?"

"Because they could alter his brain chemistry. Meds feed the body, not the spirit. Isn't that what we've just been talking about with all that ego stuff?"

"You are right, Jay, of course, but humans alter their brain chemistry on a daily basis."

"It doesn't mean my son should. He's just a kid."

"So a baby cold medicine is OK, but an SSRI is not?"

"No. Well. A baby cold medicine is harmless."

"Is it?"

"OK, Alice, you've made your point. But Maya could be doing more. Like not giving into Calder so much and finding a better therapist."

"Maya's in grief, Jay. Having the presence of mind for dealing with a difficult child right now is not easy for her. And besides, have you forgotten your own experience with therapists?"

The floor did its disappearing act and I found myself at old Dr. Al's office, a room infused with the aroma of old men, cigars, and urine. I leaned back in the tattered leather chair, my long, teenaged legs sprawled out in front of me as I pretended to sleep.

"There are many opportunities for you to sleep, Mr. Cavor. This is not one of them. Your mother is paying me good, hard-earned money for you to come see me each week."

"Yeah, well I wish she wouldn't bother. It's a waste of time."

"What makes you say that?"

"All we do is sit here and talk about dumb stuff."

"What would you prefer to talk about?"

"Anything but my dead dad."

"OK. Name it."

"Uh. I can't really think of anything right now."

"Sports?"

"Nah."

"Girls?"

"No."

"Your mom?"

"God, no."

I guess old Dr. Al finally admitted to my mom that he wasn't getting anywhere with me, and I stopped going. My mom and I both slid into a complacency around my dad's death. We didn't speak of it much, which seemed to suit us both fine.

"Another therapist might help," Alice said, popping me out of the memory, "but don't dismiss the use of medication. It could possibly help Calder. And don't forget you have the ability to help him too."

"How?"

"Talk to him."

"Alice, I know you're all into this human-as-spirit thing, but I'm not sure my ghostly conversations with Calder are getting through to him."

"Oh, Jay, you must have more faith in yourself."

"I'm just not sure he remembers our conversations. And I wish I could talk with Maya in the same way."

"He remembers on a subconscious level if not a conscious one. The child's mind can still very much access this realm. It's sad that humans lose that ability to see and hear us as they get older."

"Yeah. I hope you're right about Calder."

"I am all knowing, Jay."

This time it was my turn to laugh. "See, you have an excellent sense of humor!" Then, with a twinkle of light, she was gone.

❊ ❊ ❊

I don't know what compelled me to turn my attention to Calder at that particular moment. He was at the school playground with Maya who was distracted, talking with one of the other moms. Calder and another kid his age were practicing their "ollies", a sort of skateboard flip, at the bottom of a wheelchair ramp that led up the entrance of the school, which was perched on a hill. Beside the ramp, there was a wide, steep set of steps up to the ornate front doors. Because of the height of the incline, the wheelchair ramp was unusually long and made two hairpin turns as it made its way down to the playground. High school kids often tested their skateboard skills there by attempting to ride down the entire ramp. It was notoriously dangerous, with quite a few wipe-outs ending in visits to the ER. Calder was strictly forbidden to skateboard on the upper levels of the ramp. Lately, he'd been testing his limits with Maya and running up to try and skate with the older boys who usually made him just watch until Maya found him and marched him home. On this day, the ramp was deserted and I saw Calder look over at his mother and whisper to his friend. They picked up their skateboards and, with a last furtive glance at their moms, ran to the top. For once, none of the high school kids were around and so there were no obstacles stopping them from what they were about to do. At the top of the ramp, Calder dropped his board and stood for a moment with one foot on it.

"That's scary, dude," the other kid said. "I can't go down that."

"Why? Are you a chicken?" Calder taunted.

"No! I just don't want to die," the kid said.

"Well, I don't care if I die," Calder said.

He stood, rolling the skateboard back and forth with his foot. He seemed to be deciding whether or not to go.

Don't do it, Cald.

"I'm gonna do it!" he said suddenly, as he pushed off. He rolled down the first ramp, slowly at first, picking up speed as he came into the first curve. He managed a wobbly turn around the bend, steadying himself on the handrail, but picked up more speed along the straightaway. The second ramp was longer and the curve was backed by a brick wall. If he continued and didn't make the next turn, he would slam into the wall. If he did make it, the ramp ended in a sidewalk which opened onto the park's busy parking lot where he could go hurling into parked cars. It wouldn't be a good outcome, no matter what happened. He was going too fast and I expected him to jump off the board at any second, but a determined look came over his face. A part of me was proud of him in that moment. You had to admire the kid's courage. Just then, Maya looked up and screamed, startling him. He tilted sideways and scraped his shoulder against the side wall of the ramp as his body flew into the air.

I instinctively tried to block him from slamming his head into the wall. A white flash of light hit him in the chest causing him to rotate slightly in the air so he slammed into the wall with his shoulder instead of the full force of his head. There was a loud *crack*, and he crumpled to the ground. His skateboard bounced against the wall like a pinball and carried on down the ramp without him.

Maya arrived, crying, "Oh God. Oh God, Calder!!" He lay on the ground moaning. The other mother was already on her cell phone dialing 9-1-1. Maya tried to cover him with a jacket, but he moaned louder and so she took it off. Both mothers knew not to try and move him.

The sirens grew louder and soon three firemen climbed out of a fire truck and came over. One of them kneeled beside Calder while the other two talked with Maya quietly close by. Calder was dazed, and seemed to be in a fair amount of pain. Sarah's face was white and her hands shook.

"What's your name, kid?"

"Calder," he whispered.

"OK, Calder, the firefighter replied. "We're going to help you. Where does it hurt?"

"My shoulder."

"OK. We'll be careful then." The firefighter eased Calder's helmet off his head to more moans and felt the back of his head and neck. "Can you wiggle your fingers and toes?"

Calder complied and Maya breathed a sigh of relief.

"You may have broken your collar bone, Calder, but we'll get you to the hospital so they can take some X-rays. Sound good?"

Calder nodded, his expression serious, and I could tell he was on the verge of tears. As the firefighter checked Calder's vitals he asked, "So how'd you get yourself into this mess? Your mom says you tried to skateboard all the way down that ramp?"

"Yeah, I guess."

Maya was crouched down beside the firefighter. "Why would you do that, Calder? You know it's dangerous. And I've forbidden you to skateboard here. You could have died," she said.

"I wanted to die." Calder looked at her, his expression hard.

"Hey, hey now. Why would you want to die?" the firefighter asked.

"So I could go and see my dad." The firefighter looked up at Maya, surprised. Maya looked stricken and then started to cry. Only then did I realize how serious things with Calder had become.

Later that night I visited Calder as he drifted off to a medicated sleep.

Calder?
Mmm.
Quite a day.
Yeah.
Not a brilliant move, dude.
Maybe not.
Did you really want to die?
I don't know. Kind of. I want to be with you.
It's not your time yet, Beano.
Why not? It wasn't your time yet, was it?
Good point. I didn't think so, but it's not something any of us have any control over. For some reason, it was my time.

I hate my life.

It will get better. My dad died when I was young too, remember. I should know. If you die now, think of all the good stuff you'd miss.

Like dumb school?

No. Like fishing in the summer with grampa or growing up and getting married and having a baby.

I don't like girls. They're gross.

They won't always be gross. Someday you'll want to kiss one.

Eeww.

Haha. See all the great stuff you'd miss if you died?

But I'd be with you.

You'll be with me soon enough. Take your time buddy and enjoy this life.

I don't know how.

That therapist can help with that.

No.

You need to try and stick with it.

Why?

Because talking about my death will help.

It's stupid. It doesn't help at all. Under his eyelids, Calder's eyes were dancing their REM dance. His brain waves were in a Theta state, that state of consciousness that makes a human mind most accessible to the spirit realm.

I used to think the same thing. But now I wish I had stuck with it.

You do?

Yeah. If I had, I think I would have been a better dad to you. I wouldn't have tried to push away the sadness I had when my dad died.

I don't want to be sad. I want to be a happy person.

I know, buddy. We all do. I did too. But sometimes you have to let yourself be sad. It's OK. You won't break.

Are you sad that you died?

Of course. It was a stupid accident. And I miss you and your mom. But things here aren't so bad.

Did it hurt to die?

I didn't feel it. It was fast.

That's good.

It's so different over here. How I died doesn't really matter anymore. We're still growing and changing.

Do you have a body? Calder's breathing deepened as he slipped into a Delta wave state of sleep consciousness.

No. Not really.

What do you do there?

I'm growing up still. I'm learning how to be a better father to you.

But you're dead. How can you still be my dad?

In lots of ways. Like talking to you the way I am now. I love you, Beano.

I love you too, Daddy.

❖ ❖ ❖

"The therapist wants to put Calder on meds," Maya said, twisting a curl of hair around her finger and biting her lip, waiting for the reaction of the others. She was at Molly's house, another widowed mom in the grief support group that met once a month in each other's homes. The women gathered around Molly's living room – Maya on the couch, Molly, dwarfed by her oversized denim-covered chair, Kristie in a wicker rocker dragged in from the porch, and Chelsea on her knees near the coffee table, her back warmed by a fire in the fireplace that warded off a late November chill, with her cup of tea perched near a large plate of homemade peanut butter cookies. Of course, unbeknown to our wives, us dead husbands were there with them. Participating in these groups had become a habit for all of us, the dead and the living. When the group of widows began meeting, the husbands remained in the distance, held off by a strange mixture of regret and sadness. But the energy this group of women exuded as they talked drew us in. We became more substantive in our presence. I was able to make out a few of the human features of each husband and we developed a sort of camaraderie between us. I sat beside Maya on the couch.

"Really? He seems so young. Do you think it'll help?"

Chelsea asked, looking concerned. "Are things really that bad with him?"

"Temper tantrums, throwing things, breaking his toys, then the skateboarding accident."

"How's he doing after that?" Kristie asked.

"Oh, he's fine. He spent a few days lying around the house, but now he just wears the brace around his shoulder and he's fine. He's back at school."

"That must have been so scary!" Molly said.

"Yeah. He actually told the fireman that he wanted to die," Maya said, her eyes filling with tears.

"Oh God!" Molly said.

"Yeah. He keeps saying how much he hates his life. It's awful. I can't leave him with a babysitter without him freaking out and he's obsessed about me not being late to pick him up at school." Maya swallowed back her tears, took a deep breath and closed her eyes for a moment.

"Wow! Sounds intense," Chelsea said. "Tatiana can be difficult, but nothing like that."

"I know. It's a little extreme for an eight-year-old, right? I always thought people who put their kids on meds were copping out or something, but I'm starting to get it," Maya said as she bit her lip.

"It's not copping out. Not at all, honey," Kristie said.

"So you think I should try the meds?" Maya looked around at her friends, imploring them to help her with the decision.

I get it Lenie, but try and find another way. Meds aren't the answer! How could the woman who made her own baby food want to put our child on anti-depressants?

"It can't hurt to try, can it?" Molly interjected.

What is wrong with our wives? I looked at Declan, Molly's husband, for backup.

Don't look at me. I agree with them. What's the harm?

I just think there are alternatives to putting a kid on medication for something like grief.

But isn't this a little more than just grief? The kid tried to kill himself on a skateboard. Maybe the grief is a precursor to depression. Your son seems to be having a pretty rough time. Have you forgotten that he also pulled a knife out of a drawer and asked his mom to kill him? If that's not a cry for help, I don't know what is. I think it's more than just grief. Declan had a point.

You can't blame the kid for wanting to be with his dad. Seems like a pretty normal kid thing to me. I don't think it means he's suicidal. I'm actually impressed by his creativity and touched that he wants to be with me so badly.

A little human of you, don't you think, Jay? Ben's thought was clear. Ben, Kristie's husband, had been here the longest. He seemed to get a kick out of pointing out one's human traits, which I found hypocritical, given that it seemed like a pretty human thing to do. In life, Ben had been an extreme athlete and very particular about taking care of his body. Despite his healthy lifestyle, he dropped dead of a heart attack during a marathon. Even the kind of diligence that keeps a human body healthy is no guarantee that a body will last you through old age. I could understand his resentment towards one's humanness.

Human? Do you mean egotistical? It may be, but I think it's human nature for a child to want to be with his father, I replied.

You seem pretty convinced that Maya is wrong about this, Declan said.

I just don't like the idea of my son having his brain chemistry altered.

Fair enough, but don't you think your wife deserves your support? Ben asked.

Yeah, of course I want to support Maya, but that doesn't mean I have to agree with her, does it?

Ben seemed to shrug.

"God, this is hard. I wish I weren't doing it alone." Maya sighed as she spoke.

"Yeah, the alone part sucks," Kristie said.

Ben looked at his wife. His light blue aura dulled

somewhat by her comment, but I read no thoughts from him.

I wish they could see what we see. Ben's thought permeated the air around us.

What can we see? I responded. I sort of knew what he meant, but I wanted to hear it from him.

That the experiences we have on Earth are what shape us, the hard experiences in particular. This culture of medicating is unnecessary. Ben sounded resolute.

But there are cases where medication is helpful and can positively change neurological synapses in the brain to influence behavior. If the technology is there... Declan, the scientist, threw in his two cents.

I was no doubt emotionally invested in my son's wellbeing, but it seemed to me that Calder would emerge from this period of troubling behavior and turn out to be perfectly normal. Without meds.

But what about the toll that would take? On your son, on Maya? Declan asked. *What if the meds could just be for a little while, to help Calder over his black moods and to help him know what being happy feels like? He can always go off them if it doesn't seem to be working.*

Yeah, but having those chemicals passing through Calder's brain concerns me. We've all seen the effects of drugs on the human body. Drug addicts lose their connection to this realm completely. They become so immersed in their human bodies that they can't retain any spiritual resonance at all, I said.

Do they? Or are addicts trying to escape their human bodies, maybe trying to find their way here through drugs? What is it? Are you frightened of losing your connection with your son if he goes onto meds? Declan asked.

I could see my own aura glow with truth. Impossible to hide one's truth in this realm. Was my concern for Calder's brain really my objection to the meds? Or the fear that I would lose my late night talks with Calder, that meds would block his mind from me?

I'm with you, Jay. Declan's thought exuded warmth. *You*

don't know the effect those meds will have on Calder's mind, but you might not be able to dissuade Maya from taking this step. She's trying to help Calder and she's a desperate mom. You might need to simply support her.

Yeah. I see your point. I guess I can try.

"Thanks guys," Maya said, smiling. "I feel a little better knowing I have your support. I'm so glad for this group."

"Me too!" Molly said as she got up from her chair. "Does anyone want a glass of 'widow juice'?" She didn't wait for an answer. She disappeared into the kitchen. The women were quiet as they listened to the fridge opening and glasses being pulled from the cupboard. Kristie stood up to help. Maya kicked off her shoes and tucked her feet under her, settling into her thoughts.

The glasses clinked as they were carried out on a tray. With wine, the women all seemed to relax. Chelsea spoke suddenly, breaking the silence:

"I put a profile on Match.com… I've decided I want to see what's out there."

"Wow!" Maya said.

"I know it's only been two years since Charlie died, but I think I'm ready."

I looked at Charlie, whose normally cool blue aura glowed, the only apparent response to his wife's declaration. He seemed to shrug. *"I know, I know. I'm cool with it. She needs to move on, you know?"*

"Chelsea, that's great. That's a huge step." Kristie smiled.

"You don't think it's too soon?"

"No, not at all!" The women all spoke the same words at the same time.

"So?" Maya asked, her lips curled into a sly smile. "Any takers?"

Molly looked shocked for a moment and then laughed.

"Well, as a matter of fact, I've had quite a few responses," Chelsea said. "I've been surprised actually. I didn't think anyone would be interested in a frumpy old mom of a five-

and eight-year-old who spends most of her weekends on a soccer field. Certainly, a lot of older men responded, a couple of creepos. But one I found interesting... we're going on a date next week."

"No way!" Molly said.

"He seems really nice. A professor at Puget Sound University. Something to do with business ethics or some such thing. His name is Ken."

"Kids?" Maya asked.

"Nope. Married, but no kids. He's been divorced for about six years." Chelsea grabbed a cookie from the plate beside her.

"That's awesome, Chels. I'm proud of you. That's a huge step," Kristie said, smiling.

"Yeah, I guess I just felt ready. I'm sick of sitting around every night watching *Sex and the City* reruns. What about you guys? Are you ready?" Chelsea asked as she looked around the room.

"I'm definitely not there yet. I still cry into my pillow every night. Not exactly sex kitten material," Molly said.

"I still buy my undies at Safeway!" Kristie said. The women all laughed. "But I've thought about dating..." she continued, looking thoughtful. "I'm terrified. I haven't dated in over twenty years. I wouldn't even know where to begin."

I wish she would. The thought came from Ben. We all looked at him. *Kristie's still so closed to me in many ways. She can't seem to get beyond being my widow. I feel stuck in this place with her, tethered to her need for me to come back. I wish she could move on with her life. I just haven't been able to convince her. Kristie's very stubborn. But I need to move on as well.*

Move on? How do we move on? I asked.

We begin by relinquishing our attachments to our human selves, and to those we loved in life. It can happen at varying speeds, depending on the depth of our connections in life, or the amount of spiritual awakening we've acquired while on Earth. As we move away from earthly pursuits, we transmute into a higher spiritual level. New worlds open up to us. We can begin to plan the next phase of our journey.

"All the more reason you should try dating, Kristie," Maya said, grinning mischievously.

"Oh, sure, miss hot-to-trot, and what about you?" Kristie said.

We all looked at Maya. Perhaps I clung too tightly to my Earth life. I strove to help Maya and Calder through their grief. Perhaps that drive stemmed from my guilt of my own stupid accident, or tied up somehow in my father's death. Perhaps I still clung to Maya to prevent her from being with Marcus.

"Me, date? Uh. No. I can't imagine. It hasn't even been a year since Jay's death."

"Yeah, maybe that's too soon," Kristie said, taking a sip of wine.

"But, if you want to know the truth, I have this friend…" Maya looked down at the floor. Did she mean Marcus? Charlie looked at me now. My aura must have muddied, giving away my distress at Maya's declaration.

Chill man, it's a normal progression. Maya's just testing the waters, he said.

Yeah, I know. It's just that I'm starting to think there's something going on with this friend of Maya's. We both knew him as kids.

And that's a bad thing? Don't you want your wife to move on with her life?

Yeah, but not with this guy. He's an arrogant…

That's something she will have to discover on her own, Jay.

I'm not sure I can be as cool as you are about Chelsea dating. It's going to be difficult to see our wives with other men, isn't it?

I don't know about that. It's not like we don't know who the people are that they're going to date.

Know who they are? What are you talking about?

C'mon, Jay. Have you forgotten?

Forgotten what?

Oh, dude. It will come back to you. You must know by now that no human relationship is a coincidence. They are planned. Charlie's thoughts provoked something like a memory, one I couldn't quite reach. His truth seemed inaccessible to me in that moment.

"Friend?" Chelsea asked.

"Yeah. Someone I knew a long time ago. My first love, actually. Before Jay."

The other women looked at each other. "And?"

Maya shrugged. "He lives in Vancouver. It's not practical."

"But you obviously like this guy," Molly said.

Maya pushed a strand of her hair behind her ear. She cocked her head slightly as if she could see me sitting beside her. She looked sadder than I had ever seen her. I heard her thought:

I wish I could tell them the truth.

What is the truth, Lenie? I'm not sure I truly wanted to know.

"Yeah," Maya said. "I guess I do, but that doesn't mean it's right."

"You know, if you want, you could go and see Liz. She's that psychic my friend told me about. I haven't called her yet, but maybe she could give you some insight or something," Molly said.

"I've been thinking of seeing a psychic, actually. She might be perfect."

"It's not everyone's cup of tea, but I have to admit I'm sort of curious. I'd love to see if she gets anything about Charlie," Chelsea said.

"Ooh. That sounds fun," Chelsea said. "I'd be into getting her number."

"Not me. I think psychics are a bunch of quacks. They just make really good guesses based on what they can tell about you from how you look, the clothes you wear and that sort of thing," Kristie said. Her aura seemed to shrink with her statement.

"I don't know. This particular friend who told me about Liz is not the kind of person I imagined would be into psychics, but she raved about her. Said she picked up all sorts of stuff she couldn't possibly have known," Molly said, her brown eyes getting wider with her obvious excitement.

"Maybe, but I still think it's a crock," said Kristie, twisting her lips into a look of disapproval.

I wish Kristie would go see that psychic," Ben said. *I'd love to be able to communicate with her, tell her I love her.*

Can you really be that specific? I asked him.

I think it depends on the psychic's abilities, but, yes, I think you can. From my understanding, this Liz woman that Molly is talking about is pretty talented.

At that moment, I heard an unfamiliar voice. *I'm looking forward to meeting you, Jay.*

Who's that? I asked the voice.

What? Ben responded.

You didn't hear that voice?

No. What voice?

A woman's. Telling me she's looking forward to meeting me.

If only I could be so lucky. Sounds like you're going to get the opportunity to talk with Maya, Jay. Through Liz, the psychic. Lucky you, Ben said.

How does the psychic lady know that already? Maya hasn't even decided she's going to go see her yet.

She's psychic, Ben said.

"A psychic. What would I even ask her?" Maya said.

"It could be really emotional for you, Maya. Are you sure you want to put yourself through that?" Kristie asked.

"Yeah, I know that might be hard, but it also might be a nice kind of emotional. You know, like a happy feeling that I'm connecting with Jay."

"And maybe she'll tell you if you're going to wind up with Mr. Next Love," Molly said.

"Oh God, she could tell me that?"

"Maybe..." Molly responded.

"Then, I'm scared shitless!" Maya said, mocking a horrified look. Everyone laughed. "But, OK. I'm game. Molly, will you email me her info?"

I'm not sure I want to know about Maya's new dating life. Can a psychic really predict new love for her?

Liz can only tell Maya what she receives from you or Maya's own guardians. It will be up to you to tell Maya if she will find new love again, Ben said.

What guardians? I thought.

We all have guardians, Jay. Have you not met Maya's or Calder's yet?

No. I haven't even met mine. And how the hell is Maya's love life up to me?

You are well versed with Maya's path. You planned it together, remember?

That's the problem, Ben. I don't remember. I don't remember a thing.

All in good time, my friend. The knowledge will come to you when you're ready for it.

So I keep hearing.

Chapter Thirteen

THE PSYCHIC

Apparently anxious to connect with me in my nefarious world, it didn't take long for Maya to call the psychic. I was eager to communicate with Maya as well, excited by the prospect of being able to tell her how sorry I was, that I missed and loved her. It seemed an easier way to communicate than inserting myself into the consciousness of crows in hopes that their symbolism would be seen and understood by her. I practiced the tricks I learned from Alice and my dad to alert Maya to my presence – turning on lights by manipulating electrical circuitry with thought; selecting my favorite songs to play on the radio as she drove Calder to school using electrical thoughts to manipulate radio waves; or aligning my presence with the molecules of a particular smell (the orange blossoms of Italy).

I found ways to present myself to Maya in the form of a blackbird or crow. I could only combine my consciousness into that of an animal for very short periods of time, but I enjoyed staring into our living room window from the roof of the garage, unblinking, spying on Maya and Calder and then being able to swoop down to the ground in one swift movement, my altered weightlessness both freeing and confining at once. A heady sensation, being re-united with the yoke of gravity when one is accustomed to being matterless. I couldn't be sure if she would notice any of these signs, but grieving people seemed willing and open to any sort of connection with the newly dead.

Molly, in her email to Maya, said her friend raved about Liz's accuracy, but she admitted her nervousness about making an appointment for herself. For a few days, Maya let the email languish in her inbox, perhaps afraid of unleashing emotions she had carefully put to bed after almost a year of widowhood. I had to cajole Maya into calling Liz, visiting her in a dream and employing dream Liz to walk along the beach with me, hoping she might convince Maya of her legitimacy. I didn't anticipate that conjuring Liz for my dream was akin to calling her on the phone, pronouncing my desire to communicate with Maya.

By then Christmas arrived, and Maya forgot about the psychic idea in her effort to make it through the holiday, hosting her parents and pretending all was as it had once been. When school started up in the New Year, Maya needed time to recover, but when I sensed she was ready, I visited her in my crow form each day as she ate her breakfast, cawing at her to make the phone call. It took a few weeks for Maya to muster the courage to call, but Liz was prepared, even telling Maya that I had already visited her and that she had been expecting Maya's call.

Liz arrived at the house a few weeks later, a month or so after the one-year anniversary of my death, while Calder played at a friend's. Maya nervously escorted her into the living room. Outside, the beginnings of tiny, new yellow buds popped against a mud-gray colored sky. The weak March sun spread its ochre hues across the oak floors inside the house, back-lighting the vase of dried flowers from the garden that Maya had picked in the fall. She offered Liz tea and tried to act nonchalant as she put the kettle on to boil and tore open sachets of tea. Liz did not fit the description of a stereotypical psychic. She looked like she had just stepped off the farm, with thick, sand-colored work boots, wide-legged, faded carpenter pants, and a loose-fitting men's striped shirt. Her hair, a difficult-to-discern shade of grey-brown, shorn into a haphazard almost-mullet, was a long way from the run-of-the-mill, Bugs Bunny version of a psychic, hair pins flying as she peered into her crystal ball.

"Have you been doing this long?" Maya asked.

"I've seen dead people since I was a little girl."

"Did that freak you out?" Maya poured boiling water into the cups and handed one to Liz. Maya walked toward the living room and Liz followed.

"Not really. I didn't know that I was the only one who could see them. I thought everyone could. I guess I didn't really understand that those people were dead. To me, they seemed no different than the live ones."

"Wow. That's amazing. Would you like to sit here?" Maya gestured to a comfy chair opposite the couch.

"Perfect."

Maya couldn't see me sitting on the couch beside her, but I knew she could sense my presence, the downy hairs on her arms rising with goose bumps as they seemed to do whenever I came near her. She looked so small amongst the big brown couch pillows, where she sat clutching a smaller velvety indigo throw pillow on her lap.

"So, your husband's been very active. Apparently, he really wants to connect with you!"

"I hope so. I'm really anxious to connect with him too."

Ok, so yeah, I'm excited. I want to be with my wife.

"He's here now."

"Really, where?" Maya said, glancing around the room, looking slightly alarmed.

"He's sitting right beside you." Now Maya turned toward me and smiled nervously.

Liz took a deep breath and closed her eyes and sat quietly for several minutes. I decided to stand up in front of her and sort of dance around so she could see me.

Can you give me your name?

Liz's astral voice sounded higher pitched and more melodic than her speaking voice.

My name is Jay.

"Does his name begin with the letter J?"

"His name is Jay."

"Oh. OK. I thought 'J' was the first letter. Funny. It's his name *and* the first letter to his name. Good. Thank you." Liz took a quick intake of breath. I sat back down on the couch beside Maya.

Hello, Jay. How are you? Is there something you want to talk to your wife about today? I am at your service.

Wow. Cool. Thanks, Liz. Yes. I'm new at this, but I want to get through to Maya.

Alice appeared on the couch beside me.

"What? You don't think I can do this alone?" I asked her, a little annoyed.

"I'm just here for moral support and to help with some of the protocols. The usual way to begin when you're being read by a medium is to tell them the manner of your death. This is the easiest way they have of verifying to the person they are reading for that they have the right spirit."

How did you die? How did you die? Liz's thoughts were loud and insistent, as if she were shouting at me.

I took flight over Howe Sound locked into a BMW-cement boot, I said sarcastically.

"Isn't she supposed to know that?" I asked.

Alice shrugged. "Not unless you tell her."

I concentrated on the car, the impact, it sinking into water, my limp body trapped underwater, arms and hair floating up, dead eyes wide open.

"Oh, no. Don't show me that. I don't need to see that," Liz said aloud and visibly recoiled.

Oops. Sorry.

"Shit! This is hard. I just want to tell her that it's me!" I swiped at one of the pillows to alleviate my frustration, but the lack of impact made me more so.

"You must be careful with your thoughts," Alice said. "Sometimes certain images are just too powerful for the living to accept."

I couldn't stop my memory from continuing and I watched as they hauled my body onto the deck of the boat, zippering it into a shiny black cocoon, one with little hope of bearing new life. Liz began to tap her chest, then placed her palm over her breast.

"Something about his chest. Not breathing. And I see a great height. Did he fall?"

"Uh, yeah, I guess you could say that," Maya replied.

"See? She's pretty good," Alice said.

Moremoremore... Liz begged now.

Damn. I was so stupid. Please tell her how sorry I am.

"His passage was quick, and painless," Liz said. "He's sorry he had the accident."

"Well she got that right at least."

"Oh, give her a chance," Alice reprimanded. "She's just getting to know you. Besides, isn't that exactly what you want Maya to know?"

"He did shitty things sometimes, had a foul mouth. He was very direct, and didn't put up with a lot of crap. But he surprised you by always being truthful. He was tall, wasn't he? Very statuesque, very driven. A great sense of humor, very sarcastic."

Maya smiled. "Yes, that does describe him well."

"She has your number," Alice laughed.

"Yeah, thanks a lot," I grumbled. "But she did say 'statuesque'."

"He was also very intelligent, talented and a real charmer..."

"Ha! She *does* seem to have me figured out, all right." I

couldn't hide my smugness. Maya closed her eyes.

"Yes, he was all of that too."

I smiled, remembering our meeting in Pompeii and later having dinner in the moonlight.

"Do you have some connection to Italy?" Liz questioned. I was impressed.

"Ohmygosh! Yes! That's where Jay and I met. Wow! That's incredible!"

I thought of the grotto we swam into that day. My foreshadowed death.

"Hmm. A tomb? Why is he showing me a tomb? Or a cave? Is this maybe how he died?"

"We swam together in a grotto when we met in Italy. But he also died in the water."

"Good. OK. Thank you. Maybe that's why he showed it to me as a tomb. OK."

"He wants you to know he loves you very much," Liz said, hiccupping another quick intake of air, as if she had forgotten to breathe for the last five minutes.

"Is she just reading Maya's mind, or is she really picking up messages from me?" I asked Alice.

Alice smiled. "She picks up pure thought, pure love," she said.

"Tell him I love him very much too," Maya said, the sadness in her voice unmistakable. Her eyes welled up again with tears, and I tried to catch one in my open palm, but it splashed down onto her dark skirt. Another sunbeam broke through the clouds and streamed in through the windows, glinting against her fiery hair, casting her in a beautiful light. She gazed at the sunbeam with a look of rapture.

"Is that him? Giving me another sign?"

"Yes, it probably is. They love giving signs to let us know they're still around."

"I didn't do that!" I said.

"Go with it." Alice smiled. I looked at Maya, admiring her beauty. I wished I could talk to her directly and not through this very imprecise, indirect method."

"There is a sense of confusion with this soul – a sense of not being delivered, as if he was in the midst of something and it's been cut off and he's not sure where he is."

"I'm not confused. I'm well aware of being dead."

"I think Liz senses that you are a developing soul," Alice said.

"Developing? Is that what we call it?"

"Well, he did die unexpectedly," Maya said. She looked down into her lap, clutching a tissue.

Liz, I miss my family very much. I want to talk to Maya. It's like I can't quite connect to her.

"I feel your loss, Maya," Liz said. "He feels it too. He's worried about you. He feels you have no sense of direction. You are holding him through fear. What you need to do is hold him through reverence, through marriage, not through fear, not through pain."

Wow. Did I somehow convey all that to her? She's not that lost!

"OK." Maya sniffed. She was crying openly now. "I'm not sure I know how to do that."

"I didn't mean to upset her," I said to Alice.

"You're going to have to concentrate very hard, Jay. Think deeply about your message, and think only of it. The clarity of your communication stems from the clarity of your thought and of your love. Psychics are good at picking up the images of what is in your mind, but not the subtle ideas behind them. What might seem very obvious to you will be easily misinterpreted."

"You need to try and let him go, Maya," Liz said.

"I don't think I'm ready to."

I wished I could hug her in that moment. To realize how much I was loved.

Time to change the subject there, Liz. You're upsetting her. She might not be ready to hear this yet.

"Good, Jay. Think of Calder now," Alice suggested.

I thought of Calder sitting on this very couch.

"A boy. You have a little boy," Liz said. Maya nodded.

"He's been to see him. The boy has seen his dad." I thought of my conversation with Calder just as he fell asleep.

I entered another memory. I don't remember how our game started, but Calder and I began punching each other in the arm, ending in an all-out wrestle, with me pinning both of Calder's skinny wrists in one hand while I clutched his squirming body between my knees. "Now watchya gonna do?" I taunted. I tickled him in the armpits until he choked with laughter. Then I picked him up by both feet and threw him onto the couch, giggling. It became our game.

"He's showing me your son. I don't know if there's a chair that those two used to sit on, but he sits in this chair where he used to hold this baby. Oh my God! He's absolutely gorgeous! Those eyes! My God, that smile and the nose. What's with the nose?"

Maya smiled. "Yes, Calder is cute." *But the knife thing, Jay. What do I do about that?*

I thought of the meds that Maya wanted to put our son on and tried to convey my dislike for the plan.

"He's really concerned about Calder. Worried about his emotional state, but he feels he can't help Calder because it's you who needs to help him, Maya. Jay wants to help, but he can't put his arms around you. He can't communicate, and he's trying very hard to be with you, but can't get past your anger or your fear. He's worried because Calder needs you now."

Jeez, Liz. Kind of ad-libbing here a bit, don't you think?

"Yes, Calder's therapist wants to put him on meds," Maya said.

Don't do it, Lenie.

"Your son is young?"

"Yes, my son Calder just turned eight."

"OK. He talks to your son, is sort of his protector."

Protector. I guess that's true. I am his protector. I kind of like that.

I concentrated on the image of Calder drumming. I wanted to make sure that Maya understood how important drumming was to Calder in his healing process. Maybe she would see drumming as an alternative to meds.

"Does your son play the drums?"

"Yes! Yes, he does!"

"Good. Thank you. He's acknowledging that. He wants Calder to keep playing. It's important to him. He just wants you to know that."

"OK. I'll make sure he does."

And the meds...don't forget to tell her not to put Calder on meds.

"Nightgown. Why is he showing me a nightgown? Did he buy you a nightgown before he left this world?"

"I wasn't even thinking of a nightgown. Why did she say a nightgown?"

"Maybe she connected meds with patient and patient with nightgown. Mediums can pick up thoughts sometimes even when you might not be thinking them. They can also pick up subconscious thoughts from their subjects because most mediums are also psychic. But not all psychics are mediums."

"Really? So are psychics frauds then? Do they just read people's minds?"

"No. Mediums are just more tuned into the thoughts of the deceased while psychics are more tuned into the living. This woman seems to be fairly balanced between the two."

"He did give me a nightie for Christmas last year," Maya said, patting the velvet pillow like a kitten.

"OK. Yes. Thank you. This is his way of letting you know that he has come to see you. His concern right now is that you acknowledge his presence in your life because his concern is that you will not be able to be there for Calder."

I don't know what made me think just then of the flowers on the table at dinner that night at the *pensione* in Italy. White roses. I knew she would remember them, and if Liz mentioned them, Maya would know for certain that it was me.

"You have a garden? What is the rose he is showing me? Do you have roses in the garden?"

"I have a small garden. With a really lame rose bush."

"OK. Well, he's acknowledging that. He wants to show you it's really him."

"Damn! I tried to show her the rose in Italy! Not the stupid rose bush!"

"Calm down, Jay," Alice said.

"This is frustrating!"

"I know. It requires patience."

"There is something about a rose in the garden that means something to you and your son. He wants you to believe it's really him. Something about the rose and the nightgown. He's not giving me much more than that."

What do you need?

What are you like, Jay? Give me a sense of what you were like when you were alive. Something your wife might understand. I need to tune in and get connected to you more. You have to trust me.

OK. Well, we had a fight the night before I died. I was an asshole. Please tell her how sorry I am.

Liz did another hyper-breath and opened her eyes to look again at Maya.

"He's telling me he was an 'asshole'. That's the word he is using."

Maya laughed out loud. "That sounds like him," she said.

Alice giggled.

"Now why is that funny?"

"Hey, you said it! You need to stop swearing so much, Jay," Alice said. "It's going to interfere with the purity of your communication."

"Well, it made her laugh. She definitely knows it's me." I felt oddly elated.

Got anything else for me, Jay?

I didn't let Maya know I loved her often enough.

"He really loved you, and didn't say this as often as he should have. I think your anger at his death comes more from that than his actual loss. The loss of what wasn't completely expressed, what wasn't completely acknowledged between the two of you."

Maya nodded, more tears dripping onto the pillow in her lap. Liz leaned over and handed her a tissue.

"I know this is hard to hear. It's hard to take all this in emotionally."

Maya took the tissue and dabbed her eyes, leaning forward now, trying to regain control of the tears that were now streaming down her cheeks. "I guess I am angry. Angry that he had to go and die on us."

Suddenly I glimpsed Maya with another man. Marcus. The thought was devastating.

"Is Maya going to marry again?" I asked Alice, who said nothing. She began to annoy me. "Is she going to marry Marcus? Why can't you just tell me straight up?"

"Because that's for you to remember."

"Remember? God, if it's Marc… ugh! I can't think it!"

"He's telling me that you're going to find new love. Or maybe it's old love? Does that make sense?"

"I am? Old love? What do you mean?" Maya looked wide-eyed.

"Does the name Mark mean anything to you?"

Maya looked at Liz in surprise. "Marc? I'm going to be with Marc again? That's ridiculous! He's an old boyfriend."

"He's more than an old boyfriend. Did you have an affair with this man while you were married to Jay?"

Maya swallowed. Tears dipped onto her lap. To my shock, she nodded.

You had an affair with Marcus Pellegrino?

I'm sorry, Jay.

Why didn't you tell me?

I couldn't tell you. And you never seemed to notice. You were never around. I was lonely. It was stupid. I'm so sorry, Jay.

My thoughts were spinning. Was this why Maya was unable to let me go? She held onto me through guilt?

❖❖❖

I had come in late that night. Maya, still up, sat at the counter wearing her bathrobe, her hair disheveled as she drank a glass of wine. I was exhausted. I poured myself a glass of scotch. Maya said nothing, but watched me as I moved around the kitchen.

"What?" I said, feeling her eyes on me.

"Nothing."

"You knew I would be late tonight."

"Yes. You told me."

"Then why are you looking at me so strangely?"

"I'm not."

"You look like a cat who's just eaten a bird," I said, pulling a glass from the cupboard. "Did you ding the car or something?"

"No! That's ridiculous."

I sat down next to her. I smelled something sweet on her. "You smell nice," I said.

She looked momentarily horrified. "I do?"

"Yeah, like flowers or something."

"Must be my new hand cream," she said, quickly getting up. "I'm going to bed." She left her half-full glass of wine on the counter.

"K. I'll be up in a minute."

Maya went upstairs and I sat in the kitchen finishing my scotch, trying to figure out what had been so strange about the conversation. She seemed different somehow. Defensive. Like she was hiding something. I finished my last gulp and headed to bed, the encounter forgotten.

Oh my God, Maya! You had sex with Marcus that night? Did you do it in our house?

"I'm sorry, Jay." Tears streamed down her cheeks.

How could I not have noticed that my own wife was having an affair?

"You were busy," Maya said.

I was busy! I worked hard for you and Calder!

"He's saying he had to make sacrifices," Liz interjected.

"You came home late most nights. I was lonely," Maya said, sniffing. Liz leaned over and handed her a tissue.

I guess that's true. But that's no excuse for an affair! You broke our vows.

"I'm getting a lot of sadness and despair from him," Liz said.

"I didn't mean for it to happen. Marcus visited Seattle from Vancouver for a few days on business. We reconnected online and so I agreed to see him one night, have a drink at his hotel. It seemed harmless. But then he told me how much I took his breath away. It had been so long since anyone had told me how beautiful I looked."

He had no right!

"We had a few drinks and then when I put on my coat to leave, he just grabbed my hand and I followed him to his room. I felt so guilty afterwards. I unfriended him on Facebook. I wouldn't answer his emails."

Was that the end of it?

"I didn't mean for it to continue. He came to Seattle a few months later and called on our home phone, begging to see me. It was during one of your business trips. To me, he was exciting, Jay. He took me to a nice restaurant, and then to his hotel room. I didn't know what I was doing. It was like putting on an old shirt, familiar and comfortable. It didn't seem wrong somehow."

Oh Maya.

"You've been holding your guilt about this with you for a long time," Liz said quietly.

"Yes."

"Your affair must be why I picked up a Mark. Did Jay know about your affair?"

"I don't think so, no. I'm so sorry, Jay."

Nice way to find out. Thanks, Maya. I never imagined you would cheat on me.

Tears slid silently down Maya's cheeks.

"He says you're going to find new love," Liz said.

No, I didn't! Maya, that's not what I said. I don't want you to find new love! I'm angry. I can't believe you cheated on me and didn't tell me. And with Marcus Pellegrino of all people!

"Don't you want her to find love again, Jay?" Alice's watery blue eyes seemed to leak empathy, or pity. Either way it annoyed me.

"No, I don't. She doesn't deserve it! She cheated!"

"Perhaps you didn't give her much of a choice."

"She had a choice not to cheat on her husband."

"Just as you had a choice to love her and show her your love."

"I did love her! Maybe I wasn't a perfect husband. Maybe I was distant or distracted. Who knows? But I didn't deserve to be cheated on."

"No you didn't, Jay. But Maya was lonely. You were preoccupied."

"I worked hard for my family. Maybe I could never really love her the way she needed to be loved. Maybe she always loved Marcus."

"But she married you, Jay. She loved you," Alice smiled sweetly at me.

"Maybe. But I can't stand the thought of her finding love with Marc. The guy is a sleaze ball. He'll hurt her all over again."

"Is there no possibility that he might love Maya too?"

"No! And I just realized that if I keep thinking of Marcus, Liz is going to pick that up! I've gotta think of someone else." The first person to pop into my head was Sean Connery as 007.

"Jay says I'm going to find new love? He's telling you that? He's not mad?" Maya asked as she folded her tissue over and over.

"All I can tell you is that he's showing me someone tall.

Maybe a little older. Very handsome. Wearing a suit or maybe a tux. Maybe you meet him at some sort of function. Are you going to an art opening or fundraiser anytime soon?"

"In a few months I'm having a small showing of some of my paintings in Vancouver."

"That must be it then. Be on the lookout for someone tall and handsome. He may have an accent and I think his name sounds like Shawn. Don? John? Something like that."

Maya unfolded the tissue and blew her nose into it. "Wow. Now I'm going to be even more nervous at my reception than I would've been," she said. "So, he's not mad about Marcus?"

I'm furious.

"I guess not, if he's showing me your new love."

I'm showing you James Bond.

"This romance will be 'heaven sent'!"

It will most certainly not be heaven sent!

"Oh god, I'm not sure I'm ready. The reception's in May. Barely three months after the one year anniversary of Jay's death."

"You'll be ready. That's what he's telling me."

No I'm not. And she's not going to be meeting Sean Connery either. I had to get Sean's image out of my head. I thought of Calder instead.

"And he wants you to know he's proud of the job you're doing with your son. He knows how difficult it is."

"Does he? I can't imagine how he would've coped if it had been me who died that day. I bet he'd be remarried by now." Maya sounded angry when she said this.

"I've noticed that widowers are often quicker to marry than widows," Liz said. "But it's not because they haven't been in loving marriages. It's because they grieve differently than women. Men tend to get busy after losing a spouse, where women are less afraid of their emotions and so grieve more outwardly."

"I guess that makes sense. I'm sorry. I don't know why

I'm so angry."

"It's normal."

"I think it's the guilt I feel, knowing I had an affair with Marcus just a few months before Jay died. I feel like it's holding me back from being able to really grieve properly."

"You can't keep holding onto your guilt, Maya," Liz said. "You are going to have to find a way to forgive yourself."

"I don't know how I'm going to do that. It was a stupid mistake. I was in love with Marcus a long time ago, before I met Jay."

Are you still in love with him?

"That does make it more complicated," Liz said. "But I think it's possible to ask Jay's forgiveness."

How can I forgive that?

"Jay, this is another moment where you must learn to release your human emotions. Anger, hurt, jealousy – all the emotions you're feeling – are unnecessary here," Alice reminded me.

"But"

"Just try to let go. You are a spirit now."

With her words came an ethereal sound, a musical expression of my emotions – symphony-like sounds that began quietly and built to a crescendo of anger within me, becoming louder and faster before finally crashing like a wave against a rock, leaving me dazed and yet strangely cleansed. Those sounds eventually became hollow, like the notes on a wooden xylophone, before settling into a series of bell tones lulling me into a quieter mood until they just echoed in the silence.

Does she still love Marc?

"She might," Alice said.

Maya sat quietly wiping tears from her face. She looked up at Liz. "I'm glad you came. This has been incredibly emotional for me, but I feel like a weight has been lifted. I hadn't been willing to admit my affair to even myself before now. And now I feel like I've confessed to Jay. I hope he can forgive me."

"I'm sure Jay already does," Liz said. Maya smiled a wan sort of smile.

"I don't know about this psychic stuff, Alice. Liz doesn't seem to get much right."

"I'd say she's gotten the important things correct. And look at Maya. Do you think it's helped her?" Maya appeared to be deep in thought, folding and re-folding the now-frayed tissue on her lap. "Do you forgive her?"

"No."

"This has been amazing, Liz. I feel like he's really been here with us," Maya said.

"He is, Maya. And he loves you very much. And misses you."

I do miss you, Maya.

"Me too."

"In life, he would never have believed in someone like me..." Liz said.

You got that right!

At that moment, Calder burst through the door. He no longer wore the criss-cross shoulder brace, his collar bone having healed quickly.

"Hi Mama!"

"Oh my gosh, what time is it?"

Calder shrugged and stood in the living room looking at Liz. Molly waved from outside, not wanting to interrupt. Maya mouthed her thanks through the living room window before turning back to Calder.

"Calder, this is Liz. She's here to, uh, well..."

"You're here to talk to Daddy, right?" Both Maya and Liz looked startled.

"How did you know that, Calder?"

"Daddy told me she would be coming."

"He did? You talk to Daddy?"

"I guess."

I wanted to shout out loud. Calder actually remembered

our conversations! Liz began to laugh.

"Quite the little Indigo you have there." Maya and Calder looked confused.

"Indigo?" Maya asked.

"Children who are at the leading edge of humankind's spiritual evolution. They are often quite psychic."

All kids are psychic, Liz. Even I know that.

"I'm not indigo. What is indigo?"

"It's a color, sweetie. Sort of a dark blue."

"So, I'm going to turn blue?"

Maya laughed. "No, no. Nothing like that! Liz is a psychic medium, which means she is able to talk to Daddy."

"She can?"

"Yes. I've been telling your mom what he says."

"What does he say about me?"

Tell him how proud I am of him.

"He says he's really proud of you. He knows it's been hard for you."

And he needs to listen to his mom. And be careful on his skateboard.

"And that you need to listen to your mom a little more. Remember she is doing everything alone and that's pretty hard sometimes. He's showing me an accident you had?" Maya quickly wiped away a tear.

"Yeah. I broke my collar bone."

"He wants you to be careful."

"OK."

Tell him I love him. Tell him to trust himself. And to take chances, just not dangerous ones.

"He says he loves you and misses you. He knows you're going to be fine. Don't doubt yourself so much, Calder. Don't be afraid to take chances, take risks, but still be careful. Don't do those crazy things that put you in danger. Trust in your gut, as well as your good brains."

Calder hung his head and looked at his feet. "Uh, OK."

"Did that make sense?"

Calder nodded his head. "Is Daddy really talking to me?"

Well, she made a bunch of that stuff up, but it's what I wished I'd said.

"Yes, he is," Liz answered. "I just talk for him. I barely even know what he said. He just sort of talks through me, if that makes sense. He really loves you and wants you to know that."

Calder smiled. I could tell he'd gotten it. Maya smiled now too.

"He loves you both very much."

Chapter Fourteen

April 10th, 2007

Jay,
Was that you today, your black eyes penetrating my soul?

I left the gallery to head home and there he was, Mr. Crow sitting on top of my car. Did crows usually sit on top of cars like that? I dug around my purse for my camera and took a picture as the crow sized me up. The camera's flash did not frighten it. I finally flapped my arms at it, and it stepped back a little, clearly bemused. I flapped again, and it cackled loudly before it got the hint and spread its wings and took a step into the air. It floated up to the roof of the building and remained there. It cawed at me a couple of times before I climbed into my car and drove away.

I wish I knew, Jay, what you were trying to say to me in the guise of the "beguiling raven" from that Edgar Allen Poe poem. It makes sense in a weird way. Your punishment for my infidelity — an ominous black bird stare-down. You always did have a thing for birds. Remember the year I bought you the binoculars and the bird identification book from the Audobon Society? God, you were so obnoxious that year, pulling the car over to the side of the road so you could traipse into the woods and try and spot a rare "Rusty Blackbird"... Oh! Is that the joke?

I stopped typing and opened a browser window and Googled "Rusty Blackbird". It looked like just another crow-like bird to me, though I admired the contrast of its bright yellow eyes against the ebony sheen of its feathers. Crows seemed to have been following me since I met with Liz, but I was probably just being paranoid.

You must be angry. You deserve to be. Every night I fall asleep feeling as if a gaping crevasse has cleaved my chest in two. I feel hands holding my heart and squeezing, ringing out every last drop of emotion and strength I have left.

Crows. Counting Crows. Only now did I realize the connection. On the one-year anniversary of Jay's death, Calder and I sat together at the kitchen table silently eating dinner. I had done everything I could to forget the day, but the phone kept ringing, concerned, hushed voices asking how I was. I had no answers. I grabbed Calder and we hid in the darkness of a movie theatre watching a Teenaged Mutant Ninja Turtle movie. It was a perfect place to hide, but didn't last long enough.

Back home, Calder ate chicken strips and broccoli "trees" while I drank a glass of wine, knowing I would eat his leftovers for my own dinner. The CD player beside us on the window sill suddenly turned itself on and started playing a CD that had been there since before Jay died – Counting Crows, one of Jay's favorites that he played over a period of a few months, ad nauseam. The first words spilled out:

> "Step out the front door like a ghost
> into the fog where no one notices

the contrast of white on white.
And in between the moon and you
the angels get a better view..."

I turned to stare at the machine, whose yellow "on" light winked at me innocently. I was stunned. It felt like Jay spoke to us through those lyrics, whose meanings I had never noticed or even listened to before. Calder began to sing the chorus.

"Round here, we always stand up straight. Round here something radiates..."

Calder looked at me as he sang but didn't seem surprised. When the song ended, he said, "I think that was Daddy. He put on the CD to make you happy, Mama."

Tears burned my eyes. "Yes, I think you might be right, Cald."

We let the CD play until the end and memories washed over me – making pancakes as we listened to that CD on a Sunday morning, Calder squealing as his father chased him around the house for a tickle fight, or the sound playing through the window as we sat on the back patio watching Calder play in the treehouse built of old kitchen cabinets that Jay had found at the dump.

"Happy Anniversary, Jay," I whispered under my breath when the CD ended. "And thank you." I smiled when I realized it was probably the only time Jay had actually remembered the correct date of our anniversary without my prompting.

Crows. Another Google search took me to a website about Native American spirit animals as I search on their symbolism:

The crow, in Native American heritage, is a spirit animal representing life's mysteries and magic, a spirit guide who provides insight and supports one's intentions. The crow is seen as a sign of luck, but is also considered a trickster and can be deceiving in appearances. If the crow has chosen you as your spirit or totem animal, it supports you in developing the power of sight, transformation, and connection with life's magic.

Life's magic. Is that what all this was about? The joke was on me.

One morning I woke up to the sound of what I thought was someone walking around on the roof. I looked out to see the edge of a glossy black wing. Through the open window, I shook my fist at it. "Go away, Mr. Crow!" Later, as I walked outside to get into my car, the crow swooped to perch on the garage roof and peer down at me as I backed out of the driveway. The crows didn't frighten me, as much as they reminded me of something I was hoping to forget. Calder noticed them too and soon made it a game to name each one he saw.

"That one's Harry. Or Bob," Calder said as we walked to the store for a promised treat of candy.

"Are you sure it's not a Harriet or Bobbette?"

"No way! That's a boy one."

I don't know if Calder connected the crows to Jay the way I did, but since he noticed them too, I didn't feel as crazy. Still, it was hard not to feel like Tippi Hedren, the birds all watching her, gathering, but not yet attacking. My hell could begin at any moment.

I should have told you about Marcus, Jay. He visited Seattle for business and invited me to his hotel for a drink. I thought it would be just a drink. I didn't set out to cheat on you. But you had become so removed from our lives. And Marcus told me he still loved me all these years later. I didn't know what to make of it, but I was flattered and then a little tipsy and it became the perfect storm. I'm so sorry, Jay. I know that Marc showed up at your funeral, but I don't know why. Perhaps he feels guilty too. Or perhaps now he thinks he has a chance with me. I don't want to know. I don't want to see him. It's too painful. After you died, I couldn't continue my relationship with him on any level, even as friends. He asked to come and see me, so he could be there as a shoulder to cry on, but the thought of his presence horrified me. I am still full of guilt and remorse that I cheated on you. You didn't deserve that, Jay. Marcus coming back into my life was like discovering an old security blanket. I didn't consider myself the type of woman to cheat on her husband, but I did. I don't really have a decent explanation. I hope you can somehow forgive me. I wish I could forgive myself...

I sat back in my chair and closed my eyes and sighed deeply. Why did life have to be so complicated? I wished I knew what to do about Marcus. I needed to find someone new. I needed to forget about Marcus. Nothing good could come of it.

I assumed Jay spoke to me through crows in order to give me his opinion about Marcus, but perhaps the crows held the secret to how he viewed the meds I had started giving Calder. Was Jay trying to communicate his displeasure at my parenting skills or my adultery through shape-shifting into crows? Truly, I had to be losing it.

❊ ❊ ❊

I filled the prescription that Calder's therapist had scratched his signature onto and the next morning stood by the sink and poured a glass of water. Calder held out his hand as I tipped the bottle into his palm and a turquoise capsule rolled out. Calder eyed it suspiciously.

"We'll just give this a try for a few weeks and see what happens, K?"

Calder shrugged. He put the pill into his mouth and then took a mouthful of water, handing the glass back as he held his gulp of water. He swallowed, then without a word, turned and disappeared into the living room to watch some TV before heading off to school.

This became our routine: the glass of water and the turquoise pill, the promises that I wouldn't be late to pick him up from the school bus, but still prying his hands off my waist as soon as the bus drew near. The weather got warmer and play dates more frequent as the school year drew to a close. One sunny May Saturday, Calder called from a friend's house begging to sleep over and I agreed, trying to hide my jubilation, but around midnight I got a call from the friend's dad explaining that Calder was upset and refused to sleep over and could I please pick him up. I drove him home in his pajamas and he just shrugged when I asked him what happened.

"I changed my mind," he said. I left it at that. To me the breakthrough was tangible.

I wish I knew what you were thinking. Are you mad about Marcus? The meds? I hate these cryptic signs - CD players, crows, puzzles that I'm left to form into some kind of meaning. I always loved you, Jay. I hope you know that. I feel like I can't remember the sound of your voice, or what you looked like. I wish I could see you in the dreams I have of you, but I can never see your face. Every time I laugh or feel joy, I worry that I'm forgetting you. How silly it is that we feel we have to stay sad and in mourning in order to properly honor our dead. I guess I shouldn't worry. Your crows are always there to remind me.

I love you, Mr. Crow.
Maya

Chapter Fifteen

THE HAIRCUT

I felt helpless having to sit back and watch my family in pain. I wished I could tell Maya I wasn't angry, but in truth I didn't know how I felt about her confession through Liz. I felt sad, but my own emotional pain no longer had the same meaning in this place. I still felt Maya and Calder's pain though and felt compelled to do something to ease them through it. It was like being a parent, who watched, guided, and supported their child, but tried not to interfere even when they floundered. This was the way a child learned about the world, about life. It was no easier in spirit form to watch the loved ones you left behind struggle in the wake of your death. Only now did I understand that a human's path through life involved suffering. Why had I never learned in life that it's the hardships that teach us our innate strengths? I lived in my own little world of resentment, angry that my father died when I was young, leaving me to my lingering sense of inadequacy. A sense that I never quite possessed something that others seemed to have and take for granted. I watched others breeze through life, families intact, confidence assured, their sense of place in the world secure.

I convinced myself that I lived in an unlucky world, a view that had me seeking the negatives and blind to the tiny breadcrumb trail that led toward a life I thought had forsaken me. Only in death could I now articulate such ideas. I blundered through job after job, rising in status with each one, but ungrateful and resentful that I wasn't being paid more, or didn't have the top job. Every sprained ankle I suffered, every team I wasn't selected for, every promotion I didn't receive, I saw as proof of my luckless life. Even in my new incarnation as a dead man, I saw my death as more proof of an unlucky life. Only now could I see the life-long handicap I gave myself.

In the spirit world there could be no regret.

Death taught me that luck or unluck is merely an illusion of the human mind, a story we tell ourselves so we can blame our failures on bad luck rather than face our messy, true selves. Had I unwittingly passed such thinking onto my son during my life, causing him to hide beneath his hair, experience terror whenever Maya was not close, bang his drums incessantly for hours and rocket himself down skateboard ramps? Or had my death precipitated his anxieties, his sense of insecurity that now led his mother to medicate him?

A few weeks of Calder taking the meds, it was impossible not to notice a shift. From my vantage point on the back stairs, I watched Calder as he sat on one of the kitchen stools while his mother paid bills at the table. Calder seemed deep in thought.

"Can I get a haircut?" he asked abruptly.

"Sure. A trim again? Not too short, right?"

"No. I want a buzz cut."

Maya looked up at him. "A buzz cut? Are you sure? That's pretty extreme."

"It's what I want. Can we go right now?" Calder and I had a tradition of going together to the local barber shop, one of those slightly dingy places with a turning red, white, and blue barber pole outside and a yellowed 1966 Chrysler calendar still pinned to the wall. I usually got mine short on the sides, longer on top and when Calder was small, he copied my cut. But as he got older, he stopped going to the barber shop with me and began growing his hair into its shaggy mop. "To Daddy's barber shop."

"You're really serious this is what you want?"

"Yes."

At the barber shop, Maya sat uncomfortably on one of the three olive vinyl chairs in the waiting area while Calder perched himself on the tall burgundy leather barber chair, knobby boy knees poking out from his shorts as his legs dangled over the seat.

"What'll it be, buddy?" the barber asked. Calder looked at Maya.

"He says he wants a buzz cut," she answered.

The barber seemed nonplussed. "A buzz, eh? Would you like a one, two, three, or four?" Calder looked at Maya quizzically. She in turn looked at the barber.

"One is almost bald, four is as long as it gets. I'd recommend a three. It's what most of the kids go for."

Maya shrugged. "A three sound OK to you, Cald?" Calder nodded.

"OK, then. You ready?" the barber asked. Calder nodded again and the barber affixed the paper neck collar and cape around Calder's narrow frame. He pulled out the electric clippers and held them up. Maya's eyes grew wide. He turned it on and put it to Calder's head and a large hunk of long hair dropped to the floor. Maya gasped, but the barber caught her eye and gave her a warning shake of his head.

"What, Mom?" Calder asked.

"Nothing, sweetie, the noise of the clippers just surprised me, that's all."

I understood Maya's fear. The last time she had taken Calder to have his hair trimmed, even though they had only taken off a quarter inch of hair, Calder cried all the way home in the car. This haircut would be extreme.

Maya grabbed a magazine and held it up in front of her face to hide the sudden tears that appeared in her eyes. More long hair dropped to the floor. When the barber finished, he spun Calder around in the chair so Calder could see himself in the mirror. Calder giggled.

"Oh wow!" he said, running his hand across the top of his head. "It feels so weird!" He turned to Maya. "Mama, do you like it?"

Maya managed to collect herself. She tilted her head to the side to look at him.

"I don't think I've seen your eyes in two years!" She laughed. "It's so great to see your face. I love it Calder! I really do!" Calder smiled at the barber who peeled the cape off and pulled out a vacuum and began to suction Calder's head and neck.

On the way home in the car, Calder kept rubbing his head and leaned over so Maya could try as well.

"Why did you decide to cut your hair so short?" Maya asked him.

"Because of what the psychic said," Calder replied, matter-of-factly.

"What did she say?"

"She said that Daddy said I shouldn't be afraid to move forward. I should take risks," Calder said, looking serious.

"Wow. You remember that? And it made sense to you?"

Calder nodded. "I want to stop being afraid all the time. I think I can do a sleepover now."

"I'm happy for you. That's a big step."

Calder sat back in his seat, smiling.

The following week, Calder told Maya she didn't have to pick him up at the bus stop anymore, that he could walk home by himself. The next day he came flying into the house, slinging his backpack onto the floor like a teenaged pro. A week later, he had a new best friend, Owen, who lived down the street. The closed look he kept hidden under his hair had transformed into the happy, smiling face of an eight-year-old. Of course, Maya attributed the change in Calder to the meds, but I knew it had more to do with the message Calder had received from me, via Liz. Somehow I got a meaningful message across to Calder. Liz embellished it on my behalf, for which I was grateful.

"How can you be sure the meds didn't also have something to do with Calder's changes?" Alice's thought came before her actual presence.

"I guess I can't be sure. Except he seems pretty aware that he's changed as a result of my message through Liz."

"The medications might simply be working in conjunction with the message, but I agree, your words seem to have gotten through to him, and that's a marvelous thing. But it could also be..." Alice's thought trailed off. Then, after a while, her wry smile appeared before me.

"What?"

"Well, you're going a little overboard on the crow thing, don't you think?"

"No way! I love the crow thing! And Maya gets that it's me! Even Calder gets it, I think. That's why he always gives them names."

"Yes, I agree, Maya knows it's you, but I'm not sure you need to be quite so obvious."

"But I like being a crow!" I loved the sensation of swooping around in a strong, black bird body, being part of Maya and Calder's world, even if just peripherally.

"Now, Jay..."

"OK, Alice. I'll cool down on the crow embodiments. But honestly, it's been the best trick you've taught me. Melding minds with small creatures is awesome." I had already worked my way up the creature hierarchy - butterflies were the easiest to inhabit but died off quickly and were unavailable in the winter season, unless I wanted to be in South America. Crows and ravens seemed to fit. I appreciated their sharp eyesight, and their loud voices made it easy to attract Maya and Calder's attention. Maya would certainly understand my choice of a crow – its symbolism as a messenger of the gods in ancient Greece and a bird sacred to Athena would hardly be lost on her. In Norse legend, ravens are symbols of creative intelligence, and in Native American legends, the raven is a purveyor of light, or consciousness, a bird of creation without which human kind would forever live in darkness. I knew she would look up all the symbolism around the crow and the raven and know without a doubt that I visited her from this world. I wasn't wrong. Recently Maya had even begun painting again, crows and ravens becoming a theme.

"I know embodying creatures is a fun pastime on this side, Jay. Many newly dead like to re-experience life in that way. But you don't want to have your wife feeling as if she is being stalked by crows, now do you?"

I laughed. "No, I suppose I don't. Maybe there is someone else I can stalk…"

"Have you checked in on Marcus lately?"

"Marc? You want me to stalk Marcus? That's a good idea, actually…"

"No, no, nothing like that!"

"I'm joking, Alice. But why would you want me to check in on him? I'm trying to keep him out of Maya's life, not remind him of her."

"Your human mind speaks those words. You know the truth about Marcus, as much as you insist on denying it."

"The truth about Marc? What are you talking about, Alice?"

"You will need to figure that out for yourself, Jay. But perhaps it's time for a visit. Try a new creature on for size…" Alice chuckled as her image evaporated.

The landscape clouded with my angry thoughts about Marcus. He had preyed on Maya in her vulnerability. I should have been more attentive toward her, but there was no excuse for his taking advantage. For him to reappear after all those years, declaring his love for Maya, made me suspicious. He knew she was still married. Did he seek some sort of revenge against me for being the one to marry her?

I had no doubt that Maya loved me. And of course she deserved new love in her life. But I saw Marcus as a selfish, arrogant, even narcissistic person. I imagined he was a man focused on having expensive clothes, a slick, concrete-and-open-ductwork condo, a series of short-lived relationships with designer-clad women a decade younger than himself. I had heard very little of him over the years, but knew he worked in the restaurant business in Vancouver and had done very well for himself.

The ambient light became brighter and I found myself in what appeared to be a coffee shop. I'm not sure why, but I seemed to be sitting on the floor under a square pine table beside a youngish man wearing a grey hoodie, the hood pulled up over his head, a tangle of dark hair poking out. He slouched in his chair as if trying to hide. Marcus sat opposite the young man; a plaid shirt and jeans were all I could see from my vantage point under the table.

"I'm proud of you, man," Marcus said. The young man's mouth turned up at the corner in what might be perceived as a smile.

"I've been where you are. The first week is hell, I know, but it gets easier after that," Marcus said. A cacophony of sound in the room was unusually deafening. Chairs scraped across the linoleum floors, a line-up of teenagers held trays as they waited to proceed along a stainless steel buffet, groups of four or six gathered at tables, hunched over huge piles of food served on brightly colored dishes, all talking loudly. The walls of the space were painted in festive colors – orange, yellow, and blue decorated with sculpted letters spelling out "Forgiveness", "Grow", and "Dream".

"You just need to stick with it. Do you think you can do that, Lionel?" Lionel, the young man, shrugged in response.

Marcus pushed a business card across the table. "If you think you want to get high again, call me first."

Lionel said nothing, but a dirty hand appeared from under the gray hoodie – fingernails bloody and torn, the cuticles chewed – and slid the card into his sweatshirt's front pouch. Without a word, Lionel stood up and disappeared out the door. Another man appeared and sat in the chair that Lionel had just vacated. This man wore a tidy, striped linen shirt, khakis, and black Reeboks. Beneath his glasses, the wrinkles around his brown eyes were permanently creased into a look of worry mixed with compassion.

"Hey, Tom," Marcus said. "I don't know if I got through to him."

"Time will tell, but I'm hopeful. He obviously looks up to you. He wants to please you. I'm glad you're his mentor."

I began to realize this place was a center for homeless kids, the last place I expected to see Marcus Pellegrino.

"It's hard seeing myself in him. I was in that place once," Marcus said.

"Mentoring is difficult. But it can also be incredibly rewarding. You've come a long way yourself, Marcus."

"Fifteen years sober, this August."

"That's a real accomplishment. What changed things for you?" Tom asked.

"I lost the woman I loved and then got mixed up in a bad crowd. I performed in a band for a while in the eighties when everyone did coke. I blew away a small fortune." Tom nodded knowingly as Marcus continued.

"When I took a job at a bar, the really heavy drinking started. I went to work out of my mind half the time. One day, after a night of boozing, I couldn't remember how I'd gotten home. My car keys were flung on the floor with my jacket. I looked at myself in the mirror and saw an overweight, pasty-faced old man looking back at me and something snapped. It scared me not remembering how I'd gotten home and then realizing I had driven home during a black-out. I went to an AA meeting that afternoon. I got straightened out and wound up buying the bar. Funny business for a recovering alcoholic, right?" Tom smiled.

"A little," Tom agreed.

"Turns out I'm a pretty good businessman. And a foodie. I guess I just swapped addictions. Not that I'm addicted to food or anything, I just enjoy really good food."

Tom laughed. "No, I get it. Recovering addicts often find other passions. Some even border on obsessions. Yours sounds like a great one to have!"

Marcus smiled, but a crease appeared between his eyes making him look sad. "I should get going, Tom. I have another date tonight."

"A date? What happened to Stephanie?"

"Things didn't work out. I don't seem to have a whole lot of luck in the relationship department."

"The right one will come along," Tom said.

"Yeah. Maybe," Marc said, that same crease appearing between his eyes once more. I felt someone pat the top of my head.

"C'mon, Jericho," Marcus said and he reached toward me and hooked a leash to something around my neck. Momentarily confused, I realized I was embodied inside Marc's dog, Jericho. I shuddered and jumped free. The dog continued to shake as I hovered above them both. Marcus waited as the dog finished his all over body shake, as if he had just jumped out of a lake.

"C'mon, boy. What's all the shaking for?" The dog stopped and looked at me, cocking his head.

"Jericho, let's go. What are you looking at, boy?" Jericho seemed to wink at me before turning and heading purposefully toward the door. I hovered for a while longer. I felt Alice nearby.

"Nice work, Jay. I think that's your largest animal embodiment so far."

"That was weird. I didn't even realize I was the dog."

"Yes, that sometimes happens when you choose to enter the earth realm. You embody the closest animal in proximity to the scene you want to participate in."

"I didn't really want to participate. I was just there."

"Then there was a reason. You needed to experience that moment so you could understand a little more about Marcus."

"I guess. He seems sadder than I remember him. He used to be so cocky. I always thought he was a bit of a—"

"Marc's come a long way. It's been a difficult road for him." Alice cut off my thought.

"I find that surprising. He had it all."

"By all, what do you mean?" Alice asked.

"Good looks, intelligence, success. He seemed to make a good living, from what I heard."

Alice looked at me, waiting, saying nothing.

"I suppose you're going to tell me I should know better. That those are not necessarily the qualities of a contented human," I said.

Alice smiled, looking like she wanted to pat my head the way Marcus had patted mine, as Jericho. "You're right. That is what I was going to say. That and Marcus has endured his own form of human adversity."

"And now I'm meant to help him?"

"That's up to you, Jay. Everything you do in this realm must be done by your own volition."

"Yes, so I keep hearing."

Chapter Sixteen

Art Opening

Maya's new paintings took on a new, ethereal quality, with Mylar-colored clouds scuttling across wind-swept landscapes spun like candy floss, offset by swirls of wheaten fields. Often they contained a lone black bird, flying away in the distance. She painted Monet-style – tiny brush strokes which made up a pointillistic whole when seen from a distance. She infused each piece with meaning and gave each a name that mirrored her subconscious: Serenity, Patience, Vale of Misery, Detachment Bay. Her canvases blended sky and Earth, representations of the landscapes of Maya's mind. Her past work, mixtures of earthy browns and yellows and oranges, had a grounded feel, but lately her colors had become more deeply saturated, more vibrant, as if grief had unblocked her line of sight into the world in which I now existed and she unconsciously painted her impressions of it. She painted the dreamscapes of the dreams we shared, seeing and interpreting an afterlife's spectrum of colors at their higher vibrational frequency. The resulting paintings conveyed soothing, nourishing worlds in which to rest one's mind. The act of painting seemed to calm her, as much as it pained her. She painted with tears blurring her vision or, at times, while grinning with excitement.

Since Liz's reading, Maya began painting a series of crows, their bodies smudged into slate gray skyscapes, as if emotion had melted their wings. In some, their eyes were a piercing yellow, like tiny harvest moons against an ebony backdrop. Maya's paintings were infused with her rage, which seemed to hurl itself off the canvasses, her guilt evidenced in the lone bird portraits. But the paintings possessed an energy I had never seen before in her work. I could see the paintings' auras, the energy they exuded, and knew how much catharsis each one contained within the thick layers of paint.

While Calder was at school each day, Maya painted, trying to amass enough work for her upcoming show in Vancouver. As she worked, I occasionally stood beside her, watching, even participating as her tiny brush hovered over a color on her palette. I found I could guide her hand with my thoughts. As her brain waves relaxed into their hypnotic Theta state, I learned to merge my frequency to be more in tune with hers. I could visualize a particularly beautiful sector of my world and transfer its color and quality of light to her mind. Her interpretations of these images were stunning. I heard her tell friends that it felt as if I held her brush for her and directed her hand. "It's like I'm not even creating these paintings by myself," she explained. "I feel as if Jay is with me, guiding me. I can't believe the work I've been producing!" She knew innately that she spoke the truth. I did, in a sense, guide her hand. And her paintings were magnificent.

It was no wonder that Amalie from Crescent Knoll Gallery in Vancouver was excited to show Maya's new work. Maya and Amalie had worked together for several years, ever since Maya and I moved to the West Coast, just before Calder's birth. Amalie was a work of art in her own right with her trademark sheet of art-gallery white corkscrew hair and silken Sari-type skirts covered in tiny mirrors and jewels. If asked about her nationality, Amalie would purr the word "Persian", though no one quite knew what that meant. Maya and I laughed the first time we met her as she floated toward us and gathered Maya in an embrace with a "Daaaarlink! Finally, we meet!"

Maya was thrilled to be represented by Amalie's gallery, a coup since Amalie knew all the big players in the Canadian art world, not to mention the global one. I'd been ecstatic when one of the first of Maya's paintings to sell carried a price tag of $2,500. Since then, she commanded ever higher prices, though selling a painting did not occur every day. I knew she would do very well selling her latest paintings and that they would put her on the map artistically.

I followed Maya and Amalie around the whitewashed gallery where Maya's paintings leaned against the wall in the positions they were meant to be hung. They stood together in the middle of the room assessing one wall.

"I don't like 'Destruction' so close to 'Rusty Blackbird'. I think we should swap it out with 'Mescaline Solipsism'," Maya said, pointing and biting her lip.

"But Darlink, 'Mescaline' is so powerful! It will be lost next to the crow! You must give it the white space it deserves!"

Maya continued to bite her lip. "Maybe you're right, Amalie. I just don't know anymore. I've been looking at them all for so long. Maybe I shouldn't even be hanging the crow painting since it's not for sale."

"Trust me, Darlink, it will all be fine. I have a perfect place for your special crow." Amalie patted Maya's hand.

Later that afternoon, Maya stood in front of a mirror holding up outfits. Black. Violet. Red. Dresses I hadn't seen before.

Tonight's the night the psychic said I would meet Mr. Tall, Dark, and Handsome.

Of course. That explained the new dresses. Maya expected to meet Sean Connery. My stupid mistake of misguided thought. She was bound to be disappointed when her mystery man failed to appear. Old human emotion caused a momentary degradation of my resonance, like tiny electrical shocks of regret, guilt, jealousy. Alice popped in and took a place on the end of the bed beside me where we watched Maya hold each dress up in front of her body, and then, one by one, slip them over her head.

"I'm sure you can sense her trepidation and guilt at the prospect of meeting someone new, Jay." Maya twirled in the red dress. She looked ravishing.

"Yeah, but it doesn't make it any easier to watch."

"No. But remember, you must detach from your human emotions."

"I'm trying. I feel a low-level vibration pulling at me. Is that my emotion or hers?" Maya stood now, biting her lip, wearing the wine-colored shiny dress. Cute, but not as beautiful as the red one.

"Mostly it's a vibration emanating from her, but one that you're sensitive to. You must've felt this vibration from her at other times during her grieving."

"Yeah, but this feels different. It's not quite as low. Sure those sad, flat, grief vibrations caused Maya's aura to be a very dark navy blue, whereas this vibration carries with it something urgent, expectant. Look, her aura is pulsing with red."

"That's her sexual energy you're seeing."

"What? Really? So she pulses red when she's a horn toad? Damn, I wish I'd been able to see *that* when I was alive!" Alice smiled. Maya now wore the black dress, but tried to smooth it down against her legs, apparently unhappy with how it fell over her hips and thighs.

Dumb dress. I'm returning this one. But which dress should I wear? Red or purple?

Definitely red.

Maya put the red dress back on. *I bet you'd choose the red one.*

Thank you, Lenie. You really do look ravishing.

I look pretty good, don't I?

Absolutely!

"The new emotions Maya's experiencing will become more frequent," Alice continued.

"You mean she's going to be horny more now?"

"Yes, that's one reason for it. Her sexual energy is also healing energy. Her body is finding ways to produce more dopamine. It's beginning to rewire itself from being in a state of grief to being in more of a state of alive-ness. As a part of this process, she's also learning to resonate at higher levels spiritually as well. Grief is a transformative experience for humans. Many people who've experienced human trauma often have a spiritual awakening. Such awakenings give humans a greater ability to access our world since their brain waves resonate at levels that are more in tune with our world. The brighter hues of their auras reflect these changes."

Maya's aura throbbed. She held several hairpins between her lips as she began to pile her hair into a knot on the top of her head. I'd never seen her look more beautiful. Her curls were pulled off her face, and the dress set off the color of her eyes. She turned a little in the mirror, trying to see the V of the dress in back, apparently pleased with the result because she smiled. She slipped on a pair of gold strappy sandals and pulled a black shawl around her shoulders. Every man at the opening would have his eyes on her. It felt strange not to be jealous. As human Jay, I would've been suspicious of her new dress. I might've even teased her for looking too sexy, which would have prompted her to change or let down her hair. What a fool I'd been.

"Like jealousy, regret has no place here, Jay." Alice smiled. "But you know that." She disappeared like the Cheshire Cat, leaving just her lingering, sideways smile.

※ ※ ※

At the gallery, Amalie spotted Maya walk in and rushed to greet her.

"Daaarlink!"

Maya smiled and moved through the crowd, not noticing the looks she received from some of the other attendees, men and women alike.

"You look fabulous! Please, you must meet my friends! They *love* your work! They want to buy, Maya! It's wonderful!"

Maya shook hands and smiled as she was introduced around the gallery. Someone handed her a glass of wine and soon her pale complexion was flushed, adding to her allure. As she spoke with a small woman wearing a black dress and tall black boots, I noticed Maya's attention waned. She scoped the room for her Sean Connery. Her gaze fell upon a tall figure almost facing her, studying one of her paintings intently. He bent close and lifted his glasses to look at the brush strokes and then moved a few steps backward and tilted his head to see the painting from a distance. He wore a black suit, expensive-looking, but lassoed with a grey scarf that blended with his salt and pepper hair. His face bore deep vertical grooves, crossed by almost invisible rectangular glasses. I couldn't help noticing his perfectly manicured hands. Slowly, chatting with people along the way, Maya made her way toward him. He stayed by her painting, clearly aware of the dance.

"Do you like it?" Maya didn't often make the first move.

"Yes. Very much. I find it very relaxing to look at. You're the artist?" Maya nodded, her cheeks becoming even more pink than the wine had made them. "This is a big night for you."

"Yes. Nerve-wracking as hell."

"But why? You're very talented, Ms. Cavor."

"Thank you…"

"Dominic, but friends call me Dom."

"Dominic. Nice to meet you."

"The pleasure is all mine." Maya smiled and he held her eyes before turning back to the painting. The man pointed, circling his finger. "I love this part here. The crimson against the stormy gray sky. So much tension. It leaves you wondering."

"Wondering?"

"Wondering what might happen next."

"That hadn't occurred to me, but I think I see what you mean. Sort of an expectation."

"Precisely. Expectation." He looked at the painting in silence for a few moments, as if mining it for the secrets to Maya's soul before turning back to her. "Can I get you another glass of bad art-gallery wine?"

Maya laughed and held out her empty glass. "That would be lovely, thank you." She followed Dom towards the bar. As she drew close, another man turned around and caught sight of her.

"Maya?"

"Marcus!" Maya paled. *What's he doing here?*

Marc looked tired, his broad forehead creased with worry lines.

"Hello, Maya." He combed his dark hair off his face with his hand, nervously.

"What are you doing here?" Maya whispered as she looked over at Dom, who poured red wine from a huge liter bottle.

"I wouldn't have missed your opening, Maya."

"Why? You've never come to one of my openings before. This isn't my first."

"No, but I should have." Dom now stood behind Marcus, his chin up, trying to peer over Marcus's shoulder as he held up Maya's glass of red wine.

"Here you go." Dominic handed one of the glasses to

Maya, who took it and smiled at him.

"Thank you. Dominic, I'd like you to meet Marcus, an old childhood friend. Marcus, this is Dominic." The men shook hands.

This should be interesting. Another wrinkle in human communion I'd failed to foresee.

"Pleased to meet you, Marcus. You've known each other a long time. That's a special kind of friendship. Not enough of those in the world."

"Yes, but we haven't seen each other for a long time," Maya said quickly.

"Not since the funeral. Has it really been over a year now? How're you doing Maya? Have you been OK?"

"I'm hanging in there." Maya looked at Dom, who quickly put the puzzle pieces of her life together with these tidbits of information.

"Maya, there's something I need to talk to you about. Do you have a moment?"

"No, Marcus. Can't we do this another time?"

"It's fine," Dominic said. "Go talk to your friend."

"No. It's fine, Dominic, really. Marcus and I can talk another time. Right?" She looked pointedly at Marc.

"Will you be in Vancouver for long?" Marcus asked.

"Just overnight. I'm staying at Amalie's. I have to get back first thing in the morning. A friend is taking care of Calder tonight in Seattle."

"OK. Well, I see you're busy. Another time then. Nice to meet you…"

"Dominic."

Marc turned and shuffled his way through the crowd toward the door.

"Have I kept you from something important?" Dominic said.

"No, I don't think so. Lately, I seem to keep being reminded of my past."

"Is he a bad person?"

"No, no, nothing like that."

"So tell me, do you like photography?" Dom hooked Maya's elbow with his own and guided her towards a settee.

"Some of it. What kind do you mean?"

"My kind."

"Then of course!" Maya giggled.

Why am I blushing?

Gee, Lenie, is that so difficult to figure out? You should see your combined auras right now. This guy is just dying to get you into bed.

"You're a photographer?"

"Yes. And an architect."

"Artistic. I like artistic men."

"Do you now? Would you consider going to dinner with one?"

"I live in Seattle."

"As do I. I'm visiting Vancouver this weekend and happened to walk past this gallery so came in to check out the show. I was drawn in, if you want to know the truth."

"What drew you?"

"Your paintings. They made me want to laugh and cry at the same time. They made me very emotional. I'm not sure why but I would like to find out. How about dinner in Seattle? Or lunch even."

"Sounds perfect."

Later, after the opening, Maya sat cross-legged on a cushion on the floor of Amalie's dining room, her legs tucked under a low table. Saris draped from the ceiling gave the room a tent-like feel, flickering hues of orange and pink in the candlelight. Food sat half eaten on tiny ornate plates – olives, cheese, proscuitto, crackers. Amalie seemed pleased with the success of the night. Several of Maya's paintings sold, bringing in just under thirty thousand dollars. Excitement turned to contentment with the food and wine.

"You've done very well, my dear. We sold many of your paintings tonight." Amalie looked smug. Maya smiled.

"But not Rusty Raven, right?"

Amalie looked sheepish. "Darlink, we got the best price for that one!"

"Amalie! You knew you weren't to sell that one! That one's special. I painted it for Jay. I didn't want it sold."

"Oh my dear. I am so sorry. But truly it sold for an amazing price – twenty thousand!"

"Can you get it back?"

"No, my dear. It sold through a dealer to an anonymous buyer. I have no way of tracking it."

"Oh, Amalie. I don't know what to say."

"I'm very sorry, Maya. I truly am." Maya appeared to fight back tears. Amalie gathered plates and got up to take them to the kitchen. Maya followed her with more dishes.

"Who was that man you were talking to for so long?" Amalie placed dishes into the sink.

"A guy from Seattle. He just happened to be walking by. His name is Dom. Dominic."

"Dom? He was very handsome. He looked a little like a movie star."

"Did he? I didn't notice," Maya said, rinsing her wine glass. Amalie eyed her suspiciously.

"How could you not have noticed *that*, Darlink!"

Maya laughed. "OK, maybe I noticed a little. Do you want to know something odd?" Amalie turned and leaned against the kitchen counter as she poured herself another glass of wine, settling in for a good story. "I think the psychic I saw predicted that this man would come into my life. I think this might be the man I'm supposed to be with."

Amalie looked skeptical. "Darlink, those people, they don't really talk to the dead. They are just picking up on your intuition, the things surrounding you, the responses you give. You are paying them to tell you what you want to hear."

"I don't think so. This seemed so real. She told me things that she couldn't have possibly known."

"Like?"

"Like she knew I had a son and that Jay worried about him."

"She did the reading at your house, correct? Would there not be evidence of your son nearby?"

"I guess… She also knew that Jay was charming and intelligent."

"Things any wife would want to hear."

"And that he was a real bastard."

Amalie laughed out loud. "OK, Darlink. You have me there. What else did she say?"

"She picked up on our connection to Italy and a cave we swam in. A grotto. She couldn't have known about that."

"There were no pictures around?"

"No, I don't think so."

"OK. So what did she say about your handsome stranger?"

"She said I would meet him at some sort of art function and that he'd be tall and wearing a suit or a tux. She said he would be very handsome."

"Darlink, that could describe many people."

"She said his name would be Shawn. Oh! Dom sort of rhymes with Shawn."

"Yes. I suppose it does. My sweet, are you sure you're not reading too much into this?"

"Oh, probably. I don't know. I was attracted to him. Do you think it's too soon, Amalie?" Maya grabbed an olive from a small dish and popped it into her mouth and looked at her friend.

"No, Darlink. If you're feeling it, then you're ready. I say pursue your heart, my sweet. You deserve some love in your life. But do proceed carefully."

Chapter Seventeen

BLANK CANVAS

His indigo eyes were locked onto her as she fidgeted – nervously ripping her bread into tiny pieces and buttering each one before popping it into her mouth.

"You're very beautiful," he said, making Maya smile.

"Thank you. I should tell you that you're my first date since... for a long time."

"Am I? I find that difficult to believe. And I am honored."

This guy has all the lines.

"They're on a date, what do you expect?" Alice's voice startled me.

"Yeah, well, he's smooth."

Maya and Dominic were having lunch at Le Coq, a small French restaurant near Pike Place Market. Curiosity had me tagging along. I wanted to see what this dude was all about.

"I know we haven't really talked about our pasts yet, but are you divorced?" Dom asked.

Breath escaped Maya's lungs. Their initial emails would have been an easy way for Maya to have dropped the news, but she had apparently wanted to hide her widowhood, at least for a little while, perhaps thinking she could let him get to know her as an unencumbered single woman, as if such a thing existed in anyone over thirty.

Oh God. Here we go. Will I ever see him again after tonight?

"No. Not divorced." Her answer lingered in the air.

"Oh. Then separated?" His eyes narrowed slightly.

"Why is she being so cagey about her widowhood?" I asked Alice.

"Perhaps Maya is afraid her widowhood will intimidate Dominic."

"Why on Earth would she think that?"

"Jay," Alice said, twisting her mouth in a look of 'you should know better', "you remember how irrational fears can be on Earth."

"Right."

"She doesn't trust others to handle strong emotions such as grief, or more accurately, her grief. But she doesn't yet know she is meeting with a person who is very well versed in loss. Her status of a widow does not bother him."

"No," Maya said, looking Dom in the eye now. "I'm widowed." To his credit, his expression reflected first surprise, and then concern, but no pity. She rushed to fill the awkward silence while he digested the news.

"I'm sorry. I do recall your friend mentioning a funeral at the art opening. I didn't realize he meant your husband's."

"Just over a year now. His car went off the road on the way to Whistler."

Yup, that was me. The idiot that fell asleep at the wheel.

"I'm sorry, Maya. That must have been very difficult."

For her or for me?

"Yeah. It's been a rollercoaster, that's for sure."

"I can't imagine," Dominic said. They sat quietly for a few minutes, each taking a sip of ice water.

"I hope you don't take this the wrong way, but I am drawn to you, and this makes you more alluring, somehow. We have both endured difficult journeys, it seems."

"We have?"

"Yes. My older brother drowned when I was twelve. I couldn't save him."

"That is so weird. My husband's father drowned when he was fourteen, and he lived with the same guilt for the rest of his life."

In the silence after the waitress left with their order, his blue eyes bore into hers, challenging her.

"I don't much care about your past," he said suddenly. I could tell she was caught off guard. This wasn't something a widow normally heard. Maya had grimly borne the usual platitudes: "Sorry for your loss, that must have been so difficult, I can't imagine…" Her mouth opened in surprise at his statement.

Who is this idiot?

"It's the blank canvas that I'm interested in," he continued, his hands creating a square across the crisp white linen tablecloth, making the metaphor a literal one. This made sense coming from Dom, a photographer, a visual man, a talent that Maya admired. Before meeting again in person, she'd browsed his website, where she found samples of his work — self-portraits that cast him mysteriously in black and white shadow with an unmistakable look in his eye. I knew that look. He was a player. I watched as she scrolled through photos of sensual, curving spaces, rotundas and curling Gaudi balconies, seducing her with form, something she understood innately. At fifty-three, he was older than Maya by eleven years, but his curly salt-and-pepper hair, slim frame, and angular face were traits I knew she found attractive. In an email before their date, he told her of his desire to "have a relationship that included trust, integrity, passion, abundance, romance, sensuality, creativity, play, and miracles all inside grace and ease." If I'd been human, I would have thrown up reading it, but for some reason, Maya fell for it.

In the two weeks leading up to the date, I'd heard Maya

telling her friends about the emails he sent her with suggestive photos of himself, taken in mirrors, his shirt off, the ripples in his stomach defined. She admitted to being turned on by these images but to her sister, Bethany, admitted the photos made her slightly nervous. She knew the photos were too intimate to be sending to a virtual stranger. But she admitted to being excited for the possibility of sharing chemistry.

"Our pasts can make a frame around the edges," he continued, "but inside that framework is what I'm interested in. I want to create something new with whomever I'm with. Together we get to decide the colors and the paint strokes and although the past might influence those decisions, what we create together would be entirely new."

It seemed to dawn on her that her widowhood could become part of her framework instead of the painting itself. He was sly, using a painting metaphor. But could a person be expected to whitewash over her past? I was skeptical.

The many resemblances this man had with my Sean Connery mind burp were uncanny – curly hair, grizzled grey jawline, blue eyes, a closed, dry-lipped smile. The crepey skin on his neck disappeared into his open blue shirt, joining with a clutch of greying chest hairs. Despite his obvious fitness from a regimen of 100-mile bike rides, something he quickly disclosed, he seemed older than his stated age. His profession as a photographer was icing on the cake for Maya. I had never been creative in that way.

This could be him. This could be the man I will eventually be with.
No, Lenie. It's not him. Don't let him fool you.
He's older than I thought he would be but this must be him, right?
No, Lenie. No, it's not.

They finished lunch, talking the entire time about things Maya enjoyed – art, photography, painting, life after death, spirituality, transformation. Maya's aura pulsed.

Could I make love to this man?
Oh God, Lenie, no!

After lunch, as they walked down the street toward their cars, I noticed he walked bent over at the waist, but with a ramrod straight back – a painful looking gait. Arthritis probably. They smiled, hugged, waved. Both Maya and I watched as he got into his Mercedes.

At least he's financially secure.

It might seem that way, Lenie, but be careful.

A few nights later, Maya's friend Deirdre invited her to a play, so she asked Dom to go with her. Maya was very bold in asking him out so soon.

As the hostess showed them to their seats, Maya introduced him to Deirdre. He took a long time making conversation, leaving Maya and the hostess waiting awkwardly in the aisle for him. What was this guy pulling? Was this some sort of control thing? He stared intently at Deirdre's breasts, not seeming to notice his date's discomfort.

During the show, his hand began a mating dance – at first his pinky touched hers, and then his index finger stroked the top of her hand until his hand clasped hers, as if he were trying to claim it for his own. Eventually, their hands found some privacy under the table where they played as they rested on her thigh, as his wily index finger stroked higher and higher up her leg.

Later, when he dropped Maya off at home, they stood facing each other beside his car as she teetered on painful-looking fuchsia high heels, a new addition to her wardrobe. Their faces were inches apart.

OK. Here is where you kiss me goodnight. He gave her an awkward hug.

Rookie! You missed THAT opportunity!

"OK." She waved at him. "Well, see ya!" I almost had to laugh at the miffed look on her face. Was he being a gentleman? Was he nervous? Or did he know exactly what he was doing?

Maya let herself into the house and, after shedding her black pea coat, flopped herself onto the couch and sighed, looking like a teenager with a big grin on her face. Her thoughts were racing. *Ohmygodohmygod... Is this crazy? Did I actually feel something? Something besides grief? God I need to get laid, but I've gotta be cool.* She jumped up suddenly and dashed up the stairs, two at a time. She undressed hastily and shivered as she jumped into the sheets. She rolled over to reach into the drawer of the bedside table and remove her new "wand".

"Are you sure you want to continue watching?" Alice appeared abruptly.

"Uh, yeah. No. I mean..."

"It's understandable. It's how we try to stay connected to our loved ones, but Maya deserves her privacy."

"I know. I know. I really don't like this guy, Alice. I need to make sure he doesn't hurt her."

"Jay, you won't be able to stop this. This is Maya's journey."

"But it's my fault she's with him. And now she's thinking about having sex with him because she thinks I sent him to her!"

"Well, didn't you?"

"Yes, but not in the right way! I just made him up!"

"Did you, Jay? Perhaps his image appeared to you for a reason."

"Yeah, because I thought of Sean Connery."

"Maybe it wasn't really Sean Connery you thought of."

"You mean, Domonic *is* the person she is supposed to be with?"

"Perhaps, for the moment, yes."

"But he's a creep."

"Why do you think that?"

"Who sends a stranger naked pictures of themselves? Who tells a widow that her past doesn't matter? There's something this guy wants from Maya, and I worry he's going to do her harm, either physical or emotional."

"Perhaps Maya needs to learn that in her own time. You

can't help her in this, Jay."

"I can't help her, but I can keep an eye on her."

"Respectfully, I hope."

Dear Jay,

I think I am falling for this guy, Dominic. He's very different than Marcus. You would like him. He's smart and stylish. Not that you would care so much about the stylish part. But you might appreciate his mind. He's opened me up to new ways of looking at things. It's hard to feel sorry for my widowed self when he does not consider my past important. What a revelation! That I could turn away from my past and paint a new future. You'd think as a painter I would understand that inherently, that I could paint a new reality. I'm excited at the prospect of shedding my widow-ness, conscious that it's a place I have dwelled too long, nesting in its comfort. I fear it has become an identity of sorts — that poor single mother, widowed too young. Boo hoo. It's time to rewrite my personal narrative, piece by piece. I'm ready to dismantle my widow armor: removing that thick layer of sadness and its unexpected crying jags, shedding the guilt that comes with my increasing laughter, kicking off the loneliness that accompanies Christmas parties brimming with what I once saw as joyous couples, something I thought I would never have. I want to be a woman instead of a widow. I want to shed my loneliness and be that happy, vibrant, intelligent, alive woman I know I am. And so I am moved by Dom's unique take on my widowhood, the deep conversations we share. He is interesting and alive when he speaks, his eyes alight with an excitement I find alluring. I am allowing myself to be seduced. It's meant to be, just as Liz predicted. This is the man you told me I was destined to meet...

I wish that was true Maya.

A few nights later, Dom invited Maya out for dinner, letting her choose between his place or a restaurant. *Smooth.*

She chose the restaurant option. Good. She was taking things slow and not leaping into the sack with this guy too soon. I wanted her to take her time and see this guy for who he really was. But I also knew she needed physical companionship. Who wouldn't? She'd been single and celibate for over a year now.

I could relate. I missed sex – the sensation of skin against skin, the emotional surrender, the involuntary spasms of an orgasm – there was no equivalent in this world. But she let herself fall for this guy for the wrong reasons.

"Don't you think you should leave her alone to figure this out for herself?" Alice suddenly made one of her annoying appearances.

"Can't I tell her somehow that this guy is a fraud? I don't know what he wants from her, but he's hiding something. I sense a darkness about him and yet I can tell she's thinking about sleeping with him."

"Sex is a powerful antidote to grief, Jay. It's perfectly normal. Sex helps humans to feel alive again after a loss. In losing you, she's discovering a new part of herself."

"She's discovering her new self through sex?"

"In a way. Grief causes people to shut down emotionally. Sex can sometimes be a first step toward reclaiming life."

"So I should be happy for her?"

"Perhaps."

"Great. I'm supposed to be happy for my wife to have sex with another man. That's messed up."

At an upscale restaurant with long curtains draped between tables and linen napkins on the polished beechwood tables, a waitress asked about drinks. Maya ordered a glass of white wine, Dom ordered water.

She looked at him.

"I haven't had a drink in twelve years," he explained before turning to the menu.

"You don't mind if I have a glass of wine, do you?"

He waved his hand breezily, but a quick scowl fluttered across his face, as if he were trying to be fine with it, but wasn't quite.

"Are you sure?"

"Yes. It's fine," he said, looking at her as if challenging her to ask why. She didn't. During dinner, they seemed like strangers trying to get to know each other. She asked about his children, who were grown, one just out of high school, the other college age. He talked at length about them. She told him about Calder. Their conversation sounded stilted, slightly formal, as if neither of them was quite comfortable in their surroundings. They fell into nervous, anticipatory silences, unsure of what might happen next. But their auras became a deep burgundy red as the electricity between them built.

After dinner, in his car, he said, "Do you want to watch a movie?"

"Sure," she said. "What's playing?"

"I have a couple of Netflix movies...we could go back to my place, have some tea and watch."

I'm not ready.

No, you're not.

"Sounds dangerous," she said. He gave her a sly smile, accepting her unintended challenge.

No sex. We'll just watch a movie.

Yeah, right.

I expected a photographer's apartment to be light filled, a loft perhaps, and although Dom's ground floor condo had high ceilings with exposed ductwork and gray painted walls, the place was cast in deep shadow. His self-portraits were beautifully hung along the narrow hallway, giving it an art gallery feel. A dining table pushed against a wall was covered in trinkets – tiny bowls with ancient Roman glass beads, framed drawings, a collection of watches, more framed photographs that leaned against the wall. Against two walls of the bedroom stood giant mirrors, giving someone on the bed the ability to be seen from any angle.

"Tea?" He stood in his narrow kitchen, unwinding his signature scarf from around his neck.

"I'm good," she said, obviously trying to sound relaxed.

"OK then. Let's see. I have *The Bourne Ultimatum* or *No Country for Old Men*. Which would you prefer?"

Not the most romantic movies. I guess it's good he didn't expect me to accept his offer to come to his apartment!

"Um, *Bourne Ultimatum*," she said.

He put the movie into the DVD player and then backed up to sit on the lumpy gray leather couch beside her, causing them both to sink in toward each other.

"This couch sort of gobbles you up," he said. He took her hand and began caressing it as they watched the opening credits in silence.

Should I? Too soon?

Yes, too soon, Lenie.

I shouldn't be here.

You can always leave.

Dom seemed to sense Maya's uneasiness because he pulled her to her feet and they stood facing each other awkwardly. She prepared for the anticipated kiss. His hands were shaking.

"I thought you were going to kiss me the other night," she said, her voice gravelly.

"I wasn't sure if that was what you wanted. Is it what you want now?" His manipulation had begun. I could tell she didn't know how to answer.

Am I attracted to him, or do I just need to get laid? It's been so long and I'm so horny. I should wait. But my body is betraying me, melting like ice cream, morphing into a shape I can't control as he stares into my eyes.

You should wait.

He leaned in slightly and they kissed, awkwardly. Her ice cream apparently melted. He pulled her into his bedroom. I turned away.

Of course I wanted Maya to meet someone other than Marcus, but I hadn't banked on Dominic. His aura had a sinister darkness to it, as if he had ulterior motives for seducing Maya. Yet she appeared to blossom in her relationship with him – she smiled more, color returned to her cheeks, she ate more. My fear was that she was moving too quickly, blind to his undercurrent of danger.

"There is a purpose for everything, Jay. Maya needs to learn from this relationship." Alice's advice sometimes came without her presence. I knew her thought to be the truth, but I wanted to spare Maya inevitable pain.

...I'll admit it, Jay, I expected tears of guilt after having sex for the first time since your death, or numbness or apathy. Not spine tingling relief. Salty animal instinct transported me to a place within my brain, bereft of colour, size, darkness, light – an atrophied kernel deep inside that held proof that I am still alive, can still feel, and still love. Making love is a kind of surrender – not submission exactly, but a sense of inevitability, a release of a year-and-a-half worth of pent-up emotion. Should I fear this freshly escaped animal as a thing entirely untrustworthy? Its sweet face belies a truth about the power of sex and its relationship with grief. How easily I succumb. Maybe this is too much to be telling you, Jay, but I have no one else to tell...

I knew I should have stopped reading, but curiosity got the better of me.

He has that look. His contented smile and eyes softened in a way that tells me that his pain too has been assuaged through sex. It's a look that scared me a little, so confident and smug, his claim so firmly staked. He credits me with his happiness, but I'm uncomfortable with this responsibility for his thirst, but I know that I am thirsty too, that together we'll quench our mutual thirst, like the slave and the lion, in gratitude. Only a month ago, I cried into your bathrobe, Jay, trying to recapture the scent of your soapy fragrance that, after a year and a half, has long since turned to dust within its fibers.
I will always love you, I hope you understand that.
M.

I do understand, Maya. I will always love you too.

I knew it was a mistake when Maya invited Dom over for dinner at the house only a few weeks later, introducing him to Calder as a friend. When he arrived at the door, he stood waiting until she gave him a hug and an intimate kiss. He leaned against my kitchen counter and I saw him as Calder might – an old man with gray hair wearing a scarf. Calder came downstairs and eyed him suspiciously. Dom looked nervous.

"Calder likes to cook," Maya said, her tone upbeat.

"What do you like to cook, Calder?" Dom asked. Calder shrugged.

"He likes to make sautéed greens with onions," Maya answered for him.

"Cool," Dom said. Maya sautéed onions and Calder quietly took over the task. Dom disappeared into the living room, plopped onto the couch, and began flipping through magazines. I would have sat at the counter talking to Maya as she cooked. Often I helped with the cooking or getting the table ready. I had an instantaneous glimpse of Maya's life with this man – him on the couch ignoring her as she cooked dinner, Calder miserable.

"Don't you want to come hang out with us?" she called, poking her head into the living room.

"No, I'm fine here," he said, giving her a terse smile.

The awkward dinner was punctuated by long silences that were commented on by Calder saying in a sing-songy voice, "Awkward."

The few questions that Dom asked Calder were answered in monosyllables. Our son's instincts about this man were bang on.

When dinner finally ended and Maya had cleaned the kitchen, she collapsed onto the couch beside Dom.

"Want a foot rub?" he asked.

"Uh, OK. I guess that would be nice." Maya looked at the stairs, listening for Calder in his room.

"Do you have lotion?" Dom asked. Maya looked at him quizzically.

"You know, hand lotion or something?" Maya found a bottle of hand cream in the bathroom. Dom gently took her foot and began to apply the cream. Maya blushed.

Well, this is weird.

I'll say, Lenie.

He's just trying to be sweet.

Creepy sweet.

I watched Calder sneak down the stairs from his room to peek at the action happening in the living room. Maya caught him watching and shook her head at him. Calder dashed back up the stairs into his bedroom, slamming the door as he made a flying leap face-down on the bed.

Is he going to be my new dad?

No way, Beano.

But he's rubbing her feet. Doesn't that mean they're going to get married?

Nah. It just means he's rubbing her feet.

Calder smiled. *Are they going to do it?*

Do what?

You know, like have S.E.X.?

I don't honestly know, Calder. I'm dead, remember?

Yeah, but can't you see whatever you want? Couldn't you see them having S.E.X.?

Well maybe, but I wouldn't tell you if I did.

Why not?

Because it's none of our business.

It's my business if Mama marries this dude.

Well, that's for your mama to decide.

I hope she gets rid of him. He's creepy. He scares me.

Your mom's a smart gal. She'll do the right thing, buddy. You should get some sleep now.

Not with creepo downstairs.

Right, well, I'll just hang out here with you then.

A month later, Maya's mother, Estelle, came for a visit from Ontario so that Maya and Dom could take a weekend trip together.

"You can tell Calder you'll be on an artist's retreat," Estelle suggested. She wanted to see her daughter married again. She didn't seem to care to whom.

Maya found a bed and breakfast online in an old cannery in a town two hours outside of Seattle. They drove together in Dom's car, listening to a playlist she had downloaded onto an iPod, full of sexy-romantic love songs, most of which were too schlocky for me. I would never have listened to Dido or Jack Johnson. I always thought Maya and I had similar tastes in music, but I realized that perhaps she had just acquiesced to my music selections of Steely Dan and Stevie Ray Vaughn.

They held hands across the console of his car. As they spiraled onto a highway onramp, he turned to her and said, "I would die for you." The words shocked me. Would I have died for her? Now that I was dead, it was hard to say. It's easy to die for someone. It's much harder to let them go.

"I'd rather you didn't." She laughed.

"No really," he said. "I'm serious. I would die for you."

"OK," she said. "Wow." She turned and looked out the window, deep in thought.

They spent the day and evening locked in the room of the B&B, popping out for lunch and then dinner and again in the morning for breakfast. On their way back to Seattle the next day they took a detour and drove up to Hurricane Ridge, which even at the end of April was still covered in snow. He threw nuts to the giant black crows in the parking lot, stark against the white landscape, and for a moment the idyllic winter mountain scene took on a sinister quality, reminiscent of an Edgar Allen Poe poem. My presence was not lost on Maya. I had to warn her about this guy somehow, but she seemed to see my presence as my acceptance of her relationship rather than a warning.

Zigzagging back down the mountain, they talked about Calder.

"Calder needs to accept me for who I am," Dom said as the Mercedes careened dangerously close to the cliff's edge.

The statement hung in the air. The little crease between Maya's eyebrows appeared. I knew that perplexed look. Maya knew she couldn't expect Calder to readily accept a new guy suddenly entering their lives, and now this dude expected an eight-year-old to "accept him for who he was"? What did that even mean? Wasn't Dom the adult? Shouldn't he be accepting Calder for who he was and being sensitive to a child's needs?

"Kids are kids," Maya said. "I don't see how I'm going to get Calder to just accept our new situation overnight. It's going to take time, Dom."

"You lead by example, Maya. You need to be comfortable with our situation in order for Calder to be."

"I thought I was."

"Not entirely. You are not being completely honest with Calder. What did you tell him about where you were this weekend?"

"Well, he doesn't need to know all the details." She paused. "I told him I was on an artist's retreat."

"See what I mean? He's going to know you are not being honest with him. I was always perfectly honest with my kids and my dating. They just had to accept whatever happened."

"Yes, but your kids weren't with you 24/7," she countered. "You had opportunities to spend the night with someone while your kids were with your ex-wife. Calder will not take kindly to anyone spending the night in my bed. I don't have that freedom."

"You have to *make* that freedom. You need to set boundaries. Lock your door. Tell him what's going on."

Maybe he has a point.

What point?!
Dom is giving me the advice of someone who has experienced dating while having teenaged kids. Maybe I'm allowing Calder to rule my relationships and I'm creating a situation through my tiny lies that has left him feeling unstable, not knowing what to believe.
Hardly, Lenie. You are doing what's best for Calder. You are being a good mother.

A few weeks after their trip together, Maya sat in the Mercedes with Dom, Calder in the back seat as their ferry sliced across the Puget Sound on a sunny Mother's Day after a weekend at a friend's house on Vashon Island. Dom looked at Maya with a pained expression. The previous night, when Calder asked where they would all sleep, Maya assured him they would each sleep in separate rooms, knowing she told a white lie in an attempt to avoid a night of temper tantrums and sleeplessness.

"What is it?" she asked, Dom's face shaded by the dark hull of the boat.

"Well... I guess I'm not feeling that there has been much space in the context of your past life for me to be who I am in our relationship. You bring your husband up in conversations. A lot. I don't bring up my ex that way. I don't have photos of her around my place. It doesn't feel like there's a lot of room for me in what we are creating."

Maya looked shocked. Calder, luckily, was plugged into his iPod. "I talk about my husband to help Calder." I could hear the defensiveness in her voice. She turned then to look at Calder, to see if he could hear them. He looked up, briefly, but was oblivious to the conversation happening in the front seat. Maya turned back toward Dom. "It's my job to keep Jay's memory alive for him."

"Oh," he said, thoughtful. "I'm glad you told me that. That makes sense and makes me feel a little better."

Have I been talking about you too much, Jay?
Of course not.

"This is not really about you, exactly," Dom said. "It's my own reaction to your past, and I need to examine that. You're just being you. I need to figure out where I fit in the context of your past."

"I'm glad you recognize that because I don't think I know any other way to be in our relationship. Jay is a presence in my life. I like to think I am sensitive to you and how it must be dating someone with a ghost in their closet, but I did love him very much and that hasn't gone away. I will try and be more sensitive to your feelings," Maya said.

"I feel that love when I go to your house – the photos, your attention. You seem elsewhere when I'm at your home. I feel like we can't be ourselves at your house the way we can at mine."

Yeah, because I don't want to screw you in front of my kid!
You make me laugh, Maya!

I rejoiced at Maya's anger. Apparently, I didn't need to do anything at all to interfere with this relationship. Dom would kill it all by himself.

"When we're at my house," Maya explained as if to a child, "I have a son who needs my attention. I can't help that. We've only been going out for two months now. Calder needs time to get used to the situation."

"Yes, but it's not just that. I feel like there is this big mound of dough that is your life and your past and I'm trying to find a tiny air pocket within it to be who I am. We should be bringing ease and grace to your son and your home."

"I thought we were," she replied.

What's with all this 'ease and grace' garbage?
I think that's 'Dom speak' for 'it should all be about me', Lenie. This dude is such a narcissist!

Dom followed that stellar weekend conversation with a text and email blackout. Maya finally called him two days later. "Is everything OK? Should we talk?"

"I value integrity," he said over the phone, his voice terse. "Not being truthful with your son means you're not being truthful with me or with our relationship."

Maya closed her eyes and took a deep breath. "I'm doing my best, Dom. I'm sorry if you feel I'm not being truthful, but I have to do what I think is right for my son."

This was my fault. My stupid ego over Marcus had created more turmoil for Maya and Calder, a consequence I couldn't have foreseen when I conjured "Sean Connery" into Maya's life. I would need to find a way to undo this mess, though it looked as though it was unraveling quite successfully without my help.

Chapter Eighteen

August 7th, 2007

Jay,

It's 4 a.m. and I can't sleep. I wonder what you must think of me? Widowhood has clouded my sense of character judgment, clearly. What a catastrophe with Dom. Three months of my life I will never get back. Can I justify my idiocy in any way? I honestly thought you had sent him to me, Jay. That you, as my cosmic guardian angel, had found me a perfect new mate. Crazy, I know. But that feeling gave me a false sense of inevitability about this new relationship. God, I'm such a romantic fool sometimes. The idea that you would actually set me up from the afterlife. Foolfoolfool.

I woke up in a sweat. Those photos I allowed him to take. The videos. Oh God. How could I have done such a thing? Jay and I had a good sex life, but like many married couples, we'd fallen into a bit of a rut. Maybe only I thought that. But after Jay died, something in me snapped. I couldn't explain it. Sex with Dom filled an empty crevasse deep inside me, made me feel more alive. But I surprised myself with my sexual appetite. But now. All those external hard drives I saw on his desk were probably filled with lurid pictures of naked women. Of me. Or worse, maybe he'd sold those pictures to pornographic websites. I Googled him, too late. I paid $35 for a report, verifying addresses, family names. Everything checked out, but I was unnerved. Could I trust him now? What would he do with the photos, which until now I had seen as artistic, me playing the seductive muse?

I lay awake trying to assess his character. In his presence, everything felt fine. He seemed sane, articulate, prided himself on his honesty and talked at length about integrity. When I was with him, I had no qualms. But in the middle of the night his peculiarities woke me – the sexual photographs in particular – and yet I went along wordlessly when I went over to his place that morning to find a video camera affixed to a tripod peering at the bed. I felt extra pressure to be sexy, and to point certain parts of my body toward the camera. I wanted to trust him, to convince myself he was worthy of my trust. I wanted to be in love with him, and to do that I had to trust him. I convinced myself it must be love if I could afford that level of trust.

He seemed to sense my unease and once told me how I reminded him of a friend he had as a child of five or six, a girl who he considered to be his soul mate. I felt strangely honored by this confession, that we had a child-like friendship as well as a romantic relationship, something special, a connection that I alone shared with him. One of the defining moments of his life, he told me, happened the day he went to her house and found that her family had moved away. No one had told him. When he told me the story, I wondered if deep down, he was setting me up to hurt him the same way, creating a sort of self-fulfilling prophesy. I felt inexplicably sad.

My weekend alone with him both excited and frightened me. I hadn't had even one night away from Calder since Jay's death. I still bore the guilt of my indiscretion against him. But this man was not Jay or Marcus. What could I say? I was horny as hell. Having regular sex again made me more so. I wrote provocative emails and poems about him when we were apart and he sent me photos of us together in bed. "Naati", a derivation of the words "naughty," or "nasty". "Nasty" was my visceral reaction to each of the shots he sent of us together in bed. I didn't know how to respond to those naked photos of myself in compromising positions. They made me squeamish, but I often found myself dashing upstairs to find the vibrator. I was in dreamland, at the height of sexual addiction, riding high. I felt sexy, desired, alive. It was easy to convince myself I had fallen in love.

And then it quickly started to unravel. His comment that I still had photos of Jay around the house. What could I say? I did. It felt like a shot to the belly. I thought I had relinquished my widow mantle in the context of this new relationship, and had become a new woman, one capable of love. But now I wonder, was he right? Was I still in love with Jay? Perhaps I will always be his widow.

Calder added another complication. One night, Calder sat with me on my bed watching TV when he asked to play Angry Birds on my phone. Halfway through a game, the familiar ping of a text message sounded and Calder stopped playing.

"EEWW!! Who is texting you that?"

I took the phone and on the screen, it read: 'I want to see you naked.'

"Oh God!"

"Who is that?"

"Sorry, sweetie. It's just a friend playing a joke."

"Dominic?"

"Well, yeah."

"Why does he want to see you naked? That's so gross! Does he want to have sex with you?"

"Calder! How do you know about sex?"

"I'm not a baby anymore!"

"I know, sweetie. I'm not saying you are. It's just, I've

never heard you say that word before."

"Well, I know what it is, you know."

"Yes. Of course. Anyway, like I said, it was just meant as a joke."

"A pretty gross joke."

After Calder went to bed, I adjusted my phone so the content of my text messages would no longer pop up on the main screen. I called Bethany in a panic.

"Dominic expects Calder to simply accept him. A child traumatized was the person meant to change for him, a grown man. 'He needs to accept me for who I am.' Jesus. What a fool I am!"

"God, Maya, the guy sounds like a weirdo. Sorry to say it."

"Maybe. But he might be right about me needing to tell Calder the truth about our relationship instead of sneaking around. I should allow him to be a part of whatever Calder might dole out. Still, I'm surprised he can't be more sensitive to Calder's needs, not to mention mine."

"Calder is your number one priority right now, Maya. And any decent man would see that and be respectful of it. Are you sure about this guy?"

I didn't know what I could trust about him anymore. He seemed so enmeshed in the dogma of "ease and grace" and it made me realize that perhaps he was not as secure in himself as I thought. He needed a framework, a vocabulary to keep himself in check, as though without it he couldn't even trust himself. He believed he had "integrity" and depth, but I think now that he was so self-absorbed that his depth could only ever be skin deep. And I had apparently scratched the surface a little too hard.

I didn't see him again until he arrived at my little art show at a Seattle wine bar a week later. I needed to chat with people, so when he arrived, he hovered nearby until I turned to him. He stood waiting expectantly until the people I was talking to became uncomfortable and walked away to view another painting. Dom held out his arms for a hug, closing his eyes and pursing his lips, awaiting the kind of greeting I might give him if we were alone. Instead I gave him a peck on the cheek. He looked pained.

"I'm with some friends right now and they might be interested in buying a painting. Can you give me a few minutes?"

He moped around the bar alone, peering into my paintings as if trying to find the key to my psyche within their colors. I rejoined my friends, but watched him out of the corner of my eye. When they left, he came over and gave me a hug and tried again to kiss me on the lips, but I swiveled away from him to escape his embrace.

"Not now, Dom. I'm working."

He stepped back, chastised.

After the reception, we walked to a nearby Mexican restaurant for dinner. He tried to hold my hand as we walked, but I wiggled my hand out of his grasp. We were seated at a brightly painted table, an overflowing basket of nacho chips and a bowl of salsa between us.

"I'm sorry about not wanting to kiss you at the show."

"It's fine," he said and looked away.

"I hope you understand it was because I was working. It just didn't seem professional."

"It's fine, really. I just don't understand why you don't like being adored."

"Adored? Don't I?"

"That's all I'm trying to do, Maya. Adore you."

"OK. Well, I'm sorry." Neither of us spoke for a few minutes. I couldn't help thinking how his version of adoration felt as if he were trying to possess me. I took a warm chip and dunked it in salsa.

"I'm looking forward to meeting your daughter," I said, trying to change the subject. Despite our three months together, I still had not met any of his friends or family.

"Yes, I'm looking forward to that as well," he said,

looking away. He was leaving the next day to drive to California with his son to help his 21-year-old daughter move into his place in Seattle. His apartment was small, the second bedroom occupied by his office which he said he had no intention of moving. His daughter, Alicia, would sleep on the couch which would have a profound effect on the amount of time we would be able to spend alone together, something that didn't seem to worry him. "We'll find other ways," he assured me.

A week after his daughter's arrival in Seattle, we arranged to go out for dinner with our kids the night before his departure on one of his business trips to Hawaii. When I arrived at the restaurant, Dom waved but then turned his back to us to talk intently on his cell phone. I introduced myself and Calder to his daughter and then we all stood in awkward silence waiting for our table as Dom continued his conversation on the phone.

"Did you have a good trip up? All settled in?" I asked Alicia.

"Yes. Fine," Alicia replied. She was tall, slim, and had the same pale complexion as her father. Calder stood beside her playing on his PS2 game, ignoring the world around him. We were shown to our seats just as Dom got off the phone.

"Sorry," he said. "The hotel in Hawaii." Alicia rolled her eyes.

We sat next to our respective children, Alicia opposite me, looking bored. She clearly wanted to be elsewhere. We ate dinner in near silence, and I fumbled to make conversation. Alicia seemed to perk up only once when I told the story of my car being hit the day before and how much the shop said it would cost to fix.

"That happened to me too!" Alicia exclaimed, light in her eyes for the first time.

As we were waiting for the bill to arrive, Dom leaned over the table toward Maya and puckered his lips, an expectant gesture for a return smooch that had become his habit in public places. He appeared desperate to prove to the world, and apparently our children, his claim on me, again making me feel more possessed than loved. I gave him a withering look, hoping he would read, "Are you kidding? Our kids are sitting right here!" into it. He sat back in his chair and turned away from me, like a petulant child.

After dinner, the kids waited in our separate cars, and I stood near Dom's truck to say goodbye.

"I don't suppose you want to drop off the kids and go meet somewhere?" I asked. "I won't see you for a while."

"I still have a lot of packing to do," he said. "Why? Did you want to talk about something?"

Yes, I think I want to break up, I thought.

"It would be nice to talk, but I guess it can wait until you get back," I said instead.

"You sure?"

I nodded. He gave me a quick peck on the cheek and walked away.

During his trip to Hawaii, I had more time to think about things and wrote Dom an email:

I'm struggling right now with your expectation that Calder needs to 'accept you for who you are', as you say. He's a kid, Dom. I think it's you who needs to accept him for who he is.

Dom replied:

I'm surprised what you share with me now that I am not there to defend myself.

I sat back in my chair after reading this. I tried telling him my views, but he couldn't hear my words unless they were in black and white. I wrote back:

I've tried talking with you about this, but you don't seem to want to hear my views. I thought that I could express my side of things better in writing.

The email exchange that ensued became a volley of increasingly angry misinterpretations. I finally wrote, incredulously, "Are we breaking up over email?"

His immediate response, "I will call it — declare it as

complete," came as a shock. He had gone from "I will die for you" to "it is complete" in a matter of three months. "Complete" apparently was Dom's way of overcoming an unpleasant past experience. I had apparently been labeled "past heartbreak" and swept under the carpet – perhaps Dom's habit with any painful experience – ready for a fresh, new blank canvas to emerge. The blank canvas shimmered in all its linen whiteness, a mirage. I could no more sweep away my past than I could hold my own heart in my hands.

Our past makes us both powerful and weak, lithesome and unbending, hopeful and cynical. Our past is enmeshed into every particle of our minds and bodies, both in life and in death.

Despite my intention of only questioning myself and our relationship, I made it easy for him to read between the lines of that email. I wanted out. I knew I would never fully understand his intentions, and would always feel as if something stood in the way of us having an honest relationship. I wondered why it felt as if my own grief recovery seemed irrelevant to him. If I had dared to look deeper, my aversion to the way he tried to infiltrate my family in such a self-centered way or the fact that I had allowed my sexual relationship to cloud the way I really felt for this man would have been more obvious.

This was not at all what I intended. I thought we would be able to talk through the issues I had, face to face. I was not prepared to have the entire relationship end in an email. I learned from Dom how important it was to remain who you are in a relationship, and yet, paradoxically, he was unwilling to accept me for who I was. I suppose I too was unwilling to accept him.

This new loss has penetrated my carefully constructed shield of grief deeper than I am willing to admit. Another man present one minute and gone the next. Another round of self-recriminations.

Can you possibly still love me, wherever you are? - Maya

Chapter Nineteen

THE PLOTTING PROCESS

The invisible thread connecting me to Maya pulled taut after her breakup with Dom, accompanied by her renewed sense of loss. I was yanked back from the euphoria of being released from my humanness, as if I had just come to the end of my bungeed tether that continued to connect my soul with Maya's. I bounced back into human despair.

I had little effect on the human world, but I paid Dominic a late night visit as he sat hunched over his desk scrolling through nude pictures of women on his giant iMac screen. A photo of Maya appeared and for a moment I saw a white flash and then Dom's computer went dark. He swore, pushed the power button several times, but nothing happened. He rummaged under the desk to unplug and replug the computer and hard drives, but I didn't have to hang around to know that all his hard drives were fried by my little electrical hiccup.

After writing her letter to me, Maya lay back down and pulled the covers over her head. I surrounded her in white light as Alice had taught me to do, partly to defend myself against her sadness and partly to protect her from it.

Nicely done, Jay, my dad's thought as he appeared, wavering like heat before me.

I want you to come with me. There's a lecture I want to hear and I think you might find it enlightening as well.

Apparently it was time for an "evolvement session". My dad loved taking me to these afterlife lectures which were constant. There was nothing you couldn't learn in this realm if you wanted to know it. I had jokingly begun calling them my "evolvement sessions", but in truth I loved them. As usual, we were in a large twinkling hall with a great number of other spirits, the room resonating with a collective hum of sound, which put me in a sort of trance. It was this trance-like state that was most conducive to learning. The lecturer was a bright white entity in the center of the hall and he was lecturing – well, projecting his thoughts really – about the connection between the human and the spirit form.

"…I believe you are beginning to understand the connections that humans have with those of us who have died. Modern physicists toss around the idea of Entanglement Theory, the idea that objects made of particles such as photons, electrons, and molecules aren't necessarily separate objects. When you delve into the core of even the most solid-looking material and look at its particles, separateness dissolves. What remains after these particles interact physically and then separate into two or more objects are correlations between them that can be measured…"

"Jeez, Dad. This is awfully physics-y. Maybe a bit advanced for me, don't you think?"

"Not at all. This stuff is interesting, J.J. Pay attention."

"Since when did you become the nutty professor?"

"There's a lot to learn in the realm, if you have the desire. Are you interested or aren't you? You know it's a—"

"Choice. Yeah, Dad, so you keep saying. OK. I'm all ears. Well, not really, but you know what I mean."

"…You can measure each object's momentum, position,

and spin," the lecturer continued. "Then, by virtue of attempting to measure these qualities, when one of the objects displays a certain characteristic, such as moving clockwise, then the other object shows the opposite, corresponding characteristic; it moves counterclockwise."

I couldn't figure out where this guy was going with this reasoning.

Ah, human-Jay. Wax-on, wax-off, my son.

I laughed. My dad hadn't lost his human sense of humor.

"Humans are discovering that separation of particles is illusory. Physicists are loath to take this idea a step further, but in the same way that particles are bound, it is also possible for two living organisms to have an ongoing connection after one of them dies."

I didn't need some theory to tell me that Maya and I were still connected.

But don't you want to understand how you're connected to Maya? My Dad's thought was clear.

Apparently, I do.

The lecturer continued. "Those experiencing the loss of a loved one feel a connection to that person through memory, a kind of 'after-glow' that happens after a death occurs – a manifestation of Entanglement. Everything in the universe is linked, making an ongoing connection between life and death possible. Such connection transcends an individual completely, as so many religions decree when they talk about being connected individually to a greater whole. Entanglement theory parallels the idea behind 'collective consciousness'. If we are all a part of a universal reality, then every action we make is an event that affects all other aspects of this reality."

I would have called this Entanglement idea of connection between the living and the dead bunk if I were alive, but it all seemed pretty obvious to me now.

"Humans are so close to understanding, but are unwilling to believe the unmeasurable."

I would never have believed in being connected to Maya after my death.

And yet, you have affected her by surrounding her in white light, my dad responded.

I didn't do anything.

You did a lot. It's a good defense mechanism. You're recognizing when that needs to happen, both for her and for you. You're evolving nicely, J.J.

If I were alive, I would have smirked at my dad's comment.

You make me sound like a species of small monkey, Dad. Very Darwin.

I suppose I do. I sensed my dad's old laughter, though I couldn't hear it.

But seriously, I don't really feel as though I'm evolving. I feel like I'm weakened by Maya's grief.

As if in answer, the lecturer continued. "A spirit cannot be weakened by a human, but it's common for some spirits to be slower than others in releasing their human responses to emotion."

Now it seemed the lecturer was speaking directly to me.

"The process of a spiritual evolution is to completely free yourself from all that made you human, while at the same time remembering all you have learned from your human lifetimes. The evolution of a soul is a natural progression, but one that has no timetable. As you know, it's part of our soul's path to maturity that we help those on the earth-plane. But we need to help humans in a way that still allows us to be free of our human tendencies. You have a choice whether or not to help your loved ones. Just as they have a choice whether or not to ask for or accept your help. Each of you must express your needs, either orally or in thought. There must be free will on both sides. As humans or souls, we always have a choice about whether or not we want to evolve."

When the lecture ended, my dad and I continued our thought-conversation, though our thoughts and the lecture had been intertwined. It was impossible to hide one's thoughts to those who were attuned to them and the lecture simply interspersed our thoughts, as it did for all the spirits gathered.

So it's normal to feel weakened?

Yes, right now it is, J.J. You're still learning how to protect yourself from the negative brain waves humans express during times of heightened emotion. When you used the white light, it not only protected Maya from herself, it protected you from her as well.

That makes sense. I did feel a little better with the white light. So now what? How do I help her?

I think you have the answer to that already, but you are unwilling to consider it, since it goes against your human sense of pride.

What are you trying to tell me?

That you're getting in your own way J.J. It's time for you to remember where you came from.

I know where I came from. I came from you and Mom.

That's not what I mean. It's time for you to have a look and remind yourself of the plotting process.

You're not making any sense, Dad.

Earlier, you viewed the tablet that allowed you to recapture your meeting with Maya in Pompeii. That was me reminding you that you and the people in your life plotted your lives together before ever being born into your lives on Earth. The tablets allow you to view or recapture moments in your human life so you can decide if people, locations, and actions are in keeping with what it is you hope to achieve in your lifetime. You can recapture these moments any time you wish. Sometimes they give you perspective on events that happened in your lifetime and why they may have happened in the way that they did.

The circular room I transported to looked as if the walls were made of ice, not unlike what I imagined the inside of an igloo to look like. Light of varying colors throbbed behind the walls, giving the impression of an Aurora Borealis or a rave-club sky. I gathered with a tightly knit group of four other orbs of light, each hovering over what appeared to be a pane of glass, though I couldn't tell if it was glass or simply a hole in the atmosphere. When I looked into the hole, I watched a young Maya bounding up a set of steps, two at a time, chased by a teenaged Marcus. She flew onto a bed, and he followed her, landing beside her and rolling on top of her as they kissed. Two of the orbs, which I now realized were the spirits of Maya and Marcus, emitted auras of pink light which I felt as love, pure and innocent. The scene blackened for a moment before lighting up again.

The next scene showed Marcus facing Maya, who stood with her back against a stone wall, crying.

"I'm sorry, Maya. It didn't mean anything. You have to know I love you."

"Love? What do you know about love? Apparently you prefer blondes."

"I said I was sorry. Christ. What the hell do you expect me to do?"

"Go home, Marc, or go to Texas with your new 'friend'. I don't care."

"I followed you all the way to fucking Italy for God's sake."

"Right. So you could screw Italian whores. I didn't ask you to come, Marcus."

Marc opened his mouth as if to speak but then his face turned red and he clenched his jaw shut. "You didn't want me to come?" Maya looked down at the ground. Marcus looked incredulous. "And you wonder why I fooled around?"

"Oh, so that makes it all OK?"

"No, of course not, but..."

"Go home, Marcus."

"I thought you wanted me to be with you."

"I did, but not at the cost of my sanity. Or dignity. We don't have the same interests. I want to be a serious painter. I'm here to become that. You are just here to have fun and screw around. I think we have different values."

"What the fuck does that mean, different values?"

"I want to be in a monogamous relationship."

"C'mon, Maya, it didn't mean anything. I was drunk, and she put the pressure on."

"And you couldn't say no?" Maya asked.

"I made a mistake. It won't happen again, I promise. I love you, Maya." Marcus tried to pull her into his arms, but she pulled away. "You're what matters to me, honestly. I'm never going to see that girl again."

"I don't care what you do."

"I don't want to lose you."

"Too late." Maya began to walk away, but Marcus, grabbed her elbow.

"I want to stay here with you, Maya. I love you."

"We've grown apart, Marcus," Maya said, pulling her arm out of his grip. "You don't like my friends. You aren't interested in talking about art. You sit around my apartment all day. You go to clubs all night to pick up little Italian tartlets or Texan cowgirls, apparently. You're not a kid anymore, Marcus. Grow up."

"It only happened the one time with one girl!"

"I can't trust you anymore."

"Do you want me to get a job? I'll get a goddamned job if that's what'll make you happy." Marcus' jaw clenched.

"And that's exactly the problem. You do things you think I want, but they aren't what you want. Not deep down. You do them to make me feel like I mean something to you, and then you wind up resenting me for it, so you screw around on me. I want a man who doesn't *need* me to make him happy, one who treats me with respect, one who knows what the hell it is he wants from life."

"That's not fair, Maya."

"Go home, Marc." Maya turned away from him and walked down the darkened street, tears rolling down her face.

Marcus stood there looking stricken. "I'm going to get you back, Maya, if it's the last thing I do. I will always love you." Marcus whispered the words, so Maya didn't hear him.

I felt emotions of insecurity, helplessness, immaturity, and fear emitted from the spirit-souls of Marcus and Maya. I sensed that the third white orb hovering nearby was Calder.

It feels so painful. It's overwhelming, the Marcus-spirit communicated. *Is this what it feels like to be human?* A blanketed source of light seemed to be guiding our group through this process.

Yes. You will feel that human pain for just a moment in this realm, but as a human, it will feel much more acutely and it will last for a long duration. From that tiny moment of human pain, you must decide if you are willing to become this human. Becoming human is a choice. One that you need to make carefully. But you must understand that it is human pain that allows our spirit-souls to progress. It is the human suffering and our reaction to that suffering that become our lessons in the earth realm. Spiritual learning is something you will forget as a human. You may become victimized by your human suffering, or strengthened by it. That is your choice. Your spirit guides will be there to help you, of course. But you have to be willing to listen to their advice.

Why does any spirit-soul make the decision to become human with all that suffering? Marcus's spirit-soul asked.

It won't all be pain. Your human life will contain much joy as well, but again, you have to make the choice to notice it. Are you willing to continue?

I couldn't tell where this voice came from or whom it belonged to. I sensed it was some kind of spirit guide. The voice was soothing, possibly female, with a slight accent.

Yes. I can see how my separation from Maya might ultimately help me to understand more about myself. To become more capable of loving her.

Maya? Are you in agreement? the spirit guide asked.

I feel devastated and lost. And yet stronger for having spoken my truth. Yes. I can see how such an experience would strengthen my human-soul.

Shall we continue? The pane of glass lit up again.

This time the scene opened into a large wood-paneled room with slightly dilapidated leather wingback chairs atop blood red carpets setting off a large, jade colored tiled fireplace, with a warm fire crackling at its center. I recognized it as the lobby bar of the Sorrento Hotel in Seattle. A man sat in one of the wingbacks, visible only by gray flannel clad legs and expensive black leather shoes. The head-height wing of the chair obscured the rest of his body. Across the lobby, a hooded woman entered the hotel and smiled at the doorman who held the door for her. She stepped inside and pulled off her hood, auburn curls escaping their confinement. She looked around nervously and stepped up a few stairs into the lobby. She saw the outstretched legs, approached and whispered, "Marcus?" Marc poked his head around the wing of the chair and, seeing her, his face lit up. He stood up and faced her, smiling. His powdery blue shirt was unbuttoned and rolled at the sleeves. The stubbled creases down his cheeks gave him a rugged, masculine look on what would have otherwise been a boyish face. For a few moments neither said a word until Marcus pulled Maya into a hug she wasn't prepared for.

"It's good to see you, Maya."

She patted Marcus's back absentmindedly as she might a stranger's, before allowing herself to remember who she was with and relax. She sighed. Then she seemed to remember herself and stood back.

"It's good to see you too, Marcus. It's been a long time."

"It has. Do you want to sit here by the fire or take another seat closer to the bar?"

Maya looked toward the bar. A couple perched together on stools, leaning in close and laughing. A few more people sat at tables nearby. "This is kind of in the open," she said. "Maybe over by the bar would be more... private." Marcus gestured for Maya to proceed and followed her to a table in the corner of the room. A waiter appeared. Maya ordered a Shiraz and Marcus ordered a ginger ale for himself before he leaned back into his chair, assessing her.

"You look really good, Maya."

"I look like a drowned rat. This rain. It's impossible to keep my hair from having its way."

"You look ravishing," he said. Maya blushed.

"Thank you," she said looking down into her lap.

"I'm glad you found me on Facebook," Marcus said.

"I don't know what made me do it. I'm still married. It probably wasn't appropriate."

"Perfectly appropriate to me. I was surprised to discover that you lived in Seattle now. So close." Maya nodded her agreement and took a sip of wine. She was already halfway through her glass.

"Is Jay well?" Marcus asked.

"Yes. Busy." Maya paused. "What are you doing now? I've heard through my mom that you own a restaurant in Vancouver?"

"I'm a part owner. It's a happening place. Chaos on weekends. It's sort of Argentinian tapas. I came to check out some bars here in Seattle to get new ideas. My partners and I are thinking of opening a restaurant or bar in Seattle." Maya's eyes widened slightly. "Plus, there are some restaurant supply stores here that are cheaper than in Canada. I come down every few months or so to stock up."

"Sounds like you will be in Seattle more often then," Maya said into her nearly empty wine glass. Marcus waved the waiter over and ordered another round. When the drinks arrived, they sat in silence, each deep in thought.

"Yes. It's looking that way. So what made you contact me again, Maya? After all these years?" Marc asked. Maya looked away.

"I don't know," she whispered, still not meeting his eyes.

"Are you unhappy?" Marcus asked.

Maya looked panicked. "I shouldn't be here. I should go," Maya said, finally turning to look at him. Her eyes glistened with tears. Marcus leaned across the table and took her hand in his. Maya blinked, a look of surprise, fear and anticipation captured in her expression. Abruptly, she stood up and began to put on her coat. "I have to go."

Marc dug into his pocket for his wallet, pulled out a fifty as he stood up and left it on the table. They stood looking at each other. Maya made no move to leave, despite having her coat on and her purse slung over her shoulder. Marcus said nothing as he took her hand and led her to the elevator.

The image disappeared. I sensed Maya's reluctance, her desire, and our combined regret and shame. I felt Marc's disbelief, adoration, love. These emotions swept across my soul-spirit in an instant and then were gone. I felt weakened, understanding for the first time the ongoing resonance of my neglect of Maya in life, my inability to love her the way she needed to be loved. In recent years I had stopped really seeing Maya. I wished I had loved her more, but I was so focused on that one goal – being materialistically successful. I thought success would bring us happiness. Bring me happiness. I missed a lot of opportunities to wake up and see other people. Really see them. To have empathy for them.

Despite his behavior in Italy and his apparent disregard for Maya at that time, these were qualities that Marcus possessed, emotions I had never sensed from him when we were kids, possibly because I found them threatening. Marcus's passion had always unnerved me – his love of beauty, his expensive clothes, his ability to not care what others thought of him, his love for Maya. I never realized that perhaps Marcus had gone to Italy because he loved Maya so passionately as to follow her there. I never knew of his devastation when Maya asked him to leave, but sensed it now.

"Why does Maya marry me?"

Because I love you. Maya's thought was clear and immediate.

Calder, who until now had been hovering away from the viewing panel, not participating, came closer.

I chose you to be my father. I need to learn from you, and you specifically, to understand what drove you to work as hard as you did, to experience the effect of losing a father at a young age so that I can forge ahead and become who I am through your loss.

All I have to offer you as my son is my loss?

It is what you teach to your son after your death that becomes crucial to his life later on. Through you, he learns to take more risks. He learns to help others. Life is about being in tune, compassionate, being "other-focused" rather than self-focused. In death you are learning to have great compassion and will come to understand some of the things you did in human form. In death, you teach your son that we cannot be perfect, but we can be better — better to ourselves and to others. Life on earth moves faster and faster with advances in technology. So many people are denying their souls, not understanding the preciousness of their lives. Children are becoming aware of this and are doing amazing things to overcome the hatred in the world. They will become the teachers to the adults who have forgotten their soul-spirits. We are all pieces of the Divine or God or whatever humans want to call it, but until humans treat each other as such, feel that Divine in their very own DNA, they will not survive. Humans are made to not forget they are bound to their souls. They are reminded constantly. Calder will learn to be aware, will teach others that whatever the heart experiences, the soul experiences as well.

At that moment, I saw a human form, a woman dressed in a long, purple dress. I sensed that she was Maya's spirit guide. I wanted to know her name.

My name is Penelope. And yes, Jay, I am here as Maya's guide. I will be with her throughout her lifetime, throughout her many lifetimes. I think you have questions.

Yes. I guess I do. What was I supposed to learn from all that? I asked her.

Your inter-connections, of course.

And my father said something about my sense of pride holding me back from being able to help Maya.

Yes.

You're going to make me figure this out for myself, aren't you?

231

Penelope was silent.

OK, so my interconnections with Maya and Marcus and Calder are meant to help me help Maya?

Yes.

I wanted this riddle solved. *So how is Marcus going to help me become free from Maya?*

Penelope just smiled at me, watching as the obvious dawned upon me. I hadn't wanted to see it, but had known since my death that the reunion between Maya and Marcus was inevitable.

And you will be a part of that inevitability, Penelope's thought interrupted mine.

Me? Why?

Because it's part of your evolution.

I have to set my wife up with an old rival because it's part of my evolution? That's insane.

The problem is neither of them are ready, Marcus especially.

Why? I asked.

Jay, as you are learning the hard way, what matters in this plane is who you were on Earth. What you did – your goodness, mercy, compassion, love, joy. These states of being are all choices we make, choices about who we want to be in the world. Our earthly selves don't understand the consequences of our choices in the spiritual realm. When you cheer someone up, for instance, there is a deep spirit-level purpose that you often don't recognize when you're in human form. That is why the core of your spirit is so important, so powerful. Most humans don't realize how much of this spirit resides within them, but that's why it's so important for humans to share themselves with others, in whatever way possible. It is the community of humans that teaches their soul-spirits and allows them to truly evolve as spirits. We cannot attain that knowledge in any other way.

So you're saying Marcus and Maya have ignored their spirit selves?

In a way, yes. Maya's condition is a temporary one, brought on by grief. Marcus's is also brought on by loss – your father's death and the loss of Maya – that he used to hide with alcohol, but now hides through his sexuality and workaholism.

So he's depressed? That seems like a human condition that's not a person's fault. It's a chemical dysfunction, is it not?

Yes it is and certainly being sad and depressed makes your soul darker in vibration. But even in the midst of altered brain chemistry you have a choice. It's the striving to escape that darkness that counts. Life on Earth has nothing to do with providing for your family with money or possessions. It has to do with learning to provide for your soul-spirit. If you can't do that, you have nothing.

I can see now how bankrupt I was in my life.

Yes, Jay. That's why you're now having to learn these lessons in spirit form.

So I'm like a remedial spirit?

You could say that. You are just learning these lessons in spirit form rather than human form.

How would things be different if I had learned my lessons in human form?

Your entry back into spirit form would have been a much smoother transition. You wouldn't have had nearly as much difficulty remembering who you were before you were Jay. It's been much more difficult for you to let go of Jay and your human-ness.

What do you mean?

You are still very connected to Maya and Calder.

They need me.

They need the spirit Jay, not the human Jay.

But I want to provide for my family. Isn't that a form of love?

Of course, Jay. But your human emotions and jealousies are getting in the way. Even in life, you worked hard to provide for your family, but was it really for Maya and Calder or was it for you?

Penelope was starting to annoy me now. *I did it for my family!*

Yes, of course. But if you were to be perfectly honest with yourself, don't you think that you were also doing it for the prestige, the nice car, the respect that owning your own company afforded you?

Yeah. Maybe a little. This was a very difficult admission for me. I felt deflated.

You see, Jay, that's what so many of us spirits are trying to help people on Earth to understand. We guide the production of the books and movies and through all human creativities that help people to see the simple truth that they must care for their soul-spirits by sharing their gifts with the world, whatever those gifts may be. Most of the tangible gifts we as humans offer the world are products of our love, our passion. Through these gifts, we offer other soul-spirits a piece of our love and passion which may manifest in love and passion within them.

Sort of like passing the hot potato of love.

Very poetic. But yes, something like that.

I was pleased that Penelope had a sense of humor. *So what are we as spirits supposed to do to help humans?*

The spirit guides are the ones that set up those little connections that humans often call "good timing" or "coincidences" to ensure all the right people and ideas come together at the right time. Every voice we have out there affects different people in different ways. The exact words in those books, stories, and movies may vary, but the message is fundamentally the same: it's a passage of love from one human to another. You, Jay, have been given a voice that will help people on the earth plane. You have already spoken a little through Maya's paintings.

With the words "Maya's paintings", I transported to her. Wrapped in heavy sweaters, she stood beside her easel in the tiny sunroom that she had claimed as her "studio" for its light. Her tea was cold in its mug on the windowsill, her paintbrush hovering over the canvas. Oddly, I could see the finished painting, though the canvas was only partially painted. Maya rolled her brush in a blob of turquoise paint and applied it in just the spot I'd been looking at. After a while, her painting began to resemble the finished one I could see in my mind. This surprised me and yet the phenomenon felt completely natural, as though my seeing finished paintings before they were painted and then influencing my wife's hand as she painted them was completely normal and natural. Flecks of white and blue transformed into what looked like a speck of dust under a microscope, a black background, impossibly infused with light. Blue, red, and pink infiltrated the white blossoms, giving them both complexity and simplicity at once. Maya painted with gusto, forgetting time.

I felt most connected to her when she painted. There was little division between our thoughts and our frequencies. Her passion became embedded into the paint of each daub, its energy encapsulated within the paint's molecules. When the paintings hung on the walls at the show, I could see this energy flowing off the walls as vapors of color, and these vapors merged with the energy of the viewers in astonishing ways. At the show in Vancouver, I stood near that same painting as a woman looked at it, and the colors of the painting began to bleed into her aura, creating ripples like a stone dropped into water. The electrical energy that Maya had unwittingly infused into the painting with each brush stroke worked its magic. I saw the woman become deeply moved as she viewed Maya's painting. Something in her seemed to release and she appeared close to tears as she surrendered to her emotions in awe. I heard her thoughts: *The truth is so simple.*

Wow. I can see how powerful a painting can be. That woman in the art gallery fed her soul with Maya's painting, didn't she?

Exactly. And you helped make that happen.

I didn't really understand during my life as Jay, but I can see now how stunted I was as a human being. How much of my life had I missed? I don't think I ever experienced Maya's energy exchange by looking at her paintings. I wish now that I had noticed those paintings and their effect on me.

The important thing is that you have learned that now. Jay, you have been given special permission to connect to the earth plane in order to help Maya, Marcus, and Calder. But remember that everything you do, whether it's here or on Earth, has a consequence. Be aware of your thoughts and actions.

OK, but aren't those repercussions pre-determined by us here, during the plotting process?

The plotting process is just that, Jay. It is a plan. A look into some of the possible consequences of our actions. But the plots can change in unexpected ways, through tiny derivations — other plots that intersect with our own — so that even a serendipitous event instigated from the spiritual realm to help a human toward a greater understanding of himself might not be predicted and thus, this is merely a process, not an end result. This process provides clues as to how a possible scenario might unfold. You can help in this process of events, if you are willing. Like I keep saying, Jay, everything is a choice here.

※ ※ ※

I sat beside Maya as she lay in her bed, crying. I wanted to wipe the tears from her cheeks or feel them dripping onto my chest as she laid her head against my shoulder. Instead, I could only watch and combine my thought energy with hers. I sensed her anguish over her broken relationship with Dom and I wished I could take back my selfish thought of Sean Connery that day with the psychic, my attempt to keep Maya from Marcus. I thought I was doing her a favor. I didn't want her to be hurt again by Marcus, and instead I let her be devastated by Dominic. I wanted to help Maya, but just seemed to make things worse for her.

I can help, Jay.

How?

Liz has been called. She can help you to help Maya. Penelope smiled and disappeared as quickly as she had arrived.

Ask Maya to call Liz. Penelope's thought was clear, even if she was no longer present.

I looked at the tear-stained face of my wife and thought simply, *call Liz.*

Maya's eyes fluttered closed and she slept. The next day she called Liz and made an appointment.

A few weeks later, Maya sat tucked into the couch, Liz

across from her in a chair.

"I feel so stupid," Maya said. "I really thought Dom was the one, because he seemed to match your description of the person I would meet at the art opening. I actually thought Jay sent him to me."

"In a way he did," Liz said.

"Why would he send me someone who I wasn't meant to be with?"

"Every person that comes into our lives comes for a reason. Think about what you learned from your relationship with Dom."

Maya leaned back into the couch and seemed to be thinking. "He saw me as beautiful. After Jay died, I didn't see myself that way at all. I thought men would see me as a dried up old prune of a mom."

Liz laughed. "Hardly, Maya."

"I thought I would be scared to love again, fearful of another loss. But I fell in love with Dom. He taught me that I had the capacity to love another person and that I was worthy of being loved."

Liz nodded. "And armed with that knowledge, you are now better prepared for any new relationship that comes along."

"I hadn't thought of it that way, but I guess you're right. Are you going to tell me what's next?"

Marcus's apartment was certainly a testament to a bachelor lifestyle. At the front door he took a leash from a hook and turned toward his big, black dog, curled up sleeping in a big chair.

Suddenly I felt weird being there, watching him.

Why am I here? I asked. My dad shimmered within the frozen scene of Marcus's apartment.

To help Marcus.

Why help him? I still can't get over the fact that he slept with my wife.

It isn't obvious? Look around, J.J.

Scanning the apartment again, I noticed all the art on the walls. Every frame held one of Maya's paintings. Paintings that she had sold over the years, often not knowing who had bought them. He had no doubt chosen this apartment for its gallery-like wall space. The room resonated with her energy.

He's a creepy stalker of my wife?

That's your human speaking. What does your heart tell you?

"C'mon, Jericho," Marcus said, interrupting us. "Let's get you out for a pee." Jericho perked up his ears and looked at Marcus and then settled his head back down on the armrest, clearly not interested in a walk.

"Jericho, let's go!" Jericho took his time yawning, his big tongue curling up into his mouth before sticking his forepaws out as he slid reluctantly off the chair.

"Am I intruding on your sleep, you poor, lazy dog?" Jericho just yawned again and came sniffing around me. He sat and looked at me, cocking his head slightly as if trying to give my image meaning. "Why are you staring at the wall, ya crazy mutt? Let's go." Marcus attached Jericho's leash to his collar and together they walked out the door. They strode through Stanley Park, Jericho sniffing every tree and lifting a leg before continuing.

You will be together again. I couldn't tell if the thought was mine or someone else's.

Marcus stopped abruptly. He closed his eyes, appearing to be deep in thought. *I need her.* I heard Marc's thought clearly.

And she needs you. These words did not come easily to me. I wanted to be the one she needed.

But she doesn't want to see me.

She wasn't ready.

And what makes you think she's ready now?

I kept my thoughts silent in reply.

I think I'm going insane. Marcus shook his head as if to rid himself of his own thoughts. Jericho stopped walking and sat waiting for Marcus, his head cocked, looking at me again. "Who are you looking at? Jericho, I think we're both going insane." With that, Jericho jumped up and bounded to the end of his leash, pulling it from Marcus's hand, causing him to take off running after the dog, who, ready for a chase, kept running through trees with Marcus calling after him. I didn't follow. I knew Marcus had heard me. I didn't know how long it would take, but the seed was planted. Still, he would need more prompting to nudge him toward Maya. But this whole idea of getting Maya and Marcus together still seemed far-fetched. A little too convenient.

Dad? You still there?

Always.

Is Marcus really the right person for Maya?

All you know of Marcus is what Maya told you about a time in her life when her heart was broken by him.

Does that mean she didn't really love me? Did she always love Marcus? I hated sounding like a whining three-year-old.

Maya, like any human, has the capability to love many people. Of course she loved you. Why do you even question that?

Because I'm starting to see the inevitability of her relationship with Marcus.

Yes. You have the perspective now to see that Marcus was a pre-determined presence in her life. But then, so were you.

My father faded and I returned to the living room with Maya and Liz.

"He's showing me a dog. A man walking a black dog," Liz said. Maya looked at her blankly. Of course she would have no way of knowing that Marcus had a dog.

He's coming back to you, Maya. He will find you again.

"Someone is looking for you," Liz said. "I'm not sure what that means, but it's what I'm getting. There is someone coming, Maya."

"You mean a new relationship? God, I don't think I can do that again. Dom turned me off relationships for a while."

"The universe knows when the timing is right. You might

not be ready now, but when the timing is right, it will happen. And you will be better prepared for a new relationship because of what you learned from Dom."

"I hope you're right, Liz."

I hope so too, I thought.

At that moment I began to feel an odd sensation, one of being lifted and floating at once. I moved away from Maya and Liz. My aura changed from pale yellow to a pale purple. My father seemed to recede from me. I felt no panic at this, but instead a sense of euphoria swept over me.

What's going on? Dad? Are you doing that? At my beckoning, my father appeared.

It's not my doing. It's yours. I believe you are being absorbed into your new level. Light is absorbing your energy and as you move up, you will begin to understand more. You are becoming more of an integrated part of the collective of soul-spirits.

Why now?

You've earned it, of course. Through the renewed condition of your heart, now the universal energy has deemed you ready for more learning. Your human-ness has dropped away to such an extent that your soul-spirit is able to rise higher. You are becoming purer in soul-spirit, Jay. Embrace it.

The light around me shone with a new intensity. Colored lights surrounded me and I realized these were other soul-spirits who existed in this new realm, which I hadn't been able to see until now. I felt serene and tranquil, yet elated as well. I wished I could truly laugh, or shout or clap. I looked up and saw my dad hovering just above me, smiling. His aura pulsed a brilliant shade of emerald green I hadn't seen before because I hadn't yet achieved this level of clarity. I realized I no longer saw him in his Rolling Stone's t-shirt and I hadn't noticed the change.

That green aura matches your eyes, I thought. My dad just continued to float upwards into a realm beyond my reach. I heard his words: *Don't forget about Marcus. He needs you now.*

Chapter Twenty

The Reunion

The yellow walls, French doors out to a garden, and tightly woven grey carpet were unfamiliar. Drum equipment, an electric guitar, a small electric piano and an amp and their respective power cords snaked around the room. Calder sat behind the drums and his friend Owen stood in the center of the cords, holding a guitar and picking out the notes of a song from memory. Calder tapped his sticks against the snare lightly, trying to keep the pace and maintain a rhythm. It took a few minutes to recognize the tune as "Hey Jude". Each time Owen plucked a wrong note, he started again from the beginning. The tiny amplifier beside him reverberated.

"Hey, can I jam with you guys?" The man startled the boys, who stopped playing abruptly. He came farther down the steps and stepped over the wires to give Owen a high five. I was shocked to see it was Marcus.

What's going on?

My dad appeared. *Think of it as a little nudge, J.J.*

This is a pretty big nudge, Dad. This was not my doing. I assume it was yours? My dad seemed to shrug and vanished.

Typical.
I heard that.
"Sorry, O. Didn't mean to interrupt," Marcus said to Owen.
"It's OK."
"You want introduce me to your friend?"
"Oh yeah, sorry. This is Calder. Calder, this is Marc."
"Hey." Calder raised a drum stick.
"You guys sound pretty good. Would it be OK if I played this keyboard?"
"Sure, but it might be too low for you," Owen said.
"That's OK. I'll just get down like this." Marcus kneeled in front of the tiny electric keyboard and pushed the switch on, causing it to hum to life. "You guys start and I'll just jump in."

Owen strummed the first bar of "Hey Jude" again. Marcus quickly caught on and followed Owen's lead, playing the song perfectly, which helped Owen stumble his way through the whole song without stopping, despite his mistakes. Calder had a look of awe on his face as he pounded out an improvised rhythm.

"Wow! That was so cool!" Owen turned and said to Calder, "Dude, was that not awesome?" Calder nodded his head.

"Mind if I show you something?" Marcus asked Owen. Owen shrugged as Marc eased his way up to a standing position. He held his hand out for Owen's guitar. He held it against his thighs and positioned his hand on the frets. "If you hold your fingers like this, you'll be able to change chords faster. Here, you try." Owen took the guitar and tried to put his fingers in the positions Marcus had shown him. Marcus reached over Owen's shoulder and helped him place his fingers correctly. "It takes practice, but it really helps when you get it. Try the chord now." Owen strummed and then changed chords by sliding his finger smoothly down the strut. The next chord came perfectly as did the one after it.

"Nice!" Marcus said when Owen stumbled and stopped playing.

"Cool! That really works! Thanks!"

"No problem, buddy." Marcus then turned to Calder. "And you know, if you let your wrists go limp as you play, rather than playing with your whole arms, you won't get as tired. Also you'll be able to play faster. Can I show you?" Marcus took the sticks from Calder and wedged himself into the tiny slot against the wall as Calder vacated his seat. Marc played a long, upbeat solo that left the kids standing agape. He stopped playing and smiled. "Now you try." He got up and handed the sticks back to Calder.

Calder sat down, held the sticks over the drums, and began playing, this time mimicking the floppy wrist movement that Marcus had just demonstrated. His drumming seemed smoother. He beamed a smile at Marcus. "I wish you were my drum teacher! I've been going to him since I was seven and a half and he never taught me that!"

"Really? That's like the first rule of drumming. You might need to find a new teacher."

Seeing Calder and Marcus together seemed like the most natural thing in the world. Before now, I had never imagined them together. Why would I? And now I realized they shared a love of drumming, which of course was no coincidence.

See, son, there's a reason for everything.

Maya, at her easel, leaned in close to the canvas as she dabbed tiny blobs of rose colored paint to create the pinky slabs of rock that I recognized as a landscape view from her Georgian Bay cabin. The phone rang, and she clamped the paintbrush between her teeth so she could pick up the receiver and still hold the palette.

"Mom! Owen's mom and dad want to know if you want to come over for dinner. There's this really cool guy who's teaching me drums. Can you come now?"

"OK, well, give me a few minutes to get out of my

painting clothes…"

Maya hung up and finished adding the last of the paint to her canvas. She stood back and cocked her head to look. She shrugged and stuck her brush into a jar of turpentine, a jar already bristling with other brushes. She wiped the palette clean with a paper towel and screwed some of the lids onto the tubes of paint. She pulled her hair out of its elastic as she walked to the bedroom and opened the louvered closet door, stepped out of the old jeans smeared with paint, and put on a cleaner pair. She slipped a loose sweater over her head. In the bathroom mirror, she brushed on some blush and dragged her fingernails down a strand of hair, trying to rid it of a glob of cadmium red.

"Ugh," she said to herself, leaning into the mirror. "That's the best I can do on short notice."

From the fridge she grabbed a bottle of Prosecco, pulled on a jacket to ward off the late September chill, and walked ten minutes through the ravine to Owen's house. Patty, Owen's mom, answered the door.

"I'm so glad you could make it." Patty ushered Maya in. "We have a friend visiting from Vancouver and thought it would be lovely for you to meet him, you know, since you're both Canadian," Patty said as she winked. "Wine?" In the kitchen, Patty took down a glass from the cupboard. Maya placed her bottle on the counter.

Voices and the squeal of a guitar accompanied by a fast drumbeat floated up from the basement stairs.

"The boys are all down there 'jamming'," Patty said. "It's been so cute. Our friend Marc's been coaching them. He played in a band at one time, I gather." Patty handed Maya a glass of wine.

"The boys must be loving that."

Men's voices were heard on the basement stairs. Ian, Patty's husband, emerged and walked over to give Maya a hug. Maya wasn't paying attention to their guest. Ian let go of Maya and turned to Marcus.

"Maya, this is Marc, an old friend who's visiting from Vancouver." Maya looked up and froze. Marcus looked just as shocked.

"Hello, Marcus," Maya said, regaining her composure. Marcus seemed to be catching his breath.

"Marcus? Do you guys know each other?" Patty asked.

"Yeah, from a long time ago. And yes, Marcus is my full name, but mostly I just go by Marc. With a 'C'."

"Well, it certainly is a small world!" Patty said.

"Hello, Maya." He approached her and held out his hand. "Good to see you again." Maya seemed flustered and pulled her hand back. "Maya and I knew each other as kids," Marc said calmly, still looking at her. "Our families both had cottages on the same lake in northern Ontario."

"Yes. And Marcus attended Jay's funeral," Maya said abruptly.

"And your art opening in Vancouver," Marcus said.

"Yes," Maya said, eyeing him.

"This is just amazing!" Patty said.

"Hon," Ian said, "I think we're ready to put the burgers on." Ian held a platter of burger patties and was headed toward the door.

"Shall I join you?" Marcus asked.

Calder came bounding up the stairs. "Marc, will you come listen to us? I think we figured out what you were talking about. You gotta come!" Calder grabbed Marc's sleeve, pulling him toward the basement.

"I'll be out here if you need me," Ian said, disappearing outside.

"Calder, give Marcus a moment. He's with the adults. Maybe he doesn't want to play right now," Maya said. Calder looked at her quizzically.

"Who's Marcus?"

"It's my full name," Marc said. He looked at Calder and then at Maya.

"Calder is your son?" Marcus asked.

Maya shrugged helplessly. "Sorry. I hope he's not being annoying."

"I'm not being annoying!" Calder complained. "Marc, pleeeease?"

"I'll be there in a sec, buddy, K?"

Calder nodded and disappeared back down the basement stairs. The guitar squeals and drumbeats started up again.

"Sorry," Maya said.

"No, I just didn't connect... He looks different than he did at the funeral," Marcus said.

"Yeah, he's cut all that long hair off."

"Ah, right. I should have known. He looks a lot like you. He's a really great kid, Maya."

"Yeah, he is," Maya replied, looking at Marc directly for the first time.

"I'll just see what they need. Be back in a sec." He glanced at Maya before going down to the basement.

The series of events that led to this moment were carefully plotted, though not entirely by me. Calder's interest in drumming came from me, but my father played an obvious part in this meeting of worlds. I couldn't control the actions of either Maya or Marcus. I was still a reluctant player in this game of fate, not fully convinced that Marcus was the right person for Maya. He still had an arrogance about him that I didn't like.

"So, Patty, how do you guys know Marcus?" Maya asked as she pulled out one of the bar stools and sat at the kitchen island so she could watch Patty slice tomatoes and onions.

"It's weird, really. Ian met Marcus at Elliot Bay Bookstore of all places. They got to talking about some book and just sort of hit it off. We began getting together for dinner whenever he was in town and now, rather than stay at some nondescript hotel, he stays with us for a few nights when he's here. We all just adore him. Amazing that he's an old friend of yours. Do all you Canadians know each other?"

Maya laughed. "No. We don't. But it is amazing. He's the

last person I imagined bumping into so close to home."

"He's still single…" Patty looked at Maya with a glint in her eye. I could tell she enjoyed this matchmaking role.

Marcus re-appeared from the basement. "Who's still single?" he asked.

Patty blushed. "Maya is."

"Patty!" Maya said, blushing.

"What? I know neither of you would ever admit it, so someone has to."

Maya twisted her wedding ring, now on her right ring finger. Marcus took the stool next to Maya. Neither spoke as they watched Patty arrange buns on a plate. Marc fiddled with the tab on his Coke can.

"Did you know Jay as well, Marc?" Patty asked, breaking the silence.

"A long time ago. I hadn't seen him since we were teenagers," Marc replied. "But I know he was a good guy." Maya looked surprised. I was surprised as well. I always thought Marcus had nothing but contempt for me, being the one Maya chose to marry.

"Such a tragic accident," Patty said. "Just so meaningless."

"It sucked," Maya said.

"That's one way of putting it," Marcus said, smiling slightly.

"I have no better words," Maya said. Another awkward pause followed.

"Are you two OK here for a moment?" Patty said. "I just have to go grab some paper towels from the garage. Be right back."

Maya turned to Marcus. "What are you doing here?"

"I could ask you the same thing."

"Did you just become friends with these people so you could get to me?" Maya asked, sounding accusatory.

"What? That's ridiculous and you know it. I had no idea you knew Patty and Ian. How would I?"

"Because they live in my neighborhood and have a boy the same age as Calder?"

"I had no idea what neighborhood you lived in, Maya. I don't even know how old Calder is at this point."

"Well, it just seems awfully coincidental!" Maya said, her voice shrill.

"I'm back!" Patty pulled the wrapping off a roll and fiddled it onto the holder attached to the wall. Marc and Maya remained silent.

"Hope I'm not interrupting anything. Is everything OK?" she asked.

"Yes, of course." Maya's face flushed.

"Maya and I were just getting caught up," Marcus said and smiled at Maya. Maya looked uncomfortable.

Ian came through the door with the empty burger platter and placed it in the sink. "Burgers are on. It'll be just a few minutes," he said. Marcus and Maya sipped their drinks as they watched Patty and Ian do the dinner prep dance around the kitchen.

"Is there anything I can do?" Marcus asked.

"I think we have it under control, Marc. Thanks," Ian said.

"We just need to set the table," Patty said, juggling a bowl of green salad and another of pasta salad toward the open deck door.

"Here, let me," Maya said, grabbing the bowl of pasta salad. Marc followed with the platter of buns and a tray of condiments. Ian called the boys from the top of the basement steps and grabbed the wine and another couple bottles of beer. The usual dinner frenzy of items being passed around the table, drinks being poured, all punctuated with laughter made me miss dinner with friends, the smell of meat on the barbecue, the taste of a cold beer.

"So, Maya," Patty said, "tell me about the cottage where you and Marcus know each other from."

Maya took a deep breath. "Well, it's on Georgian Bay, a

beautiful part of northern Ontario, where the pine trees have all been blown in the direction of the prevailing wind and there is a lot of rock—"

"Canadian Shield," Marcus corrected.

"Right," Maya said, annoyed. "Canadian Shield rock, so there are lots of little islands everywhere. I used to love going there. My family spent entire summers there."

"Our families were friends," Marcus interjected. "Our cottages were just down the road from one another."

"Oh, so you've known each other for a long time then," Ian said.

"My family bought our cottage when I was about ten, and Maya was, what?" Marcus turned to Maya. "Seven?"

"Eight."

"Eight. Right. I didn't really meet you until a few years later, but I used to spy on you," Marcus said.

"You did? You never told me that."

"I didn't? Yeah, well I used to swim under my dock and stay there and watch you and your family swimming."

"Did you have a little puppy crush on Maya?" Patty asked. Both Maya and Marcus blushed.

"I guess I did," Marc said, grinning before biting down on a burger.

"As we got older, the people on the road got together on the beach and had these huge bonfires…" Maya said, looking wistful.

"Corn roasts," Marcus interjected. "We would wrap cobs of corn in tin foil and stick them into the coals. They were to die for!"

"Can we try that with the corn next time, Mom?" Owen asked.

"Sounds like fun," Patty answered.

Maya seemed lost in reverie. I remembered the photograph of her being held by Marcus around one of those bonfires and knew her thoughts were there too.

"Do you remember counting the shooting stars that

night?" Maya asked, looking at Marcus.

Marc closed his eyes. "Yeah. An amazing night. I don't think I've ever seen so many stars. We counted, what? Fifteen shooting stars?"

"Something like that. A lot." Everyone else around the table was quiet as they listened to Maya and Marcus.

"We had some good times, didn't we, Maya?"

"We did. We really did," Maya agreed. She looked up at Marc and then around the table at everyone watching her. "Oh! Well, it looks like maybe it's time to clear the table," Maya said as she stood up and gathered plates. Patty rushed to help. Marcus and Ian and the boys stayed at the table talking about whether there were people living on Mars. In the kitchen, Maya stood beside Patty as she rinsed the dishes and put them into the dishwasher.

"You and Marcus have quite the history together," Patty said, taking another dish from Maya.

"Yeah, we've known each other a long time. Actually, Marcus was my first love if you want to know the truth."

"Really?" Patty stopped to look at Maya. "Your first love?"

"Yeah."

"No wonder you guys were getting all googlie-eyed with each other out there."

"What are you talking about? I wasn't googlie-eyed!" Maya said.

"Oh yes you were. And so was he."

"No! I'm not at all interested in Marcus!" Maya's voice came across sharply and she looked to be close to tears.

"Oh! I'm sorry, Maya, I didn't mean to imply anything. It's just..." Patty stammered.

"I am not interested in Marcus Pellegrino! Really."

"OK," Patty said. "I'm sorry. I didn't mean to upset you, Maya." Patty put her hand on Maya's back.

"Sorry," Maya said, regaining her composure. "It's just—"

"No need to explain. Will you take these out?" Patty

handed Maya the dessert plates and forks and then followed her out with the pie. Marcus's eyes were on Maya as she leaned over the table to set a plate and a fork down at each place setting. She sat and took another sip of wine, avoiding eye contact with Marcus. Patty sliced the blackberry pie.

"Homemade from blackberries picked from our own garden. I froze them last summer."

"This looks amazing, Patty, as usual," Marcus said as he put a forkful into his mouth and closed his eyes, savoring and letting out an audible moan. "Delicious."

"Thank you, Marc. I'm so glad you like it. You're always so easy to please."

"When are you leaving?" Maya asked abruptly.

"Leaving?" Marcus seemed lost for words. "The day after tomorrow. Why?"

"No reason," Maya said and dug into her pie. Marcus turned away from Maya and asked Ian about a book they had obviously discussed before. Maya and Patty talked about the upcoming school auction. The boys jumped up from their half-eaten plates of pie and disappeared back to the basement. When everyone had finished, Marcus stood up and began collecting dishes. Patty started to help him.

"Maya and I have this, Patty. You sit. Have a moment with your husband."

"That's very sweet, Marcus. Thanks."

Maya stood and glared at Marc, obviously not pleased to be in his company. In the kitchen, Maya took Patty's place by the sink and rinsed plates before putting them into the dishwasher.

"What's going on here, Maya?"

"What do you mean?"

"You're acting awfully strange."

"Am I? I guess I'm just not very comfortable having the man I committed adultery with being friends with the family of one of my son's friends. You might say it feels a little awkward for me."

"You're not acting like it's awkward."

"What do you mean?" Maya asked.

Marcus took a step toward her. "All that talk about the bonfire. You were reminiscing. We were in love then, Maya, remember?" Marcus touched the top of Maya's hand with his finger.

Maya pulled her hand away like she'd been stung. "That was a long time ago, Marcus."

"I can understand you're feeling guilty, but you're not married anymore," Marc said quietly.

"What happened between us is done. It was a mistake on my part, and it didn't mean anything. I love Jay."

"Of course you loved Jay. But I don't believe I meant nothing to you. We had something real. Just like there was something real all those years ago. Something I think about every day and I have a feeling you do as well."

Maya hiccupped a quick intake of breath. "Don't do this, Marcus."

"Do what?"

Patty walked into the kitchen with a pie plate, a mangled slice pooled in the center, two empty glasses of milk, and an empty bottle of wine.

"Uh, we can't keep talking about the past!" Maya grabbed another one of the glasses that Patty had set on the counter and jammed it into the dishwasher. Patty gave Marc a wide eyed expression that said, "Did I interrupt something?" and Marcus shook his head.

"Patty, this has been a lovely evening, thank you so much, but we really have to get going. It's a school night."

"I'm so glad you and Marc were able to meet and reconnect!"

"Me too," Marcus said. "It's been great for Maya and I to revisit our past."

Maya said nothing and went to the top of the basement stairs to call Calder, who came up, reluctantly.

"Aww, why do we have to go?"

"It's a school night. You have an early morning," she said.

"Just another half an hour?"

"No. We're going *now*, Calder. Did you have a coat?"

Hugs were exchanged between Maya and Patty and Ian, and Marcus gave Calder a high five.

"Hope to see you again soon, K, buddy?"

"Yeah. Sure," Calder said. Maya stood waiting for the exchange to be over and then ushered Calder out the door. When she turned back to say her final farewell, Marcus stepped forward and pulled her into an embrace. He held her tight. At first she stiffened, but then she seemed to just let go.

"It's good to see you again, Marcus," she said, her voice wavering. "Have a good trip back to Van." She turned quickly and put her hand into the air for a wave without turning around. Outside on the sidewalk, Maya followed Calder, who raced down the street toward the path into the ravine. She blotted her eye with a fingertip as she walked. Calder waited for Maya and by the time she caught up to him, she had calmed herself.

"I wish we had a friend like Marcus who would come to visit us," he said, now dragging a stick along the damp path, lit by moonlight.

"Why?"

"Dunno. He's cool I guess."

Maya looked up at the full moon and closed her eyes as she walked.

The next day, Maya stood in front of her half finished painting, her brush hovering. The pristine Georgian Bay scene with mounds of coral rock that looked like the backs of submerged tortoises in inky water, and a sky wispy with clouds. She dabbed her brush in paint and began to stroke a thin layer of white across the sky. I thought of that view, standing on her deck, and remembered the scene in the bunkhouse playing air guitar. With that thought, Pat Benatar singing "You're a Heartbreaker" came on the radio.

"Seriously?" Maya said aloud.
Jay, is that you?
Yeah, sorry. I didn't mean to do that.
Christ. Are you trying to tell me something?
Just remembering.
Is this about Marcus?
I didn't know the answer to that question. Was it?
Is this some sort of cruel sign I am meant to be with Marcus?
I don't know, Maya. But it might be.

She scooped white paint onto her brush and smeared it across the sky, obliterating the entire scene with big white globs. She stabbed at the canvas with her brush, piercing it with what looked like bullet holes. She stabbed over and over, tears taking over, and then she grabbed the painting off the easel, which crashed to the floor, spilling the jars of brushes, glass smashing. She screamed and tried to break the painting over her knee, the canvas giving way but the wooden frame remaining intact. She stomped on the frame to break it apart, crying, "Stupid, stupid, stupid! I can't do this!"

Maya sat amid the wreckage in a corner of the sunroom, hugging her knees to her chest until the crying stopped and her face, streaked with tears and white paint, slackened.

Chapter Twenty-One

PONDER

Maya dabbed a tissue on the corners of her eyes as she sat in a utilitarian leather chair of vaguely Scandinavian design.

"I can't stop crying." She looked out at a seventeen-story view of Seattle with Puget Sound visible in stripes between sleek grey buildings. I kept to the corner of the room, wishing I wasn't culpable in her distress, or that I could do something to excise it. The story of her encounter with Marcus spilled out through tears and hiccups as her therapist, Dr. Haslett, sat across from her, silent but attentive, his suit looking both tailored and relaxed. She leaned over and pulled another tissue from the box on the table beside her, the spent ones littered like a collection of snowballs across her lap.

I was to blame for Maya's breakdown. Pat Benatar could send anyone over the edge. I needed some way of conveying my apology and my forgiveness to Maya. I only had my presence and my thoughts.

"You sound angry that you encountered Marcus this way," Dr. Haslett said.

"I was unprepared. I wasn't expecting to see him."

"You weren't happy to see an old childhood friend?"

"Well, I might not have mentioned that he was also my first love."

"You did mention that. But it still seems like you would be happier to see him than you were. Why the anger?"

You may as well tell him, Lenie.

"We had a bad break-up." Maya looked at the clock.

"A long time ago," Dr. Haslett reminded her.

"Yes." She looked up at the doctor as she said this, perhaps challenging him to probe further, but willing him not to.

"That still doesn't explain your strong emotions. Is there more about Marcus you haven't told me?"

It's OK, Maya. Speak the truth.

Tears dropped into her lap and she made no effort to wipe them away. She didn't speak for a long time. The doctor waited patiently.

"We had an affair," she whispered, finally. "While Jay was alive." She blew her nose loudly and wiped away the tears, crumpling another tissue and adding it to her collection.

Good, Lenie.

"I see. That does make for a complicated grief."

"Complicated is a good word for it, yes."

The doctor smiled at her remark. "It would make sense for you to feel guilty about your affair. When Jay died, you had no way to set things straight. You were robbed of the chance to discuss the affair with Jay and get through it together, whatever might come."

Would you have left me? Her thought pleaded.

I would have stuck by you.

"Yes, that's the problem. I don't know what to do with it. How do I get over the guilt? And the shame?"

"You have already begun by speaking the truth to me. I expect there will be some forgiveness that needs to happen as well."

"Forgiveness? I need to forgive Marcus?"

"Yes, but more importantly, you need to forgive yourself."

Yes!

"Oh." Maya twisted her tissue into a snake-like shape. "I don't know if I can do that."

"It's not an easy thing to do. Forgiving others is the easy work. But Maya, Jay was also to blame for your affair, through his neglect of you, or at least his perceived indifference."

I wish I could go back and change that, Lenie. I regret how I treated you.

"He was busy. It wasn't his fault."

Busy, yes, but that was no excuse. I hardly participated in our marriage. I see that now.

"Not entirely, but his actions or lack of action played a part." Dr. Haslett set aside his notebook and folded his hands into his lap. "How do you feel about Marcus now?"

"I don't know. Why?" Maya sounded tentative.

"Are you in love with Marcus?"

A part of me didn't want to hear the answer to this question.

"In love with him? I was once."

"I mean now."

"I don't know."

I think you do, Maya.

Am I still in love with Marcus?

"When you were having the affair with Marcus, how did you feel?"

Maya closed her eyes and took a deep breath, as if trying to place herself back at that hotel. "Alive," she said at last, opening her eyes. Dr. Haslett nodded.

I can't compete with 'alive', Lenie.

"Something to ponder," he said.

The four women sat on the floor on Kilim cushions in

Chelsea's sunny living room, sipping jasmine tea. It was her turn to host the monthly support group.

"This is a pretty room, Chels," Kristie said, "but it's such a gorgeous day, do you think we could sit in your garden? I just love it out there."

"And can I make a suggestion as well?" Molly asked. She didn't wait for an answer but waved her hands over the tea and cookies arranged on the table. "Tea is nice and all, but can we have wine?" They all laughed.

"I was trying to be good," Chelsea said in mock pout. "I'll get the glasses. Sheesh, you widow types!"

The women moved out back to sit around an antique iron table under a trellis dripping with pale purple wisteria. Us husbands lingered nearby, congregated by a low stone wall bordering an extensive garden.

"Who wants to start?" Kristie asked.

"Chelsea, we are living vicariously through you. How's your romance with Ken going?" Molly said.

Chelsea smiled. "It's going great! I really like him. He gets along great with Tatiana. He's really good with her. It's cute to watch."

"How long's it been now?" Maya asked.

"About a year and a half, I think," Chelsea said as she flipped through photos on her phone, finally handing it over to Molly.

"Look at this. That's Ken with Tatiana at the zoo." The women took turns passing the phone around, smiling at the photo.

"Do you think you'll get married?" Kristie asked as Chelsea took her phone back and tucked it into her purse.

"Married? I don't know. I don't feel a huge need to get married. I have a kid, enough money, a house, a job. I like how things are with Ken now. I don't really want to rock the boat, you know? Plus, I don't think he's in any great rush. He had a pretty messy divorce," Chelsea added. "There are also financial implications if we get married."

"Your survivor's benefits would stop, I think," said Kristie.

"I don't even know," Chelsea said. "I would never let that be part of my decision to get married though."

"I think I feel the same way about marriage, Chels," Maya said. "Why bother?"

"And what about your old flame, Missy?" Molly said to Maya.

"Yeah! We want an update! Have you seen Marcus since you met him at your neighbor's house?" Kristie asked. Maya had told the story of her encounter with Marcus in the previous month's meeting and the women had quizzed her. Maya's reserve in talking about him had obviously raised their suspicion that something was going on.

"Hang on!" Chelsea said. "If this is going to get juicy, we need more wine! Let me grab another bottle." When Chelsea returned and poured the wine, Molly prompted Maya to continue.

"OK, so Marcus. I think we were waiting to hear if you've seen him again."

"Right." Maya laughed. "No. And I don't expect to. I was so mean to him that night. It's been two months since then and we've had no communication. I think if he was really interested he would've called." Kristie gave Maya a thoughtful look. "What?" Maya asked.

"From what you told us last time, I think you made it pretty clear you didn't want to hear from him," Kristie said.

"Yeah, I guess that's true."

"Are you expecting him to call you?" Chelsea asked. "It sounds like it's in your court."

"Guys, this is a romance that is going nowhere, I promise you," Maya said. She took a sip of wine.

"Are you in love with him?" Molly, who had been unusually quiet, asked.

The husbands all looked at me.

What? I thought. *I'm cool.*

Quite a departure from the first meeting, then, Ben said.

I'm coming around.

"In love with Marcus? That's the second time this week someone's asked me that."

"Well, are you?" Molly asked again. "He was your first love, after all."

"And the way you talk about him…" Chelsea interjected.

"It's very complicated with Marcus," Maya said before pausing and then blushing.

"How?" Kristie asked.

"You know, because we were childhood sweethearts," she said quickly. "Plus, I'm pretty burned out on relationships after Dominic."

"Ugh." Chelsea grunted. "I never liked that guy."

Me neither, Chelsea. I felt Declan, Ben, and Charlie's agreement of my thought.

"I got caught up into thinking I loved Dom because I thought Jay had 'sent' him to me. I fell under the spell of a psychic prediction. When it happened, I told myself it was meant to be and ignored all the red flags. Plus, I think I mixed up sex with love."

"Oh, I miss sex!" Molly moaned.

What I'd give for just one more time, Declan, Molly's husband, thought, glowing with a deep pink aura.

"Tell me about it," Kristie agreed.

Ben's aura changed when she said this, but his thoughts were blocked, so it was impossible to guess his opinion of his wife's statement.

"Sex is nice," Chelsea said, smiling. She took a sip of wine coquettishly and everyone laughed.

"Stop that!" Molly said, giving her a playful slap.

She's definitely found her solace in sex, Charlie laughed. We all looked at him.

You don't watch, do you? Ben asked.

Nah. I give her privacy, of course. But it's impossible to not see it in her aura. Indeed, Chelsea's aura gave off a glow that had a unique energy to it that registered as heat to us.

It doesn't bother you? Declan asked Charlie. *Knowing?*

Nah. It's freeing me. The more alive she becomes after her grief, the more she lives her life, the more energy I feel. Almost as if I become more alive as well.

I hadn't thought of it that way. I noticed a slight change in my own energy when Maya began seeing Dominic, but it never occurred to me to attribute it to, well, Maya having sex.

Yes, it's sort of as if two souls merge during sex, Charlie thought in response. *And in a way they do. The human brain is closest to spirit at the moment of release.*

"Quit gloating, be-otch!" Molly said, laughing.

"It's weird. I never liked sex this much with Charlie. I feel so guilty about that. But now, it's like I'm a wild thing. It makes me feel so alive," Chelsea said, eyes wide. Her passion was obvious.

Is there an equivalent to sexual release in the spirit world? I asked Charlie.

Sort of. You can "merge" with another entity to emit a unique form of energy. I think of it as being like the clashing of light sabers in Star Wars. At least, that's my understanding. It's an experience that none of us are apparently ready for. It can only happen at the higher frequencies. Why do you think we all reincarnate into humans over and over? We ALL miss sex! The mirth felt from the husbands at this thought was palpable.

"Yeah, I think that's what happened with me and Dominic," Maya said. "I just craved that intimacy. Oh god, how wonderful it felt to be touched!"

"There's always Marcus…" Chelsea prodded.

"No!" Maya said loudly. We were all surprised by her tone. "I just mean… well there's something about Marcus I haven't told you." Maya's face turned pink, and tears gathered, welling in her lower lids. "I had an affair with Marcus while Jay was still alive," she whispered and looked down into her lap to avoid eye contact with the group.

"Oh, Maya," Molly said, grabbing a napkin and handing

it to Maya, who dabbed her eyes with it. "Why didn't you tell us before?" Molly reached out and put her hand on Maya's shoulder.

"I don't know. I feel so ashamed. So guilty." Maya's tears fell down her cheeks. Molly took her hand. Maya seemed so small and her aura faded to the color of weak tea.

"It's OK, honey. We all still love you."

It's true, Maya. We all do.

"It must be so hard to grieve with all that guilt," Chelsea said.

"I think I just blocked it out and pretended the affair never happened, but that fell apart the night I met him at Patty and Ian's. I haven't been able to stop crying since. It's been awful. I had a total temper tantrum and wrecked one of my paintings and haven't painted since. I just can't seem to get motivated."

I feel so helpless. How do I help her?

We all do, Charlie responded to me. *You can't help her. Living is a struggle, remember?*

I smiled. *Nobody tells you that death is a struggle too.*

"Maybe you should call him," Molly said.

"Who, Marcus? Oh god, no. I couldn't do that."

"Why not? You're obviously in love with him."

"I am? I loved him once, but now, I don't know. I have love for him as my first love, but 'in' love? I'm not so sure about that."

"I think you should just move on," Kristie said abruptly.

"What? Why? There's obviously a deep love there. Don't you think that's worth checking out?" Molly said.

Kristie reached over and took a square of dark chocolate from the plate and bit into a corner. "Not really. From what you've told me about Marcus, I'm not sure I like him." She savored another bite of the chocolate and then popped the rest of the piece into her mouth.

"Why's that?" Molly asked, still holding Maya's hand, but her look challenging.

"Why would you want to have a relationship with someone who would start an affair with a married woman, even if that woman was you?" Kristie said. Everyone sat in shocked silence.

"That's something to consider," Maya said quietly. "I think I need to remain single for a while. I need to figure all of this out."

"That's not fair, Kristie," Chelsea said. "Maya was in love with this man once."

"I'm just saying, you might want to step back and question his integrity a little. Just trying to be the voice of reason here," Kristie said.

"No, I'm glad you're saying this, Kristie. You're right. I really do need to think about this carefully. My history with Marcus complicates things and it's difficult to see things clearly."

"But Maya, there's really only one question here," Chelsea persisted. Everyone looked at her. "Do you love him?"

Maya closed her eyes in thought. She took a deep breath and then opened them again. The setting sun lit her from behind, casting her features in shadow.

"If I'm totally honest with myself, then I think the answer is yes. I do love him. I always have."

"OK then. How often does one person fall in love in a lifetime? Not that many, right?"

"I always thought it was only once, but now I'm not so sure," Maya said.

"I just don't think you can walk away from this. Why would you deprive yourself of love?" Molly talked quickly now, excited by the idea of romance.

"But the guy has no morals," Kristie interjected.

"Perhaps it seems that way simply because he loves her and always has," Molly countered.

"So what are you going to do, Maya?" Chelsea asked.

"I honestly don't know. But probably nothing. If it's

meant to be, then I guess I'll let the Universe make it happen."

You know what that means, don't you? Ben asked me. My confusion must have been evident. *You're up to bat, Mr. Universe.*

What if I'm with Kristie? What if he's a total schmo? I countered.

Is he? Charlie asked.

I wished I had the ability to lie, but when you can only communicate with thought, the little white lie becomes a lost skill. *No. I do believe Marcus really is in love with Maya.*

Welcome to death, kid, Declan teased.

A few weeks later, I watched Maya in the sunroom picking up the broken easel, pushing the brushes back into their jars, and arranging her paints on the table. She stretched a new canvas and with a thick brush swashed it with Gesso, readying it for her next masterpiece.

Chapter Twenty-Two

AUGUST 22, 2008

Dear Jay,

    I had a dream last night that my wedding ring, that thick gold band that you slipped onto my left hand all those years ago, had been grotesquely mangled, as though someone had taken huge steel cutters to it. The gold all torn up and sharp.
    I don't have many dreams about you. At the beginning I used to dream about you, but could never see your face. Your face was always hidden by a hat, or by the fact that I am riding behind you on the back of a motorcycle and can only feel your shoulders, but not see your eyes. Lately in my dreams about you, I'm angry at you because you keep telling me you are leaving me, that you want a divorce. After two and half years of mourning, I feel as if I am mourning a new sort of loss. I wake up with that anguished, angry, heartsick feeling, something I imagine people go through when their spouse leaves them. But it also feels like good pain, that last scratch that removes the scab revealing the tender pink skin underneath. The scar is tender and fragile, but in no danger of bursting open. It tells me I am ready to jump back into the fray and risk new scars.
    I can't help be struck by the thought that my mind is helping me

divorce you. Or are you the one doing this? Deep down, it feels like I need to 'divorce' you in order to truly get beyond my grief and open up to whatever might be next. Perhaps too, it's what your ghost needs to do in order to untether yourself from my grip.

The only thing I changed about our bedroom after Jay died was our bed. The sprawling king size, I decided, even before his death, was too big. "A marriage wrecker," I used to insist. We held hands across its expanse as we fell asleep, but we both depended on the gap for a good night's sleep. Any closer to Jay and I would awaken to the wind tunnel of his heavy breathing in my face. The new Queen-sized pillow top that I purchased at Macy's replaced a ten-year-old two-piece IKEA wonder we had bought as newlyweds.

The new bed had a plush, mushroom-colored velvet headboard and footboard. I bought a down-filled duvet, with a subtle blue striped cover in soft jersey. Down had made Jay sneeze, and so I had resigned myself to synthetic during our marriage. I replaced the pillows with down as well.

Today I decided it was time to clean out Jay's side of the closet. His closet remained untouched and still smelled faintly of mothballs. His dress shirts hung at attention, stiff from all the starch he insisted the dry cleaners use. Thousands of dollars worth of gray and navy wool suits, tailored to fit his broad shoulders, their cuffs turned perfectly, looked forlorn and seemed embarrassed by their slip in stature. Jay's shoes were still lined up neatly under the suits, a little dusty now. The black Brogues and the caramel-colored horsehides had me remembering the little pony jig he used to do when he put them on, making me laugh. And then there was the black body bag holding Jay's tux. He had spent a fortune on it, for a black tie event put on by the New York office. He rationalized that it would be a good investment, that he would need it again someday. I shoved it to the side so I could get at the wire mesh drawers that held his undershirts, boxers, and socks. I began stuffing them into a garbage bag, trying not to see what I was putting in, so I could avoid emotion.

I pulled a sweater off the shelf and remembered him wearing it that day we worked in the garden, him raking, me weeding, each content to work silently near the other. I refolded it and added it to the top of the pile inside the garbage bag. With each sweater and shirt came another memory – a vacation in Mexico, skiing at Whistler, him asleep on the couch with a book abandoned on his flannel-covered chest. The tears came, but I worked despite them, folding more clothes, flicking open another garbage bag. Maybe I would have a yard sale, but then I imagined watching strangers walk away with one of his suits or pairs of shoes and shuddered. Perhaps I should save some of this stuff for Calder, but these things would likely be out of fashion long before they would fit him. I decided the only thing I would save for Calder was the tuxedo.

I tied the tops of the bags and dragged them down the stairs. When I got them to the back door, I bent down to pick one up, hugging it to my chest, puffing with effort as I lugged it to the car and pushed it into the trunk where it looked like a disposed body in a bad late-night crime movie.

Later I swept the closet and hung up a few of my long, rarely worn dresses, which looked lonely and out of place in the big empty space. I walked past the dresser on my way to putting the broom back and stood staring at our wedding photo. We looked so happy, frozen in a long-ago kiss. I touched Jay's face behind the glass and then opened a drawer and lay the frame on the bottom under my socks.

I think I need to let you go now, Jay. And perhaps you too are hanging on a little too tightly to me. I'm not sure. I hope you can forgive me. I always loved you. I always will. I hope you know that.

All my love, M.

Chapter Twenty-Three

Full Circle

Marcus shuffled around his apartment, absently opening the fridge and closing it, flipping through channels in the living room, sitting on the bed and running his hand through his hair. Jericho watched quietly from his chair, head on paws on the armrest, but eyes following Marcus everywhere. Only when Marcus disappeared into another room did Jericho close his eyes. In the bedroom, Marcus abruptly pulled a leather satchel out from under the bed and began to fill it with a change of clothes. He grabbed a toothbrush from the bathroom and then sat on the bed again.

What am I doing?
You need to see her, Marcus. You're doing the right thing.
This is crazy!
You're still in love with Maya.
She's not in love with me.
You're meant to be in each other's lives.
Is she in love with me?

"Jericho, I think I'm going starkers." Jericho perked his ears up at his name and slid off the chair to amble his way into the bedroom, where he placed his big square head onto Marcus's lap. Marc patted him behind the ears until Jericho turned toward me and cocked his head. "Are you seeing ghosts again, Jer? Haha. Jay, is that you, creeping out my dog?"

Yup.

Jericho whined. Marcus turned his head abruptly toward the dog.

"Whoa." Marcus scratched the dog behind his ears and looked around, as if trying to determine where I stood. "You must be pissed at me."

I'm over it.

Jericho whined again. Marcus looked at him pointedly.

"Shit, dog. That's weird." Jericho just looked back at Marcus. "Are you talking to a ghost, boy?"

Jericho whined a third time.

"This is crazy. Jay, is that you, man?"

Yup

Whine.

"Man, I'm sorry. I didn't mean for it to happen. I hope you can forgive me."

I think I do.

Jericho pawed the floor, sniffing around.

"OK. Well, the thing is, I think I'm in love with her."

Yes.

"Are you cool with that?"

I'm cool.

Jericho barked.

"This is nuts! C'mon, Jericho. I need a coffee or something to wake up." Marcus and the dog walked into the kitchen and started the coffee maker. I needed to get his attention somehow. I wanted him to follow through on his plan to visit Maya, but he needed an excuse to see her. I concentrated on the painting above the couch until it swung slightly off kilter. Marc walked into the living room with his coffee cup, about to sit down on the couch when he noticed the skewed painting. He reached over, about to straighten it, but then stopped. He stared at it a long time.

Suddenly, he stepped onto the couch, lifted the painting, and leaned it against a wall. In the storage locker in the basement of the condo, he rummaged around until he found the wooden crate that the painting had been shipped in, hauled it up in the elevator, and slid the painting inside.

"Tomorrow, Jericho, we'll go experience our fate, whatever that may be." He grabbed the leash from the hook near the door, clipped it to Jericho's collar, and they headed out for their nightly walk under a late September harvest moon.

* * *

Maya and I drifted together across an ether sky, bright in its blackness, like India ink splashed across a light box. The light became blinding and then dimmed until we were inside some sort of cavern. There was a familiar sound of water plinking on stone, with a rush of waves off to the left. As my vision cleared, I saw that we were inside the very same grotto in Italy that Maya and I swam into all those years ago. The water lapped clear and blue on either side of us, and the stalactites were just as menacing as I remembered them. Tiny flecks of gold twinkled from above.

Where are we, Jay?

Do you remember our swim into the grotto that day?

Maya took in her surroundings, a look of awe on her face.

Why are we here? And why do I hear singing?

I'm not sure, but I think it's because I have to go now.

The tunnels we had seen that day, branching off from the main chamber, were now pulsing with lights of varying colors, beckoning me.

Where will you go?

I don't know, Maya.

Will I see you again?

I don't think you need me anymore.
I need you. Can't I come with you?
Calder needs you. Marcus needs you too. The tugging of the tunnel became more insistent. I heard the singing grow louder from within and my father and Alice waited for me just inside the entrance.
Do you want to go, Jay?
Yes, and I want you to live.
You want me to be with Marcus? After everything that happened?
Marcus was always meant to be in your life, Maya, just as I was.
So you're going to be OK, if Marcus and I...
Yes, Maya, as long as that is what you want. Things are unfolding as they should. I don't know how I know that, but I do.
I have no other choice but to trust you, Jay.
You always have a choice, Maya.
I suppose I do. You look so happy, Jay. Happier than I've ever seen you.
Yes. I think I finally understand that I need to go.
Go where?
I need to let go of my life as Jay. Let go of you and of Calder. I know it's all going to be OK.
Water rushed into the grotto.
What do we do now?
I guess we just have to leap. Like we did that day in the grotto. Jump as the wave recedes, and then swim like crazy back to the rock.
Maya set her gaze at the water washing around her feet.
Ready? The wave began to move out of the grotto. Maya nodded.
I love you, Jay.
I will always love you, Maya.
We stood together in the threshold of light looking into the swirling eddies. I smiled at her and she smiled back at me.
Now!
Re-emerging into blinding sunshine, I saw Maya already scrambling back onto the rock, but no matter how hard I swam, I could not reach her. Instead, I stopped swimming

and found myself floating toward the sound of singing, which became louder as I drew near the tunnel entrance where my father and Alice still waited.

    I turned to see Maya one last time. She lay on the rock in the red underwear bikini looking as beautiful as I remembered her, but this time, instead of lying in bright sunlight, the bluish tone of a full moon illuminated her pale skin. We waved a final farewell before I drifted back inside the grotto. The gold flecks on the ceiling were so similar to the cat's eyes that Maya had shown me on the streets of Pompeii all those years ago, leading me precisely, I realized, in the direction I was always meant to go.

    Marcus and Jericho sat in the front seats of his gleaming red MG, watching Maya's front door. He'd called Patty that morning to get Maya's address.

    Calder came out onto the porch carrying a skateboard and wearing a helmet. His collar bone had healed and he became more cautious about riding. He hadn't gone to the school to watch the high school kids speed down the ramp in months. This was the first time he'd taken out the skateboard in several weeks.

    "I guess this is it, Jer." Marcus opened the car door and waited as Jericho leapt over the console and out onto the sidewalk. The dog dashed up the steps and onto the porch, letting out one large bark. Calder turned as Jericho jumped up to put his paws on Calder's chest and lick his face. Calder laughed and then saw Marcus coming up the steps behind Jericho.

    "Marc!" Calder pushed Jericho down and stepped forward to hug Marcus around his hips. I felt a pang of regret. Or maybe it was envy. Had Calder ever greeted me so enthusiastically?

    "Hi, bud."

    "Is this your dog?"

    "Yup. That's Jericho." As the dog licked Calder's face,

Calder turned his head away and scrunched up his face. "I think he likes you," Marcus said, laughing.

"He's awesome. I wish we had a dog." Jericho now sat beside Calder and panted as Calder stroked his ears.

"Yeah. He's a good pup."

"How come you're here?"

"I came to give your mom a present."

"A present? Did you bring me a present too?"

"What, are you kidding? Does Jericho here not qualify?"

"Oh, well. Yeah. I guess. I'll go get Mom. She's painting."

Calder opened the door and yelled, "Moooommmm! Marc's here!" Calder had not stepped more than a foot inside the door.

Marcus smiled. "Dude, I could have done that!" he said.

For good measure, Calder called once more. "Mooooommmmm!"

"Coming!" A faint voice came from the back of the house.

"She's coming."

"Yeah, I heard."

"Well, I'm going over to Owen's. We're going to the park to skateboard."

"Have fun. Say hi to Owen for me."

"K!" Calder leapt down the porch steps onto the sidewalk, throwing his board to the pavement as he did a running step onto it and sped off. Marcus stood on the porch, the door wide open, as Jericho sat obediently at his feet. Maya came from the back of the house, wiping her hands on a rag. When she looked up and saw Marcus, she stopped. A blush crept up her neck from under her crumpled grey t-shirt.

"Hi," she said, barely audible.

"Hello, Maya."

"What are you doing here?" she asked. Marcus seemed to be at a loss for words. He looked down and saw Jericho sitting obediently beside him, as if Jericho knew it was his job to be polite.

"Uh...I wanted you to meet Jericho," Marcus said, patting the top of the dog's head.

"Hello, Jericho." Maya smirked. "You came all this way to introduce me to your dog?"

"Well..." Jericho took the opportunity of Marcus's hesitation to bound into the house, almost knocking Maya over. "Whoa! Jericho, get back here!" Marcus hesitated at the door.

"I guess you'd better come in." Maya stepped back so Marcus could get past her.

"Yeah, OK." Marcus walked in and squeezed past Maya, his hand accidentally brushing her waist, creating an awkward closeness between them. Their auras merged into a molten light and they both hesitated in the moment before Marcus took another step inside.

"Jericho!" The dog bounded into the kitchen, sniffing around under the kitchen table. "Jeez, Jericho. That wasn't very polite of you."

"It's fine," Maya said. "I was about to make myself a pot of tea. Do you want some?"

"Yeah, OK, sure. That would be great."

"You still drink it black?" Maya asked, looking back at him as she filled the kettle with water and flipped the switch.

Marcus nodded. "Electric kettle. Nice," he noted.

"You know me and my tea..." Maya said.

"Yeah. I do."

Maya turned around and watched as Jericho sniffed his way around the kitchen and adjoining dining room. Marcus pulled one of the rustic wooden stools up to the cool, gray soapstone counter and sat. He looked around at the white walls, tiled with a variety of brightly colored, framed artwork. An open shelf above the sink contained a display of ornate cobalt blue glass jars and bottles. A couple of Calder's paintings were taped to the fridge. A vase of wilting pink tulips sat forlornly in the kitchen window that looked out onto a side garden.

"This is a great house, Maya. Really homey. Very you."

"Thanks. It's kind of a mess at the moment. I wasn't really expecting company."

"I'm sorry I didn't call first. I wanted to surprise you. I have something for you."

"For me?"

"Stay where you are. I'll be right back." Marcus stood up abruptly and dashed out the door, Jericho bounding after him. They came back a few minutes later, Marc carrying the large, long, flat wooden box that had been poking out of the back seat of the car.

Marcus placed the box on the island as Maya shoved a butter dish and a loaf of bread out of the way.

"What's this?"

"I bought this not too long ago, but I think it really belongs to you."

"OK..." Maya said as she began to slide the painting out from the crate. It faced down, and as she pulled it out, she recognized her own signature and the gallery's insignia glued to the back.

"What the...?" Maya said as she turned the painting over and saw the crow.

"*You* bought this? I was so mad at Amalie for selling it, since it was not for sale. But she sold it to you? I don't understand," Maya said, looking confused.

"I bought it through Amalie's assistant. I guess neither of us knew it wasn't for sale. Honestly. I never would have bought it if I'd known."

"But Amalie told me she had no record of who had bought it... My God. This is astonishing. What made you buy this one in particular?"

"I'm not really sure," Marcus said. "I liked the crow, I guess."

"And why bring the painting back to me now?"

"I don't know that either. Just a feeling." The kettle clicked off, startling them. I enjoyed making my presence known.

"A feeling? Do you know what this painting represents to me, Marcus?"

"Not really. Maybe something about Jay?"

Maya looked surprised. "How did you know?"

Marcus shrugged. "Just guessed, since you didn't want to sell it."

"I keep seeing blackbirds and ravens in really strange places and in unusual circumstances, and so they've come to represent Jay to me in a way. They have such knowing eyes. I tried to capture that in this painting." Maya held the painting up to look at it more closely.

"You did a great job. I couldn't take my eyes off it. Something made me buy it and I guess circumstances allowed that to happen. And now circumstances are bringing the painting back to you." Marcus looked serious as he spoke.

"Yeah. That is pretty odd, isn't it?" Maya said.

"Maybe not. Perhaps it's all a grand plan to get us back together," Marcus said with a smirk. Maya rolled her eyes.

"Are you going all woo-woo on me, Marcus? That's not like you." Still holding the painting, she walked over to the other side of the kitchen, placed it on the floor, and leaned it against the wall. She removed one of the paintings hanging on the wall and put it on the floor. Then she hung the crow painting in its place.

"Looks like it belongs there," Marcus said.

Maya stepped back to take a look. "Yeah, he seems pretty at home there. I think I like it. He can watch while I paint and make dinner."

"Do you miss him?" Marcus looked down at his hands, picking at a well-manicured fingernail.

Maya turned and poured hot water from the kettle into the teapot. "Of course I miss him. But it's been two and a half years now, and I'm learning to live my life without him." Maya looked up at Marcus as she answered.

"I'm sorry, Maya. I really am."

"What are you apologizing for exactly?"

"I don't know. Jay's death. Our infidelity. How I treated you all those years ago."

"There's no need. But thank you. That means a lot." Maya distracted herself by pouring the tea into cups, pushing Marcus's cup toward him and adding milk and sugar to her own. She took the stool next to Marcus and they sat together in silence, sipping tea, each in silent contemplation.

What's going on here? Her thought startled me.

Maya, he's still in love with you.

This is crazy. She looked over at Marcus's hands and noticed they were trembling slightly as he brought the cup to his lips.

Marcus can't be in love with me. After all these years?

He'd be good for you, Maya.

You always hated him, Jay.

Yeah, well now I don't. I've grown up.

Maybe you're finally growing up.

Finally.

Well I believe you've grown up if you've brought Marcus back into my life. The question now is, am I in love with him?

That is the question. I think you already know the answer.

Calder came crashing through the door, Owen following in his wake. They both ran over to Marcus.

"Hey dudes, back so soon? What's going on?" Marcus said. Jericho, who had been lying under the table, got up and walked over to Calder, who started patting him absently.

"When Owen found out you were here, he wanted to come and see if you can come over to his house with us so we can play," he said.

Owen nodded vigorously. "Pleeeease! You can say hi to my mom and dad."

"Whoa. I just got here. Can't you guys play here?"

"No! All the instruments are at Owen's place!" Calder said.

277

"Please, Marc, pllllleeeeaaaase?" The boys begged in unison. Marcus looked pleadingly over at Maya.

"Go. I'll clean up here and then put something on for dinner. You'll stay?"

"If you'll have me," Marcus said as a boy on each hand led him toward the door. Jericho followed, his tail wagging. Maya looked up at the crow painting and smiled. Through his gleaming yellow eye I smiled back.

Very cunning, you. Very cunning.

Thank you. I'm pretty pleased with myself.

Maya took another sip of tea and headed to the sunroom to clean her brushes. Outside the window in the twilit sky rose a perfectly round, salmon-colored moon. Maya stopped dunking her brush in turpentine and watched the moon rise for a long time. She looked back at her painting in progress - the entry to our grotto, its interior dark and mysterious while outside its entrance waves crashed violently around the flat rock where Maya lay in her red bikini. Thick slabs of paint slashed through the wispy shades of white, gray, and purple that created the waves. A lavender sunset similar to the one we had witnessed that evening at the *pensione* brushed across the sky.

Maya wiped clean a brush on a cloth and dabbed it into some paint, and as she peered out the window, she smiled as she painted the pale coral moon that now glowed in the inky sky.

OTHER TITLES BY ABIGAIL CARTER

If you enjoyed *Remember the Moon*, and are inspired to post a review on Amazon or Goodreads, the author would be eternally grateful.

Also by Abigail Carter:
The Alchemy of Loss: A Young Widow's Transformation

Like *A Year of Magical Thinking*, this powerful and touching book is both an inspirational read and a comfort to those who are looking for help in overcoming loss.

"What an eloquent, brave and (even) occasionally comic account Abigail Carter has given us of her zigzagging odyssey through the country of mourning. No mourner has it easy, but Carter's tasks were daunting — to mother two suddenly fatherless children, to find her own way through the strife that bereavement brings to her parents and mother-in-law, and to disentangle her personal grief from the national mourning. Through it all, she is a generous, nuanced and admirably honest guide."
— Katherine Ashenburg, author of *The Mourner's Dance*

ACKNOWLEDGEMENTS

After my memoir, *The Alchemy of Loss* was published, it became evident that a second memoir might be difficult for a publisher to sell. I tried a few different tactics, but in the end I simply poured all that material into this fictional story about a life I imagined Arron might have after his death. I was no more an experienced fiction writer than I was a memoir writer and so many people have had a hand in guiding me along the way. The first of those is Scott Driscoll, literary fiction instructor at the University of Washington Continuing Education Department, who helped me lay down the foundations of this story and encouraged me with his thoughtful comments and ideas in his nearly impossible-to-read scrawl.

    The early chapters were also carefully read by the members of my writing group who were all writing memoir, but suffered my fiction gracefully. They helped me eek out the various plot twists. Before you all think that I had an affair on Arron before his death, please know that I place this twist squarely on the shoulders of Paul Boardman who questioned Marcus's presence at Jay's funeral with the innocent question, "Was she having an affair with him?" Invaluable feedback also came from Kellini Walter, who was one of the first to read the entire manuscript and had some wonderful ideas based on her own experience with loss. Wendy Colbert helped with her astute comments regarding Maya's character, Dana Montanari and Linda Bigley were my enthusiastic cheerleaders, and comments from Anne-Phyfe Palmer (Lady Phyfe) and Natalie Singer-Velush always had me thinking hard and re-writing.

This novel might not have ever seen the light of day had it not been suggested by Margaret Bendet, my advisor during the Whidbey Island Writer's Association Lockdown Retreat, that I put away the paranormal memoir I was struggling with and return to *Remember The Moon* instead. A few of her simple plot suggestions had me off and running again after my long stall.

All the writers at the Seattle Daylight Writer's Group who listened as I stumbled and sometimes cried as I read passages out loud, who always provided me with ideas and thoughts that were valuable for their immediacy and authenticity. In particular, the founder of this group, Kelsye Nelson, who is another ardent cheerleader and my astute business partner at Writer.ly, wisely suggested I intersperse scenes into Maya's letters to Jay.

I was heartened when I put out a call on my blog for Beta readers and had 37 people sign up. Of those, 17 actually provided me with incredibly insightful feedback from which I made several major and minor edits. I would like to thank those 17: Nancy Orlikow, Nancy Schatz Alton, Marganne Glasser, Kerry Donahue, Kylie Eklund, Melissa Schwartz, Tony Kwok, Karen daSilva, Kim Nymark, Alexandre Rocha Lima e Marcondes, Lisa Norley, Rachel Kodanaz, Margie Waldo Simon, Tammie Lewis, Susan Wong, Barnaby Guthrie, Marny Williams-Balodis. I am indebted to you all. A special thank you goes to Nancy Orlikow, one of my dearest friends and great Beta reader – any likenesses found in this book are purely subconscious.

My angel-sister Sheri Bakes found me after she read *Alchemy*. Her beautiful paintings inspired all of the descriptions of Maya's paintings in the book and when on a whim I asked her if I could commission her to do a painting for the book cover, she graciously obliged and insisted it be a gift. I now have the pleasure of seeing her work on both my office wall and on the cover of this book.

Jennifer Munro, my valiant editor whose invaluable suggestions, edits and questions all contributed to making this a profoundly more cohesive and engaging book. And Michelle Dias, my valiant copyeditor (discovered on Writer.ly) whose effusive comments made me smile and bolstered my confidence at the same time.

Deirdre Timmons, my best friend, reader, cheerleader, and inspiration helped me realize that dead husbands watching their wives having sex was downright creepy, advice perhaps only a good friend would be brave enough to say.

An early manuscript undertook a motorcycle trip across the country with Jim Evans who proudly pulled it out of his bag and read it at greasy spoons and diners along lonely highways. I received it back beat-up and coffee-stained, his insightful comments scrawled in margins and shyly articulated (coaxed by me) during cherished moments.

And finally, to Carter and Olivia who suffered a consistent view of my hunched back, but conveyed their pride in my dilatory profession. You are my inspiration, always.

About the Author

Abigail Carter wrote *The Alchemy of Loss: A Young Widow's Transformation* (HCI, 2008) as a form of catharsis after her husband's death in the World Trade Center on September 11th, 2001. Her work has also appeared in SELF magazine, Reader's Digest Canada, MSN.com and More.com and she maintains blogs at abigailcarter.com and alchemyofloss.com. Abigail is also the co-Founder of Writer.ly an online marketplace where writers can find the people they need to publish successfully. She can be found on Facebook and Twitter (@abigailcarter).

Abigail teaches memoir writing at Camp Widow, a yearly retreat for widows and at The Recovery Cafe in Seattle, a community center for people recovering from addiction. She has extensive Board experience: Executive Board of The Healing Center, a Seattle-based bereavement center for children and their parents; Executive Board, Hedgebrook, a women's writing retreat on Whidbey Island, WA; Executive Board, The Seattle Freelances Association, a respected professional writer's association based in Seattle; Advisory Board, University of Washington Digital Publishing Program.

Abigail moved from New Jersey to Seattle in 2005, where she now lives with her two children.